The Limits of Nationali‹

MW00805538

This book discusses the justifications and limits of cultural nationalism from a liberal perspective. It begins by presenting a normative typology of nationalist ideologies. The main distinction in this typology is between cultural nationalisms and statist nationalisms. According to statist nationalisms, states have an interest in the cultural homogeneity of their citizenries. According to cultural nationalisms, people have interests in adhering to their cultures (the adherence thesis) and in sustaining these cultures for generations (the historical thesis). Gans argues that freedom- and identity-based justifications for cultural nationalism common in the literature can only support the adherence thesis, while the historical thesis could only be justified by the interest people have in the long-term endurance of their personal and group endeavours.

The Limits of Nationalism examines demands often made in the name of cultural nationalism. Gans argues that national self-determination should be constitutionally interpreted in sub-statist rather than statist forms. The book presents two conceptions of the notion of historical rights. It also discusses the demands entailed by cultural particularism as opposed to cultural cosmopolitanism.

CHAIM GANS is Professor of Law at Tel Aviv University, Israel. His previous publications include *Philosophical Anarchism and Political Disobedience* (Cambridge, 1992).

The Limits of Nationalism

Chaim Gans

Tel Aviv University

CAMBRIDGE
UNIVERSITY PRESS

PUBLISHED BY THE PRESS SYNDICATE OF THE UNIVERSITY OF CAMBRIDGE
The Pitt Building, Trumpington Street, Cambridge CB2 1RP, United Kingdom

CAMBRIDGE UNIVERSITY PRESS
The Edinburgh Building, Cambridge CB2 2RU, UK
40 West 20th Street, New York, NY 10011-4211, USA
477 Williamstown Road, Port Melbourne, VIC 3207, Australia
Ruiz de Alarcón 13, 28014 Madrid, Spain
Dock House, The Waterfront, Cape Town 8001, South Africa

http://www.cambridge.org

First published 2003

Printed in the United Kingdom at the University Press, Cambridge

Typeface Plantin 10/12 pt   *System* LaTeX 2$_\varepsilon$ [TB]

A catalogue record for this book is available from the British Library

ISBN 0 521 80864 2 hardback
ISBN 0 521 00467 5 paperback

For my father

Contents

Acknowledgements

In the course of writing this book I received aid and support from many people and institutions. My greatest debt is to my friends Meir Dan-Cohen and Andrei Marmor who read earlier drafts of most of this book. Daniel Kofman, Alon Harel, David Heyd, Ariel Porat, David Enoch, Will Kymlicka, Sammy Smooha, Zvi Gitelman, Rainer Bauböck, Thomas Pogge and Yael Tamir commented on various sections of this book.

I began the research for this project at the Max Planck Institute for Public International Law and the Law of Nations in Heidelberg in 1995, and completed most of it at the Yitzhak Rabin Center for Israel Studies in Tel Aviv in 2001. Both institutions provided me with financial support and with a supportive and congenial environment. I would like to express my appreciation to the staff of these institutions, especially Jochen A. Frowein and Rüdiger Wolfrum, directors of the Max Planck Institute and Naomi Vered, director of the research programme at the Rabin Center.

Most of the work on this book was done while fulfilling, and sometimes neglecting, my regular duties at the Faculty of Law at Tel Aviv University. I am grateful to my colleagues for their patience. I would also like to thank the Minerva Center for Human Rights and the Zegla Center at the Tel Aviv University Faculty of Law for their financial support.

Several people provided me with valuable research assistance. First, I would like to note Amos Kfir, an outstanding and beloved student, whose recent tragic death left everyone who knew him grieving. A group of equally dedicated and able students subsequently provided me with invaluable help: Einat Fisher, Tally Kritzman, Keren Brown and Michal Saliternik. Michal Kirschner edited my English and contributed not only to improving the style, but in the process also helped me to clarify my thinking.

I presented earlier drafts of chapters of this book at several colloquia and workshops where I received helpful comments. I am especially indebted to the following: the participants of the Netherlands–Israel Academy Colloquium on nationalism and multiculturalism which was organised by Govert A. den Hartogh and took place in Amsterdam in November 1997; the participants of the colloquium on historical justice which was organized by Lukas H. Meyer and was held at the Einstein Forum in Potsdam, in July 2001; the participants of David Miller's political philosophy workshop at Nuffield College where I presented earlier drafts of Chapters 2 and 4 in October 1998 and in May 2000.

Earlier versions of some of the chapters of this book were published in several journals. Substantial parts of Chapter 2 were published under the title 'The Liberal Foundations of Cultural Nationalism', in the *Canadian Journal of Philosophy* 30/3 (2000), 441–66. A large part of Chapter 3 was published under the title 'National Self-Determination: A Sub- and Inter-Statist Conception', in *The Canadian Journal of Law and Jurisprudence* 13/2 (2000), 185–205. Earlier drafts of Chapter 4 were published under the title 'Historical Rights' in *Mishpatim* 21 (1992), 193–220 (Hebrew) and under the title 'Historical Rights: The Evaluation of Nationalist Claims to Sovereignty' in *Political Theory* 29/1 (2001), 58–79 (copyright 2001 by Sage Publications; reprinted by permission of Sage Publications). Earlier versions of some of the arguments presented in Chapter 5 appeared in the article 'Nationalism and Immigration', published by Kluwer Academic Publishers in *Ethical Theory and Moral Practice* 1/2 (1998), 159–80, reprinted with kind permission of Kluwer Academic Publishers. I am indebted to the anonymous readers of these journals for their comments. I am grateful to these journals for permission to use the material in this book. In addition, I would like to thank the anonymous reviewers of Cambridge University Press for their detailed comments which made the book better than it would have been otherwise.

Introduction

Cultural nationalism is a nationalism according to which members of groups sharing a common history and societal culture have a fundamental, morally significant interest in adhering to their culture and in sustaining it for generations. In the name of the thesis that members of national groups have such interests, nationalist movements often voice specific practical demands in both the public and private spheres. Their main demand is for national self-determination. However, national groups also make claims with regard to territories with which they are historically linked. They demand that their members be granted priority in immigrating to their homelands. They further make claims concerning the special responsibilities that exist among their members, and assert the superiority of particularistic national ways of life compared to other lifestyles such as cosmopolitanism. The purpose of this book is to examine these theses and claims. I shall first examine the possibility of providing a liberal justification for the abstract tenet of cultural nationalism, namely, that members of national groups have an interest in adhering to their culture and preserving it for generations. After discussing this theoretical thesis, I shall move on to examine the more practical demands of cultural nationalism, namely, those relating to national self-determination, historical rights, priority in immigration and the like. It is a well-known fact that cultural nationalism has enjoyed a revival in many parts of the world in the last fifteen years. The present book joins a steady stream of philosophical writing on nationalism, both liberal and from other orientations, which has accompanied this revival.

In Chapter 1 I shall further elucidate the nature of cultural nationalism and attempt to situate its liberal version within nationalism in general. I shall argue that the liberal version of cultural nationalism must be distinguished from non-liberal cultural nationalism on the one hand, and on the other hand, from a liberal nationalism that is not cultural but rather statist. Unlike cultural nationalism, which focuses on the interests people have in their own culture, statist nationalism focuses on the interests states have in the cultural homogeneity of their citizenries. Unlike cultural

1

nationalism, statist nationalism does not focus on the protection that states can provide for national cultures and those of their members who are interested in adhering to them. Rather, it focuses on the contribution that national cultures can make towards the realization of political values that are neither derived from nor directed at the protection of particular national cultures. I shall argue that this distinction between cultural nationalism and statist nationalism forms the normative essence of the well-known distinction suggested by historians and sociologists between ethnocultural nationalism and territorial-civic nationalism. It is common among students of nationalism to associate its liberal versions with civic nationalism and its non-liberal versions with cultural nationalism. Several writers have criticized this linkage.[1] I concur with them, especially with regard to the normative distinction that I propose between cultural and statist nationalism. I will claim that distinctions between liberal and non-liberal versions of nationalism could be made both within the cultural and the statist types. In addition, I shall discuss the possible logical and empirical relationships between the various types of nationalism and the state and how these types of nationalism relate to ethnicity. Some contemporary writers do not seem to be fully aware of the normative significance of the distinction between cultural and statist nationalism. In my opinion this has caused some confusion in their discussions of nationalism. I shall try to demonstrate this with regard to several of these writers.

The distinctions between the various types of nationalism to be presented in Chapter 1 will enable me to isolate and delimit the specific topic of this book which is a *liberal* (as opposed to non-liberal) version of *cultural* (as opposed to statist) *nationalism*. If the way in which I have formulated above the normative essence of this nationalism is correct, then it seems to comprise three main theses. The first thesis is the *adherence* thesis which concerns the basic interest people have in adhering to their culture. The second thesis is the *historical* thesis and it concerns the basic interest people have in recognizing and protecting the multigenerational dimension of their culture. The third thesis, a *political* one, holds that the interests people have in living their lives within their culture, and in sustaining this culture for generations, should be protected politically. In Chapter 2 I will discuss possible justifications for these theses. Contemporary writers who support what seem to be liberal versions of cultural nationalism do so mainly by arguing that people have an interest

---

[1] See for example Will Kymlicka, *Politics in the Vernacular: Nationalism, Multiculturalism, and Citizenship* (Oxford University Press, 2001), chap. 12 and Rogers Brubaker, 'Myths and misconceptions in the study of nationalism', in M. Moore (ed.), *National Self-Determination and Secession* (Oxford University Press, 1998), pp. 257–60.

in culture because it is a prerequisite for their freedom and because it is a component of their identity. I will try to show that these arguments could provide an adequate basis at most for the adherence thesis, but not for the historical thesis. I shall then offer a third argument based on the interest people have in their endeavour which could serve to support the historical thesis. According to this argument, people undertake projects, express their personalities and live their lives on the assumption that their lives have meaning and some impact on the world outside them, which exists independently of their own existence. I will argue that the interest people have in the existence of the world where their endeavours leave their mark could provide support for the historical thesis of cultural nationalism. I will also argue that this argument provides part of the justification for the distinction between the two types of rights advocated by contemporary writers for the protection of people's interests in their culture: rights to self-government on the one hand, and polyethnic or multicultural rights on the other.

Many people living today are interested in adhering to their national culture, in living their lives within it, and in its continuation in history. Whether or not the attempts to provide liberal justifications to these interests succeed, the question remains whether the more concrete and practical demands that are made in the name of cultural nationalism are reconcilable with liberalism. Usually these demands have a rather ambitious character. National groups and those who speak in their name when demanding self-determination want it to have the form of independent statehood. When they claim historical rights to territories, they mean rights to territorial sovereignty. When they require priority in immigration for their members, they want it to have the form of individual rights granted to each and every member of their group, that is, rights that entail the state's corresponding duty to admit these individuals. When they argue for the existence of particularistic obligations that members of national groups owe one another, they sometimes deny the derivative nature of such obligations and their subordination to moral universalism. When they argue that it is good for people to be immersed in their own nation's culture, they sometimes deny the legitimacy of non-nationalist, cosmopolitan lifestyles. In the chapters dealing with these demands, I shall show that if they are at all acceptable, then this would only be in much more modest form. Specifically, the demand for national self-determination, if it is indeed acceptable, should be realized universally in sub-statist rather than statist forms. Claims to historical rights, if acceptable, cannot serve as a basis for territorial sovereignty. At most, they can serve as a basis for determining the location of national self-determination under its sub-statist conception, which does not include the right of national groups to territorial sovereignty. I shall further claim that nationality-based priorities in immigration should not have the form of individual rights granted to each and every member of a given national group. Rather, they should have the form of nationality-based quotas within general immigration quotas that are also based on a variety of other considerations. I shall argue that some sorts of particularistic obligations among members of national groups should be acknowledged, but only to a limited extent and under the auspices of moral universalism. I shall also argue that accepting particularistic national lifestyles does not imply rejecting the possibility of a cosmopolitan lifestyle. These lifestyles can coexist side by side.

The right to self-determination, which is the main practical demand made by cultural nationalism regarding the public sphere, will be discussed in Chapter 3. It is usually interpreted as the right of national groups to secede from existing states and to form new ones. However, I shall discuss it mainly as a question concerning the proper institutional framework for protecting the interests of national groups in their self-preservation and collective self-rule; in particular, whether these interests should be protected by means of independent statehood or by less drastic means. I shall present several arguments against a statist interpretation of self-determination and for a sub- and sometimes inter-statist interpretation. According to the sub- and inter-statist conception, the right of national groups to self-determination should be conceived of as a package of privileges to which each national group is entitled in its main geographic location, normally within the state that coincides with its homeland. This package should include self-government rights, special representation rights and rights to cultural preservation. This sub-statist conception of self-determination differs from the statist conception in mainly two matters: first, it represents the right to self-determination as a right within the state, never as a right to independent statehood. Secondly, according to this sub-statist conception, self-determination is not a right of majority nations within states *vis-à-vis* national minorities, but rather a right to which each national group in the world is entitled. This right must be realized at least in one place, usually the historic homeland of the national group enjoying it. Accordingly, it is a right of homeland groups *vis-à-vis* non-homeland groups.

National groups quite often make demands to territorial sovereignty in the name of what they call 'historical rights'. I shall discuss these demands in Chapter 4. The framework for my discussion will be provided by a distinction between two conceptions of historical rights. One conception focuses on the primacy of the national group in the history of the territory over which it demands sovereignty (the first occupancy conception), while the other conception focuses on the primacy of that territory in the history of the national group demanding the sovereignty (the formative territories conception). I shall argue that despite the fact that historical rights cannot serve as a basis for territorial sovereignty in either conception, they are not entirely void of normative significance. Especially under their formative territories conception, they are connected with the notion of *homeland*, and in this sense they might have some normative importance. Historical rights could be a source for considerations on the basis of which the location of self-determination under its sub-statist conception should be determined.

Chapter 5 discusses the question of whether nationality-based priorities in immigration could be justified. Prima facie, such priorities seem to contradict the United Nations International Convention on the Elimination of All Forms of Racial Discrimination that prohibits racial discrimination and states that this term applies, among other things, to 'any ... preference based on ... national or ethnic origin ...'. After arguing that nationality-based priorities in immigration are not necessarily racist, I shall propose three principles for regulating such priorities which follow from or could be justified by the sub- and inter-statist conception of self-determination. The immigration rights asserted by these principles will be an embodiment of the inter-statist dimension of this conception. In addition, they will also constitute the most detailed example provided in this study for another component of this conception, namely, cultural preservation rights which are meant to enable members of national groups to continue living major parts of their lives within their own culture. Other major examples of such rights are the collective language rights that were granted to the Francophone majority in Quebec, the collective land rights of the native Fijians and the restrictions imposed on non-aboriginal people in the reservations of Canada. When such rights are being granted, it is easy for them to slide beyond their appropriate limits. For example, the current form of Israel's Law of Return, which grants every individual Jew a personal right to immigrate to Israel, does indeed seem to exceed such limits. It does so at least if we read it (as many Zionists in fact do) as granting advantages which should be realized by most of their potential beneficiaries and not just as a historical declaration, part of the value of which is mainly symbolic and not practical. The principles for regulating nationality-based priorities in immigration that I shall propose in Chapter 5 are intended to demonstrate the desirable limits of such priorities.

Chapters 3–5 discuss the demands which cultural nationalism makes in the public domain. The purpose of Chapter 6 is mainly to consider some demands that cultural nationalism makes in the private domain.

I will first discuss the position according to which people are permitted or even required to demonstrate a measure of partiality and special concern for their national group and its members. I will argue that this partiality can be accommodated within the framework of ethical universalism, and reject the thesis according to which it is only ethical particularism that can account for it. I shall then discuss the relationship between cultural particularism and cultural cosmopolitanism. The former is the view that it is good for people to be immersed in one particular culture while the latter is the view that it is good for them to shape their lives by means of ideas, texts, customs etc. that they have collected from different cultures. I will argue for at least one sense in which these doctrines could be compatible. In the concluding chapter of this book, I will make some remarks regarding how this book relates to other recent writings on nationalism and address some objections that could be raised regarding some of its theses.

1   Nationalist ideologies – a normative typology

Cultural nationalism and statist nationalism

The terms 'socialism', 'liberalism' and 'conservatism' have been said to be 'like surnames and the theories, principles and parties that share one of these names often do not have much more in common with one another than the members of a widely extended family'.[1] The term 'nationalism' is even more complex, for it is the surname not only of one family of ideas, but of two. One family is that of *statist nationalism*. According to this type of nationalism, in order for states to realize political values such as democracy, economic welfare and distributive justice, the citizenries of states must share a homogeneous national culture. It must be noted that the values in question do not derive from specific national cultures. Nor are they aimed at their protection. The second family is that of *cultural nationalism*. According to this nationalism, members of groups sharing a common history and societal culture have a fundamental, morally significant interest in adhering to their culture and in sustaining it across generations. This interest warrants the protection of states. The two families of nationalism share a common name, and there are cases, as we shall see below, in which members of both families were or could have been happily married. Yet, their genealogies, at least their philosophical-normative genealogies, do not share one common origin. Within statist nationalism, the national culture is the means, and the values of the state are the aims. Within cultural nationalism, however, the national culture is the aim, and the state is the means. Moreover, within statist nationalism, as I shall further clarify below, any national culture, not necessarily the national culture of the states' citizenries or a part of their citizenries, could in principle be the means for realizing the political values of the state. Within cultural nationalism, on the other hand, states are the means or the providers of the means for preserving the specific national cultures of their citizenry or parts thereof.

---

[1] Jeremy Waldron, 'Theoretical Foundations of Liberalism', *The Philosophical Quarterly* 37 (1987), 127–50.

The nationalism I have here called *statist* expresses the normative essence of a nationalism that historians and sociologists call *territorial-civic*, while the type of nationalism I have here termed *cultural* expresses the normative essence of the type of nationalism that historians and sociologists call *ethnocultural*. The historian Hans Kohn, who was the first to make this distinction in the literature after World War II, characterized the territorial-civic nationalism as 'predominantly a political movement to limit governmental power and to secure civic rights'.[2] Kohn claimed that 'its purpose was to create a liberal and rational civil society representing the middle-class...'.[3] He argued that it developed mainly in the advanced countries of the West, England, the United States and France, during the age of Enlightenment. According to Kohn, ethnocultural nationalism was characteristic of less advanced countries, mainly in Central and Eastern Europe (but also in Spain and Ireland). Because the middle class of these countries was weak, he claimed that nationalism in these countries was less political and more cultural. It was 'the dream and hope of scholars and poets',[4] a dream and hope that was based on past heritage and ancient traditions. Unlike the nationalism of the advanced West, which was inspired by the legal and rational concept of citizenship, the nationalism of Central and Eastern Europe was inspired by imagination and emotions, and by the unconscious development of the *Volk* and its primordial and atavistic spirit. Kohn believed that the ethnocultural nationalism of the Eastern European countries was a reaction of the elites of underdeveloped societies to the territorial-civic nationalism of the advanced societies of the West. A dichotomy similar to that between ethnocultural nationalism and territorial-civic nationalism, that was adopted by many scholars after Kohn,[5] was also used much earlier, for example, by Marx and Engels in their accounts of the nineteenth-century nationalist movements. In order to express their attitude towards these movements, they used Hegel's

---

[2] Hans Kohn, *Nationalism: Its Meaning and History* (Princeton: D. Van Nostrand Company, 1955), pp. 29–30.

[3] *Ibid.*, p. 29.   [4] *Ibid.*, p. 30.

[5] While criticizing some of its details and developing it. See Anthony D. Smith, *The Ethnic Origins of Nations* (Oxford and Cambridge, MA: Blackwell, 1986); Anthony D. Smith, *National Identity* (London: Penguin Books, 1991), pp. 80–4; Anthony D. Smith, *Nationalism and Modernism: A Critical Survey of Recent Theories of Nations and Nationalism* (London and New York: Routledge, 1998), pp. 177–80; John Hutchinson, *The Dynamics of Cultural Nationalism* (London: Allen and Unwin, 1987), pp. 12–49, 30–6. Hutchinson calls civic nationalism 'political'. Deutsch suggests an analogous distinction between patriotism and nationalism: 'Patriotism appeals to all residents of a country, regardless of their ethnic background. Nationalism appeals to all members of an ethnic group, regardless of their country of residence.' See Karl Wolfgang Deutsch, *Nationalism and Social Communication: An Inquiry into the Foundations of Nationality* (Cambridge, MA: Technology Press of Massachusetts Institute of Technology, 1953), p. 232.

distinction between historical nations and non-historical nationalities. The former, the main manifestations of which are England and France, were led by strong middle classes which aspired and were able to bring about the cultural unity which is required for consolidating the conditions for capitalism. The latter, the main examples of which are the national movements of the southern Slavs, lack a strong middle class. Marx and Engels believed that the fact that such nationalities insisted on not assimilating played a reactionary role, because it impeded the transition to capitalism, which they considered a necessary stage in the progress of history.[6]

In making the distinction between territorial-civic nationalism and ethnocultural nationalism, Kohn and other historians and sociologists have mixed geographical, sociological, judgemental and normative parameters. Territorial-civic nationalism is Western and ethnocultural nationalism is Eastern. The former involves a strong middle class whereas the latter involves intellectuals operating in a society whose middle class is weak or which lacks a middle class. The former is progressive and is inspired by the legal and rational concept of citizenship while the latter is regressive and is inspired by the *Volk's* unconscious development. How should the normative essence of this multidisciplinary distinction be interpreted? An attempt to answer this question has recently been undertaken by the editors of a collection of essays called *Rethinking Nationalism*.[7] They characterize territorial-civic nationalism as a type of nationalism within which 'individuals give themselves a state, and the state is what binds together the nation . . . That concept of nation is subjective since it emphasizes the will of individuals. And it is individualistic since the nation is nothing over and above willing *individuals*.'[8] Voluntarism, subjectivism and individualism thus characterize this type of nationalism. Ethnocultural nationalism, which the editors choose to call *ethnic* rather than *ethnocultural*, is based on a conception of the nation as the product of objective facts pertaining to social life. These facts are that members of the nation share a common language, culture and tradition. In this type of nationalism, the nation exists prior to the state. It is also a collective that transcends and is prior to the individuals of which it consists. Objectivism, collectivism and a lack of individual choice characterize this form of nationalism.

---

[6] Ephraim Nimni, *Marxism and Nationalism* (London: Pluto Press, 1991), chap. 1.

[7] Michel Seymour, with the collaboration of Jocelyne Couture and Kai Nielsen, 'Introduction: Questioning the Ethnic/Civic Dichotomy', in Jocelyne Couture, Kai Nielsen and Michel Seymour (eds.), *Rethinking Nationalism* (University of Calgary Press, 1998), pp. 1–61.

[8] *Ibid.*, pp. 2–3.

If this formulation of the distinction is meant to convey its normative essence, and if it attempts to represent the basic principles of each family of nationalism at a level of abstraction that allows them to include their many different and peculiar descendants, then it seems to fail. The fact that the editors of *Rethinking Nationalism* have chosen to call the nationalism which historians called ethnocultural *ethnic* without the further qualification of *cultural* means that they regard common descent, or the myth of common descent (as opposed to a shared history, language and culture) as the most important component of this nationalism. This is because common descent (or a myth of common descent) is an essential characteristic of ethnic groups but not of national groups which only share a common language, religion, customs, history or ties with a particular territory (none of which is necessary).[9] Many movements of cultural nationalism did indeed grant the myth of common descent an important practical role in their agendas. This perhaps justifies calling the present nationalism 'ethnic' for purposes of historical classification. However, from the viewpoint of the normative classification, ethnicity certainly need not be the focal point of this type of nationalism. This is the case particularly if one describes the nationalism introduced by Herder, as the editors of *Rethinking Nationalism* do,[10] as ascribing importance to people's belonging to groups that share language, culture and traditions.[11] For then it is language, culture and traditions, and not common descent, which are the focal point of this type of nationalism. Similar criticism can be directed at the characterization of cultural nationalism as a nationalism that takes nations to ontologically precede their members. The editors of *Rethinking Nationalism* here attribute to the whole family a trait which characterizes only some of its members. It

---

[9] According to Max Weber, ethnic groups are defined by means of a myth of common descent. According to him these groups are 'those human groups that entertain a subjective belief in their common descent . . .' (Max Weber, *Economy and Society*, eds. G. Roth and C. Wittich (New York: Bedminster Press, 1968), p. 389). In this definition, the original meaning of the notion of an ethnic group, which according to Walker Connor is 'a group characterized by common descent' becomes a matter of subjective belief. Connor criticizes authors who used the concept of ethnicity in a broader and less accurate sense (Walker Connor, *Ethnonationalism: The Quest for Understanding* (Princeton University Press, 1994), pp. 100–3). Anthony D. Smith also acknowledges the loose meaning that ethnicity has acquired in the writings of some recent writers, but says that the myth of common descent is the *sine qua non* of ethnicity (Smith, *The Ethnic Origins of Nations*, p. 24). It is a necessary feature of ethnic groups that does not necessarily characterize national groups. (Both immigrant nations such as the United States or Canada and non-immigrant nations such as Great Britain exemplify this.) Thus, ethnic nationalism means a nationalism that grants common descent a central role in its agenda.

[10] Seymour, Couture and Nielsen, 'Ethnic/Civic Dichotomy', p. 3.

[11] F. M. Barnard (trans. and ed.), *J. G. Herder on Social and Political Culture* (Cambridge University Press, 1969).

is doubtful whether the prophets of cultural nationalism were all aware of the question of whether nations precede their members or vice versa, either morally or ontologically.[12] The editors of the collection themselves mention some contemporary writers whom they take to be advocates of cultural nationalism who hold the opposite view, namely, that at least morally, individuals are prior to their nations.[13]

The way the editors of *Rethinking Nationalism* represent the philosophical essence of territorial-civic nationalism suffers from similar drawbacks. The editors chose Ernest Renan to represent the principles of civic nationalism. Renan emphasizes that nations are a matter of 'daily plebiscite'. Yet, as the editors note, Renan himself thought that nations are also 'legacies of remembrances'.[14] This point is of great importance, because it stresses the central role which culture has in civic nationalism. Some contemporary writers, the most prominent among them being Jürgen Habermas, argue for an entirely non-cultural and purely civic conception of political communities. According to him, all that citizenries of states need to share is loyalty to a set of political and constitutional principles.[15] As long as this is intended to specify one possible conception of the social cohesion of states' citizenries, I would concur.[16] However, some writers identify this conception of social cohesion with civic nationalism.[17] They speak of civic nationalism as if it were exhausted by loyalty to a set of political principles. Habermas himself could be viewed as lending support to this usage by proposing to interpret German identity after the reunification of the Federal Republic with East Germany on the basis of such loyalty. Moreover, he suggests justifying this reunification not on the basis of restoring 'the pre-political unity of a community with a shared historical destiny', but on the basis of restoring 'democracy and a constitutional state in a territory where civil rights had been suspended . . . since 1933'.[18] Bernard Yack comments that the latter justification of the reunification of West and East Germany would have applied with equal force

---

[12] For example, I doubt whether Ahad Ha'am, the father of 'spiritual Zionism' thought about this matter.

[13] Specifically, they mentioned Tamir and Kymlicka. Seymour, Couture and Nielsen, 'Ethnic/Civic Dichotomy', sections 5 and 6.

[14] Seymour, Couture and Nielsen, 'Ethnic/Civic Dichotomy', p. 3.

[15] Jürgen Habermas, 'Citizenship and National Identity: Some Reflections on the Future of Europe', in Ronald Beiner (ed.), *Theorizing Citizenship* (Albany: State University of New York Press, 1995), pp. 255–81.

[16] See Chapter 3, pp. 91–6, below.

[17] Michael Ignatieff, *Blood and Belonging: Journeys into the New Nationalism* (New York: The Noonday Press, 1993), p. 6.

[18] Habermas, 'Citizenship and National Identity', p. 256. See also Seymour, Couture and Nielsen, 'Ethnic/Civic Dichotomy', p. 26; Bernard Yack, 'The Myth of the Civic Nation', in Ronald Beiner (ed.), *Theorizing Nationalism* (Albany: State University of New York Press, 1999), pp. 107–8.

to a possible unification of the Federal Republic with Czechoslovakia or Poland.[19] Without resorting to common culture and history, loyalty to common political principles cannot be considered nationalism, not even civic nationalism. This is demonstrated by the French and British nationalisms which are the historical paradigms of civic nationalism. These states did not merely attempt to inculcate constitutional principles, but have insisted that their citizenries, who already shared a common religion, should also share further complex cultural contours, such as language, tradition and a sense of common history and destiny.[20]

As we shall see below, the philosophical rationale of civic nationalism also implies the need to instil in citizenries of states a pervasive common culture, and not merely a constitutional culture. However, ideas of the sort expressed by Habermas, according to which the loyalty of the members of political communities to constitutional principles is sufficient for applying to them concepts which are typically associated with nationalism, were expressed as early as the seventeenth and eighteenth centuries. When they spoke of patriotism and love of one's country, many thinkers then did not necessarily refer to communities sharing specific cultures and/or territories, but rather to specific sets of political ideals. 'Patriotism is the affection that a people feel for their country understood not as native soil, but as a community of free men living together for the common good', says Maurizio Viroli when discussing the principle of patriotism as understood by Shaftesbury at the beginning of the eighteenth century, following a similar interpretation expressed by Milton in the middle of the seventeenth century.[21] However, this sort of republican patriotism, which is a form of patriotism without any cultural content, the sources of which can be found in the ancient world[22] and to which Habermas

---

[19] Yack, 'Myth of Civic Nation', p. 108. See also Maurizio Viroli, *For Love of Country: An Essay on Patriotism and Nationalism* (Oxford University Press, 1995), p. 175: 'the very story of unification seems to indicate that to be German meant something else beyond allegiance to political ideals'.

[20] On Britain see Linda Colley, *Britons: Forging the Nation 1707–1837* (New Haven: Yale University Press, 1992). On France see Eugene Weber, *Peasants into Frenchmen: The Modernization of Rural France 1870–1914* (London: Chatto & Windus, 1976). Some writers believe that the US nationalism consists in loyalty to certain constitutional principles and nothing else. See: Viroli, *For Love of Country*, pp. 178–82; Paul Gilbert, *The Philosophy of Nationalism* (Oxford: Westview Press, 1998), p. 8. However, other writers believe otherwise. See: Smith, *National Identity*, pp. 149–50; M. Lind, *The Next American Nation* (New York: Free Press, 1995).

[21] Viroli, *For Love of Country*, p. 57. Viroli discusses Shaftesbury in pp. 57–60, and Milton in pp. 52–6.

[22] Viroli, *For Love of Country*, especially chaps. 1 and 3; Charles Taylor, *Reconciling the Solitudes: Essays on Canadian Federalism and Nationalism* (Montreal: McGill-Queen's University Press, 1993), pp. 41–2; Charles Taylor, 'Nationalism and Modernity', in Robert McKim and Jeff McMahan (eds.), *The Morality of Nationalism* (New York: Oxford University Press, 1997), pp. 40–1.

wishes to return, proved to lack sufficient appeal during the last few centuries. Rousseau believed it was impossible without cultural unity.[23] At the end of the eighteenth century and during the nineteenth and most of the twentieth centuries, the belief in the necessity of cultural unity as a condition for the realization of political goals and values became prominent, both among political thinkers and political activists.[24] This unity was sometimes achieved by establishing states around groups which already enjoyed such unity. However, it was quite often achieved by assimilating culturally distinct populations. Such assimilation was in many cases brought about by methods which were far from civil and for which politicians could draw support from the writings of political thinkers.[25]

These far from civil methods with which civic nationalism was implemented brings us to another problematic characteristic which the editors of *Rethinking Nationalism* attribute to territorial-civic nationalism. They characterize this nationalism as based on the free will of the individuals who comprise the state's population. However, it is not true that all the historical instances of civic nationalism, namely, those in which the state preceded the nation, were based on the voluntary acceptance of the national culture by all the individuals living in these states. Furthermore, in many cases, states attempted to force individuals and groups to assimilate into the majority. For example, in France at the end of the nineteenth century and the beginning of the twentieth, individuals were not asked whether they accepted French culture. The United States and Australia tried to force their respective aboriginal populations that had survived genocide to assimilate into the majority. Turkey has also recently attempted to do this to its Kurd population, as have post-colonial African states with respect to their populations.[26] Moreover, the practices under discussion were not only adopted by states that are identified with civic nationalism but were also justified by many thinkers who could be associated with this type of nationalism.[27]

---

[23] Michael Walzer holds this view. According to him republican patriotism and political participation 'were the political expression of a homogeneous people' and 'rested and could only rest on social, religious and cultural unity' (Viroli, *For Love of Country*, p. 85).

[24] See the Neapolitan thinkers mentioned in Viroli, *For Love of Country*, pp. 108ff.; James Tully, *Strange Multiplicity: Constitutionalism in an Age of Diversity* (Cambridge University Press, 1995), pp. 161–2 about J.S. Mill and Lord Durham; Smith, *The Ethnic Origins of Nations*, chap. 6; Smith, *National Identity*, pp. 40–1.

[25] I already mentioned Mill in the previous note. Some texts by Hobbes and Locke could also be interpreted as implying some support for such methods (Tully, *Strange Multiplicity*, pp. 89–91).

[26] See Smith, *National Identity*, p. 41.

[27] Viroli, *For Love of Country*, pp. 85, 108ff.; Tully, *Strange Multiplicity*, pp. 161–2; Smith, *The Ethnic Origins of Nations*, chap. 6; Smith, *National Identity*, pp. 40–1; Will Kymlicka,

In contrast to other ideologies such as socialism and liberalism, one of the main sources of difficulty in characterizing the essence of both kinds of nationalism is the scant philosophical treatment it has received compared to the enormous extent of its political influence. As Benedict Anderson observed, 'unlike most other isms, nationalism has never produced its own grand thinkers: no Hobbeses, Tocquevilles, Marxes, or Webers'.[28] Isaiah Berlin made similar observations.[29] The difficulty of abstracting the tenets of nationalism is aggravated by the multitude of concrete historical manifestations of nationalist movements. An abstraction of the tenets of nationalism should not be completely divorced from these historical manifestations.

A second difficulty in abstracting the essence of both kinds of nationalism is moral. Great evils and atrocities have been committed in the name of liberal and socialist ideals, but their scope and intensity do not equal the evils and crimes that have been committed in the name of nationalist ideals. An abstraction of the tenets of nationalism based only on the texts of nationalist writers risks ignoring this particular fact about nationalism as a historical and social phenomenon. However, despite these difficulties, it seems to me that it is both possible and desirable to abstract tenets of nationalism from texts and from history that could but need not necessarily lead to its monstrous manifestations. In order to interpret the dichotomy between civic and cultural nationalism as a normative dichotomy sufficiently abstract to apply to many specific historical cases of nationalist movements and positions, it ought to be regarded as a distinction between the two positions presented at the beginning of this chapter. According to one position, the citizenries of any given state must share a homogeneous national culture in order for each state to realize political values such as democracy, economic welfare and distributive justice. According to the second position, members of groups sharing a common history and societal culture have a fundamental, morally significant interest in adhering to their culture and in sustaining it across generations.

Multicultural Citizenship: A Liberal Theory of Minority Rights (Oxford: Clarendon Press, 1995), pp. 49–74; Will Kymlicka, *Liberalism, Community and Culture* (Oxford: Clarendon Press, 1989), pp. 206–19. Kymlicka mentions Mill, Durham and Marx as thinkers who believed that people belonging to cultural minorities should be forced to assimilate.

[28] Benedict Anderson, *Imagined Communities: Reflections on the Origin and Spread of Nationalism*, revised edition (London: Verso, 1991), p. 5; Ernest Gellner, *Nations and Nationalism* (Oxford: Basil Blackwell, 1983), p. 124; Ronald S. Beiner (ed.), *Theorizing Nationalism* (Albany: State University of New York Press, 1999), pp. 2, 3, 17.

[29] Though his complaints refer not so much to the fact that nationalism has never produced its own grand thinkers, but rather to the fact that no grand thinker of the nineteenth century predicted its powerful role in twentieth-century history and politics. Isaiah Berlin, 'Nationalism: Past Neglect and Present Power', in Isaiah Berlin, *Against the Current: Essays in the History of Ideas*, ed. Henry Hardy (New York: Viking Press, 1980), p. 337.

The first position, according to which a common national culture is a condition or means for the realization of political values which neither derive from national cultures nor are intended for their protection, should be called *statist* nationalism rather than *civic*. This might help to eliminate the positive connotation of the term *civic nationalism* and would perhaps highlight the fact that the process of the national homogenization of the respective populations of nation-states has not always been justified by liberal values and has often been carried out in ways that are far from civil. With regard to the second position, I would like to suggest that it be called *cultural* nationalism rather than *ethnic*, despite the fact that in most cases, both in its historical manifestations and its philosophical versions, there are elements that pertain to ethnicity.[30] The term *cultural* would, first, serve to discard the negative connotation of the term *ethnic nationalism*. However, this form of nationalism should be called *cultural* first and foremost because any serious justifications for it focus primarily on the culture and history of the group in question. Common descent often goes together with a shared culture and history but may not be required. As noted above, however, in many cases in which cultural nationalism was historically realized, common descent turned out to be the main focus of attention. Yet this does not constitute a sufficient reason to make it the central characteristic of the class from the normative point of view.

The social and historical phenomena of civic and cultural nationalisms prompted and influenced one another. Sociologists, anthropologists and historians are divided as to which of the two preceded the other. Some scholars believe that civic nationalism came first, and was the main factor in awakening ethnocultural nationalism. Others claim that the historical process occurred in the reverse order.[31] If either of these positions is correct, then from the historical and sociological viewpoint both nationalisms share not just a name but also their origin. However, the interpretations I have offered here show why, from the normative point of view, there are in effect two different families of nationalism rather than one. Cultural nationalism, according to which members of national groups have a morally significant interest in adhering to their culture and preserving it for generations, is not concerned with how a national culture can contribute to the realization of the state's values but rather with the support which states should extend to national cultures. Statist nationalism, according to which citizenries of states must share a homogeneous national culture in order for their states to realize political values, is not concerned with the support which states should extend to national cultures.

---

[30] See also pp. 26–9 below and Chapter 2 note 27.
[31] Seymour, Couture and Nielsen, 'Ethnic/Civic Dichotomy', pp. 10–23.

Rather, it is concerned with the support which national cultures should extend to states. It is important to emphasize that calling the one type of nationalism 'cultural', and the other nationalism 'statist', does not mean that cultural nationalism is a-political, and that statist nationalism is a-cultural. Cultural nationalism is political, for it seeks political protection for national cultures. Statist nationalism is cultural, for as noted earlier with regard to civic nationalism, it requires that citizenries of states share not merely a set of political principles, but also a common language, tradition and a sense of common history. In other words, the difference between statist and cultural nationalism is not due to the fact that the former is purely political and the latter is purely cultural but rather because of their entirely different normative and practical concerns. The goal of cultural nationalism is for people to adhere to their culture. The state is a means for achieving this purpose. Statist nationalism differs in that the national culture is the means, while the realization of political values that do not have anything to do with particular national cultures is the goal. As noted above, statist nationalism could attempt to instil *a common national culture*, whether it is the culture of the citizens of the state or not. For in accordance with the logic of statist nationalism, if a common national culture is important as a means of enabling everyone's participation in government, in assuring everyone their fair share and in fostering everyone's economic welfare, then it is not important *which* national culture ultimately becomes the common culture. Of course, the culture of the majority of the state's citizens would normally be chosen as the common national culture. However, this is not because the majority has an interest in adhering to its own culture, but rather because, *ceteris paribus*, it is more efficient that the majority's culture be chosen as the one to serve the ends of the state. (However, if, for example, the minority in the state speaks a language used globally which serves as the language of science and technology and international communications, and the majority happens to speak a local and esoteric language, then it might be best for the state to organize itself around the minority culture).[32]

If the map of the world's states corresponded to that of its peoples, or if such correspondence could easily be achieved, then distinguishing between the two forms of nationalism would be of theoretical importance only and would have no practical urgency. The two types of nationalism

[32] This is in line with Mill who argues that assimilation is generally worthwhile for minorities who are members of 'one of the backward parts of the human race'. J. S. Mill, 'Representative Government', in Geraint Williams (ed.), *Utilitarianism, On Liberty, Considerations on Representative Government, Remarks on Bentham's Philosophy* (London: Dent, 1993), chap. 16. If this is valid with respect to minorities, it must also be valid for majority groups. See David Miller, *On Nationality* (Oxford: Clarendon Press, 1995), p. 86.

would complement one another. The state would satisfy the desire of all its citizens to adhere to their common national culture and would protect this culture. Similarly, the common national culture of all its citizens would benefit the state in its efforts to implement the values of self-rule, distributive justice and solidarity. This is possible, for example, in Iceland. The state of Iceland can serve all its citizens who wish to adhere to their culture and preserve it for generations, for all its citizens share one culture. At the same time, Icelandic culture can serve the state in implementing its values, for it is the only culture in that country. However, Iceland is a rare exception. The two maps, namely, that of the states of the world and that of its peoples, do not correspond in most cases. This adds practical urgency to the distinction between statist and cultural nationalism. Due to the current geodemographic conditions in most parts of the world these two types of nationalism are bound to clash, each impeding the realization of the other. On the one hand, in most places, statist nationalism has been interpreted as requiring the engagement of the state in 'nation-building', whereby many people must relinquish their own culture. In effect, this entails acting against cultural nationalism. On the other hand, acting in the name of cultural nationalism has been interpreted by many states as requiring them to assist the various cultures of their citizens and to relinquish the ideal of cultural homogeneity in the state, which, of course, counters statist nationalism. Regardless of whether it is the first route or the second that should be taken, and of whether some kind of compromise between the two should be found, it must be emphasized that cultural nationalism and statist nationalism are two distinct ideologies with different normative concerns, and that these concerns conflict with each other in most places.[33] I will return to this point, and to the way some prominent contemporary writers treat it, at the end of this chapter.

Liberal and non-liberal nationalisms

The distinction between statist and cultural nationalism and the interpretation proposed here for the main principles of these nationalisms suggest that the term *nationalism* could be regarded as a homonym for two different ideologies that lack a common normative origin and which need not necessarily be compatible in their implementation. This interpretation also allows us to see that each of them might and in fact did

---

[33] Anthony D. Smith, 'States and Homelands: The Social and Geopolitical Implications of National Territory', *Millennium: Journal of International Studies* 10 (1981), 194–5; Walker Connor, 'Ethno-nationalism in the First World', in Milton J. Esman (ed.), *Ethnic Conflict in the Western World* (Ithaca and London: Cornell University Press, 1975), p. 19.

have various descendants that are very different from one another. For example, cultural nationalism had various forms that included liberal and fascist, socialist and conservative, humanist and anti-humanist versions as well as chauvinist and egalitarian, collectivist and individualist, ethnocentric and non-ethnocentric, state-seeking and non-state-seeking forms of nationalism. As shown below, statist nationalism also had a variety of versions, though not as rich as that of cultural nationalism.

John Stuart Mill's famous arguments in chapter 16 of *Representative Government* seem to be liberal-democratic arguments for statist nationalism. Mill argues that a citizenry that shares one common national culture is necessary for representative government. 'Free institutions are next to impossible in a country made up of different nationalities. Among a people without fellow-feeling, especially if they read and speak different languages, the united public opinion, necessary to the working of representative government, cannot exist.'[34] Similarly, it could be argued that a common national culture is instrumental in furthering other aspects of democracy. It increases the probability that a greater number of citizens will be able to comprehend the issues that are on the political agenda and in this way also enhances their own informed self-rule. It is possible to show that cultural homogeneity could contribute to the realization of other state values such as distributive justice and economic welfare. Cultural homogeneity is a prerequisite or at least a facilitator for the development of the state's economy.[35] In fostering economic growth, it also bolsters material welfare. A common national culture also contributes to developing a sense of fraternity among citizens of the state, which then allows the machinery of distributive justice to operate more efficiently. On the basis of all or some of these points, liberal thinkers have concluded that states should aspire for their citizenries to have a common culture – a thesis that is the basic thesis of statist nationalism.[36]

However, it must be noted that non-liberal versions of statist nationalism are also possible and have in fact been advocated by certain thinkers. Like the liberal versions of this type of nationalism, such versions share its basic tenet, namely, that the citizenries of states must have a homogeneous national culture because such a culture contributes to the realization of certain political values. These values are not derived from specific

---

[34] Mill, 'Representative Government', chap. 16.

[35] At least it was of help during the nineteenth and early twentieth centuries under the technological conditions of the time.

[36] D. Miller, *On Nationality*, chap. 4. All these arguments may be supplemented by social and historical explanations for the emergence of the nation-state. These explanations focus on the instrumentality of national cultures to the industrial revolutions of the nineteenth century and the first half of the twentieth (Gellner, *Nations and Nationalism*).

national cultures and do not serve to protect them. Non-liberal statist nationalisms would obviously select values that are not liberal as those values to be promoted by the common national culture. Non-liberal versions of statist nationalism seem to be possible to the left of liberalism. If a common national culture is conducive to the realization of the liberal conceptions of participation in government, solidarity and distributive justice, it might also be conducive for the realization of the socialist conceptions of these values, especially the value of distributive justice.[37] Such versions of nationalism have in fact existed. The most prominent example is that of Marx and Engels mentioned earlier. Of course, these thinkers could hardly be classified as either nationalists or as supporters of the state. Their ultimate ideal is the withering of both nations and states. However, in order to facilitate the process which would lead to the withering of states and nations, Marx and Engels supported statist nationalism and repudiated cultural nationalism. They supported the cultural homogenization of states and the nationalist movements that could advance such homogenization – mainly the nationalist movements of Western Europe. They believed that these movements would pave the way to social progress by consolidating the conditions for capitalism. They repudiated the nationalist movements of small nationalities that hindered the achievement of the national homogenization of large states. In the case of such small nationalities, and for the reasons just mentioned, they held a view similar to that of John Stuart Mill, namely, that such communities should assimilate into the large national communities in whose vicinity they lived. In other words, Marx and Engels ignored or even denied the thesis according to which people have interests in adhering to their culture and preserving it for generations. For their socialist reasons, they supported the idea that the state should have one homogeneous culture.[38]

Is statist nationalism also possible to the right of liberalism? It seems clear that right-wing individualist ideologies cannot support such nationalism. Their individualism is hardly compatible with the existence of the state. They would therefore not support claims concerning the means that would enable states to achieve their goals. It would also be difficult to attribute statist nationalism to many collectivist right-wing ideologies. As repeatedly emphasized above, statist nationalism presupposes that there are political values that are not derived from the nation and are not aimed at the preservation of the nation. Many right-wing collectivist ideologies reject this presupposition. They define the state and the cultural nation

[37] Kymlicka attributes this position to D. Miller within a socialist framework (Kymlicka, *Multicultural Citizenship*, pp. 72–3).
[38] Nimni, *Marxism and Nationalism*, pp. 17–43.

in terms of each other.[39] They believe that there are no political values apart from those derived from the nation and aimed at its preservation. Therefore, it seems that the proponents of such ideologies are not likely to think of a common national culture as conducive to the implementation of political values that are *independent of the ethnocultural nation*. I am trying to be cautious here, because conservatism, for example, could in some sense espouse a statist nationalism, since one of its central values is stability. The validity of this value does not necessarily derive from the values of particular nations or the need to preserve them. Conservatives could in principle view the cultural homogeneity of the state as a means to preserve its stability and therefore justify statist nationalism. However, despite the centrality of the value of stability within conservative worldviews, and despite the possibility that this value might be valid without being derived from the nation, it is still the case that conservatives define the state in terms of the nation. The nation precedes the state, and the latter is just an organ of the former and does not exist independently of the nation.[40] Conservative nationalism is therefore mainly cultural rather than statist. Fascism is problematic from the viewpoint of the present discussion for different reasons. As it is not a very systematic and coherent ideology and because demagogy often obscures its ideological essence, it is difficult to determine if the state is conceived by fascism as a tool in the service of the nation or if the reverse is the case. However, it does not seem entirely groundless to associate fascism with a position close to that of statist nationalism.[41]

Cultural nationalism is widely believed, or has been until recently, to be possible only within collectivist right-wing ideologies. Cultural nationalism is sometimes considered a synonym for such ideologies, or at least to always coincide with them. Moreover, it was also widely believed that liberal nationalism is necessarily civic (just as it was commonly believed that civic nationalism is necessarily liberal). The association of cultural nationalism with collectivist right-wing ideologies and that of civic nationalism with liberalism is demonstrated in the introduction to *Rethinking Nationalism*, for the authors characterize civic nationalism as individualistic and as depending on people's choice, while characterizing ethnocultural nationalism as collectivist and independent of individual

---

[39] For example, Karl Schmitt defines the state as 'a specific entity of the people'. See Karl Schmitt, *The Concept of the Political*, trans. George Schwab (Chicago and London: University of Chicago Press, 1996), p. 19.

[40] On the precedence of the nation to the state according to conservatism, see Roger Scruton, *The Philosopher on Dover Beach* (Manchester: Carcanet, 1990), chap. 28.

[41] Benito Mussolini, 'Fascism', in Omar Dahbour and Micheline R. Ishay (eds.), *The Nationalism Reader* (New York: Humanities Press, 1995), pp. 224–5.

choice. The characterization of nationalism by an influential intellectual such as Isaiah Berlin constitutes another example of the view that cultural nationalism is necessarily a right-wing collectivist ideology.[42] According to Berlin, nationalism is a doctrine according to which, first, 'men belong to a particular human group . . . that the characters of the individuals who compose the group are shaped by, and cannot be understood apart from, those of the group defined in terms of common history, customs, laws, memories, beliefs, language . . . ways of life . . . ' of the group.[43] Secondly, according to nationalism, 'the essential human unit in which man's nature is fully realized is not the individual, or a voluntary association which can be dissolved or altered or abandoned at will, but a nation . . . '[44] Berlin further presents nationalism as including the view that nations are like biological organisms the needs of which constitute their common goals, which in turn are supreme goals. Berlin also maintains that according to nationalism, the most compelling reason 'for holding a particular belief, pursuing a particular policy . . . living a particular life, is that these beliefs, policies . . . lives, are *ours*', namely, they are the beliefs, policies and lifestyles of the nation to which we belong.[45]

Another example of an interpretation of cultural nationalism according to which it is necessarily anti-liberal has been provided recently in Brian Barry's *Culture and Equality*.[46] Barry characterizes cultural nationalism mainly by ascribing to it the view according to which people belonging to different nations are like animals belonging to different species. According to this view, what is common to human beings belonging to different nations is of secondary importance. The differences among them, on the other hand, are of utmost importance. This has anti-liberal implications such as that universal norms for humanity as such are either almost impossible or of negligible value, that every national group needs a different system of laws, or that national cultures must preserve their own purity because accepting influence from other cultures would not suit their members, just as the behaviour patterns that characterize one species are not necessarily appropriate for members of other species.

Berlin and Barry's characterizations are undoubtedly consistent with various ideas expressed by major proponents of cultural nationalism,

---

[42] Berlin, 'Nationalism', in Berlin, *Against the Current*, pp. 341–3.

[43] *Ibid.*, p. 341.   [44] *Ibid.*, p. 342.

[45] *Ibid.*, p. 342. It must, however, be noted that Berlin distinguishes between what he calls 'nationalism' and which he describes by means of the four characteristics listed above, and what he calls 'national sentiment', 'the pride of ancestry' (*ibid.*, p. 341), 'the need to belong' (*ibid.*, p. 338). The latter, according to him, could be perfectly compatible with liberalism.

[46] Brian Barry, *Culture and Equality: An Egalitarian Critique of Multiculturalism* (Cambridge: Polity Press, 2001).

mainly proponents of the romantic versions of cultural nationalism. Examples are inherent in Joseph de Maistre's famous saying that he had seen Frenchmen, Italians and Russians, but that 'as for *man*, I declare that I have never in my life met him',[47] and Herder's comment that 'the Arab of the desert belongs to it, as much as his noble horse and his patient indefatigable camel'.[48] There is also no doubt that if we accept these narrow characterizations of nationalism, a liberal cultural nationalism would hardly be possible. However, these characterizations should not be accepted as exclusive characterizations of cultural nationalism. Many liberals throughout the nineteenth century and the first half of the twentieth believed that people have interests in their national culture and that states must protect these interests. They did so without holding views such as that people's national affiliation explains their character, and that their national affiliation is a source for the validity of views, policies or lifestyles.[49] Furthermore, in the last few years many authors have attempted to show that certain liberal values such as freedom and autonomy can serve as bases for nationalism. Other scholars have tried to show that liberalism can be reconciled with certain theses predominantly associated with nationalism. For example, they believe that the thesis that nationality may be considered an important part of personal identity does not necessarily contradict liberalism. The same holds for the thesis that national communities are those whose members are committed to each other more extensively than to other human beings as such, or that 'people who form a national community in a particular territory have a good claim to political self-determination'.[50] The authors who defend these propositions do so without assuming the normative priority of the national group over its individual members, and without assuming the normative priority of one national group over others. On the contrary, these writers presuppose individualistic assumptions concerning the relationship between national groups and their members, and egalitarian assumptions concerning the relationship among different national groups. The broad characterization of cultural nationalism proposed here, that is, its characterization as a nationalism attributing value to groups sharing a common culture and history, to their existence across generations, and to the protection states owe to such groups, makes it possible for these attempts to be included within cultural nationalism.

[47] Joseph De Maistre, *Considerations on France*, trans. and ed. R. A. Lebrun (Cambridge University Press, 1994), p. 53.

[48] J. G. Herder, quoted in R. R. Ergang, *Herder and the Foundations of German Nationalism* (New York: Columbia University Press, 1931), p. 91.

[49] For specific examples see Kymlicka, *Liberalism, Community and Culture*, pp. 206–19; Kymlicka, *Multicultural Citizemship*, pp. 49–74.

[50] D. Miller, *On Nationality*, pp. 10–11.

Nationalisms and the state

One of the most salient characteristics of contemporary liberal writing on cultural nationalism is the complex position it takes with regard to the way in which states should protect the interests people have in their culture and in its existence across generations. Contemporary writers believe that this protection must be realized mainly by means of two types of rights: rights to self-government, and polyethnic rights. The former enable members of a national group to live their lives, at least major parts of their economic and political lives, within their national culture. Multicultural or polyethnic rights enable groups of common national origin to express their original culture while integrating with another culture and living at least their political and economic lives within that other culture. Furthermore, many contemporary liberal proponents of cultural nationalism believe that from the perspective of the interests people have in their nationality, independent statehood is the best way to realize self-government rights. However, they also believe that from a wider perspective this is not the case. These writers believe that self-government rights must at least sometimes take a sub-statist form, which is not easily reconciled with one very widely accepted characterization of nationalism. This characterization is expressed in Ernest Gellner's definition of nationalism. 'Nationalism', he says, 'is primarily a political principle, which holds that the political and the national unit should be congruent.'[51] If we take this definition seriously, then the liberal versions of cultural nationalism that I have just mentioned are not really versions of nationalism. However, Gellner seems to ignore the fact that 'nationalism' is a surname, as it were. His definition clearly applies to statist nationalism. This follows from the basic tenet of this kind of nationalism, which focuses on how cultural homogeneity is instrumental in the implementation of state values. According to statist nationalism, there is no doubt that 'the political and the national unit should be congruent'. As a matter of historical fact, it is also true that the aspiration to achieve congruence between nations and states has also characterized many movements of cultural nationalism.[52] Ultimately, however, Gellner's definition is

---

[51] Gellner, *Nations and Nationalism*, p. 1. See also Anthony D. Smith, *Nations and Nationalism in a Global Era* (Cambridge: Polity Press, 1995), p. 112; John Breuilly, *Nationalism and the State*, 2nd edition (Chicago University Press, 1992), p. 2; Eli Kedourie, *Nationalism*, 4th, expanded edition (Oxford: Blackwell, 1993), p. 1.

[52] 'There were national movements which developed the goal of independence very early – for example, the Norwegian, Greek or Serb. But there were many more that came to it rather late, and in the exceptional circumstances of the First World War – among them the Czech, Finnish, Estonian, Latvian and Lithuanian movements...' See Miroslav Hroch, 'From National Movement to the Fully-Formed Nation: The Nation-Building

misconceived, for it is a fact that not all national movements and not all versions of cultural nationalism aspired to bring about the convergence of national and political units.[53] Otto Bauer's theory of nationalism, and Ahad Ha'am's 'spiritual Zionism', are prominent examples.[54] Moreover, if my abstraction of the normative tenets of cultural nationalism correctly represents its normative concerns, then state-seeking need not be an essential component of this nationalism. This is so because institutional arrangements can hardly be regarded as defining features of political moralities. Such arrangements depend on the basic values of these moralities on the one hand, and on the moral and empirical constraints imposed by the circumstances within which these values have to be implemented, on the other hand. Since such circumstances are fluid and could change over time, the institutional arrangements following from a given political morality could also change. If this is correct, the principle of the congruence between states and national groups cannot be a defining feature of nationalism as a political morality.[55] At most, it could follow from the values of nationalism under certain empirical conditions. The contemporary authors who defend principles that are associated with cultural nationalism, and who do not insist on the convergence between state and nation, can thus be said to concur with earlier exceptions to the general aspiration that national movements did have to bring about the convergence between state and nation. We thus need to give up the claim that cultural nationalism necessarily seeks this convergence. Within cultural nationalism one must distinguish between state-seeking versions, according to which nations must aspire to have a state of their own, and

Process in Europe', in Geoff Eley and Ronald G. Suny (eds.), *Becoming National: A Reader* (New York: Oxford University Press, 1996), p. 76.

53 Kymlicka, *Liberalism, Community and Culture*, pp. 206–19; Kymlicka, *Multicultural Citizenship*, pp. 49–74. For doubts similar to those expressed here in relation to the centrality ascribed by Gellner to the state in his definition of modern nationalism, see also Taylor, 'Nationalism and Modernity', p. 35.

54 On Bauer see Nimni, *Marxism and Nationalism*, chaps. 5–7. On Ahad Ha'am see Steven J. Zipperstein, *Elusive Prophet* (Berkeley: University of California Press, 1993).

55 See Brubaker, 'Myths and Misconceptions', pp. 235–41 for arguments demonstrating that nationalism, not just as a political morality, but also as a social-historical movement, is not in principle state-seeking. Let me also continue the quote from Hroch, 'From National Movement to Nation', p. 76, the beginning of which appears above: 'the Slovene or Byelorussian – did not formulate [the goal of independence] even [in the exceptional circumstances of the First World War]. The Catalan case provides a vivid example of the way in which even a powerful national movement need not make the demand of an independent state.' See also Smith, *National Identity*, p. 74; Jeff McMahan, 'The Limits of National Partiality', in McKim and McMahan (eds.), *The Morality of Nationalism*, pp. 108–9; Stephen Nathanson, 'Nationalism and the Limits of Global Humanism', in McKim and McMahan (eds.), *The Morality of Nationalism*, pp. 177–8; Judith Lichtenberg, 'Nationalism, For and (Mainly) Against', in McKim and McMahan (eds.), *The Morality of Nationalism*, p. 165.

non-state-seeking versions, which at most regard states as desirable, but not as necessary.

Incidentally, I would like to note that certain writers call the state-seeking nationalism in this latter distinction *political nationalism* while referring to the second nationalism as *cultural*.[56] From the viewpoint of the distinction I have suggested here between statist and cultural nationalism, both the state-seeking and the non-state-seeking versions of nationalism are cultural rather than statist versions of nationalism, for they are concerned with people's interests in adhering to their culture and preserving it for generations. The difference between them lies in the nature of the political measures they require for the protection of these interests. As noted earlier, the distinction between what I have called *statist nationalism*, and *cultural nationalism*, is a more fundamental one. It is a distinction not between two descendants of one family, but rather between two families whose normative genealogies cannot be traced to one source. Cultural nationalism is concerned with the services that states can and ought to provide for nations, while statist nationalism is concerned with the services which a common national culture could provide for states.[57]

What has been said so far could and perhaps should also be clarified in terms of the ideal of the nation-state. Both families of nationalism have produced this ideal. Yet it is important to stress that the notion of the nation-state has an entirely different meaning within each of them. According to statist nationalism, the ideal of nation-states is that sovereign political units should strive not only for legal but also for cultural unity. According to cultural nationalism, the ideal of nation-states means that

---

[56] On Alfred Zimmern, see Kymlicka, *Multicultural Citizenship*, p. 207. See also Avishai Margalit, 'The Moral Psychology of Nationalism', in McKim and McMahan (eds.), *The Morality of Nationalism*, pp. 74–87, and my remarks on Tamir on pp. 32–4 below. Within the Zionist movement there was some debate between what was called Political Zionism and Ahad Ha'am Spiritual Zionism. Most adherents of the former aspired to establish a Jewish state in Palestine. The latter was content with much less, and is an example of what Margalit calls cultural nationalism. However, within the framework of the distinction between statist nationalism and cultural nationalism elaborated in this chapter, most brands of Zionism belong to cultural nationalism rather than statist nationalism. Most of them were motivated by the interests that Jews had in adhering to their culture and in preserving it for generations. However, it should be noted that in some sense Zionism had some characteristics of statist nationalism. For example, with respect to the various cultural groups of Jews that immigrated to Israel, the state of Israel has acted in accordance with statist nationalism, trying to mould them into one culture.

[57] The confusion is even further amplified by the fact that some writers use the terms political nationalism or cultural nationalism not to designate the distinction between *state-seeking* and *non-state seeking* nationalism, but rather the distinction between civic nationalism and cultural one (Hutchinson, *The Dynamics of Cultural Nationalism*).

cultural groups should have states of their own.[58] One could hold the latter position because it is a means for realizing the former position. In other words, it is desirable that sovereign political units should also be cultural units. However, this is not the only way to realize the latter ideal. 'Nation-building' and 'melting pots' are also means to turn sovereign political units into cultural units. In any case, those who subscribe to the thesis of cultural nationalism merely because it is a means for implementing the ideal of statist nationalism, obviously subscribe to statist nationalism rather than to cultural nationalism. Only those who adhere to the ideal of the nation-state for the reason that this is the proper way to protect people's interests in their own national culture, subscribe to it as a position of cultural nationalism. As noted, not all the manifestations of cultural nationalism subscribe to this ideal. At least in some cases, some of them support the ideal of multicultural states.

Nationalisms and ethnicity

I have so far sub-divided cultural and statist nationalisms, first, according to the political ideologies with which they were or could be associated, that is, liberal ideologies and those ideologies to the left and to the right of liberalism, and secondly, according to their stance towards the state. It might also be useful to comment on the different classifications of the various nationalisms according to their position on ethnicity. Again, it is important first to distinguish between historical and sociological questions concerning the actual motivation of any particular national movement, and philosophical questions concerning what is implied by or is compatible with the basic normative positions of statist nationalism on the one hand, and cultural nationalism on the other. In considering the historical and sociological issues regarding the relationship between nationalism and ethnicity, three questions must be discerned. The first issue is motivation: Was a given national movement or a particular nationalist thinker actually motivated by the goal of preserving the culture of a given ethnic group? Or were they perhaps motivated by the goal of preserving a given ethnic group in the sense of keeping its blood 'pure'? The second question concerns the composition of a given population led by a

---

[58] The ideal of the nation-state has perhaps a third meaning according to which the world should be organized so that its sovereign units are not the size of entire empires or continents. This position could result from attempts to implement one or both the other positions. This is because most national groups are not the size of entire continents or empires, and because nation-building is a project which has a better chance of succeeding if it does not cover territories of such size. However, the present position can also be held for reasons which have nothing to do with the other two positions.

particular nationalist movement: Did this population consist of one particular ethnic group, or did it consist of various ethnic groups? The third
question concerns the conception of the nation held by a given nationalist movement or ideology. Is it a purely ethnic conception according to
which all the members of the ethnic group and only the members of that
group belong to the nation, and according to which anyone who does
not belong to the ethnic group cannot become a member of that nation?
Many movements of civic nationalism, which is the historical counterpart
of the normative position I have here called statist nationalism, were in
fact mainly motivated by the wish of certain ethnic groups to preserve
their culture. In order to do so, they engulfed other ethnic groups that
either did or could have threatened their culture, or which they perceived
or pretended to perceive as threatening their culture. It is obvious that
the ethnic groups leading these nationalist movements did not in fact
preserve the so-called purity of their blood, and it is also obvious that
they did not and could not have held an ethnic conception of the nation.
None the less, it seems that despite the fact that these nationalist movements looked and behaved like civic nationalisms, the desire to preserve
the culture of their dominant ethnic group could have been a major force
motivating them. All these facts are irrelevant from the viewpoint of the
philosophical-normative counterpart of civic nationalism, namely, statist
nationalism. As a philosophical position, this type of nationalism is purely
non-ethnic, first, because questions concerning the actual motives of
those who subscribed to it, and concerning the composition of the population to which it was applied, are philosophically irrelevant. Secondly,
though it is logically compatible with an ethnic conception of the nation,
this philosophical position does not logically entail it. As noted earlier,
this nationalism focuses on the fact that the homogeneous cultural composition of the citizenries of states is instrumental for the realization of
political values which have little to do with the preservation of cultural
groups, certainly not with the preservation of ethnic groups. In states in
which the citizenries are not ethnically homogeneous, statist nationalism
can be applied by melting different ethnic and cultural groups into one
cultural group, as has indeed been the case in many countries.

The situation regarding cultural nationalism is somewhat different. As
an *historical movement* it was clearly associated with ethnicity both in the
sense that many movements of cultural nationalism were actually motivated by the desire to preserve the culture or even 'pureness' of the
blood of a particular ethnic group, and in the sense that many held an
ethnic conception of the nation. However, can cultural nationalism as a
normative position imply or be compatible with ethnicity in the latter sense,
that is, as subscribing to an ethnic conception of the nation? The answer

to this question depends on the particular justifications one provides for the fundamental thesis underlying this type of nationalism, that is, the thesis that people have interests in adhering to their cultural group and in preserving it for generations. Cultural nationalisms which are to the right of liberalism could perhaps regard the common culture of an ethnic group as of secondary importance compared to the common ancestry or kinship ties that supposedly exist among their members, and could be motivated mainly by the interest in the continued existence of this ethnic group as such. Nationalisms that fit Isaiah Berlin's characterization of nationalism seem to be of this sort and would probably hold a purely ethnic conception of the nation. However, as seen above, a nationalism need not carry all the characteristics Berlin attributes to it in order to be cultural. Cultural nationalism is characterized by ascribing importance mainly to the interests people have in the common language, traditions and history of their national groups. Some national movements adhering to this ideology were ethnic at least in the factual sense. That is, they were the national movements of cultural groups whose members did indeed share or regard themselves as sharing a common ancestry. Yet, could they also *justify* the attribution of practical importance to ethnic descent?

There are three ways in which ethnicity might have practical consequences. First, it could serve as a basis for excluding people who share the culture but not the ethnicity of the group. Secondly, it could serve as a basis for including people who share the ethnicity but not the culture of the group. Thirdly, it could serve for both of the above purposes, as it did in Germany until recently. On the one hand, Germany did not allow the naturalization of its residents of Turkish origin whose culture was German in the sense that they had grown up and lived in Germany all or most of their lives. On the other hand, it allowed the naturalization of ethnic Germans who had not really been part of the German culture and who had immigrated to Germany from various places such as Romania, Russia, the Baltic states, Central Asia and Caucasia. The question of whether cultural nationalism as a normative position can allow the use of ethnicity for such purposes depends, as noted above, on how the thesis that people have interests in adhering to their culture and preserving it for generations is justified. For example, if this thesis is based on the idea of a national culture as an intergenerational project, or on the idea that people's individual endeavours have meaning mainly within their cultures, it is possible that descent will have some limited role to play within cultural nationalism. This is so if one ascribes moral value to intergenerational relations, that is, if one subscribes to views such as that people have some obligations to their ancestors, or that they might legitimately consider themselves as having such obligations. If their ancestors' endeavours were realized within a given culture, this might constitute a reason to allow them to join this culture in order to take part in the continuation and/or memory of these endeavours. In Chapter 5, which deals with nationalism and immigration, I shall argue that this might sometimes constitute a reason to consider ethnic origin in order to include members in the group (but not for the purpose of excluding anyone).[59] The tree-diagram

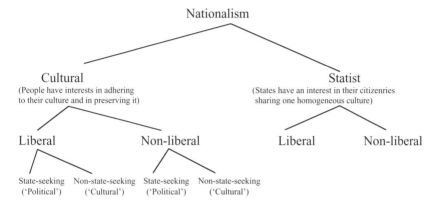

above summarizes the distinctions outlined above. To ensure the simplicity of this diagram, I have avoided including all the possible divisions of the various nationalisms according to their stance on ethnicity. The categories of cultural and statist nationalism were only sub-divided into 'liberal' and 'non-liberal', though many other divisions such as 'humanist – non-humanist', 'socialist – non-socialist', etc., could be added. Since the purpose of this book is to examine a liberal version of cultural nationalism, this necessitates the 'liberal – non-liberal' distinction. In light of the distinctions made so far and as indicated in the diagram, a liberal version of cultural nationalism should be distinguished both from forms of liberal nationalism which are not cultural but statist, and from cultural nationalisms which are not liberal.

Some sociological and normative theories of nationalism

Some sociologists of nationalism, such as Ernest Gellner and Charles Taylor, as well as some writers who have dealt with normative aspects of cultural nationalism such as Yael Tamir and David Miller, do not make the distinction between cultural and statist nationalism or at least refrain

---

[59] See also Chapter 2 note 27.

from giving it its proper weight. In my opinion, this causes some confusion in their theories. Despite the fact that Gellner attempts to account for the rise of nationalism without distinguishing between statist nationalism and cultural nationalism, he inadvertently provides explanations for the rise of two kinds of nationalism. In addition to his definition of nationalism as 'primarily a political principle, which holds that the political and the national unit should be congruent', and which I have already referred to above, he attributes additional meanings to the nationalist principle. In one place he notes that nationalism means 'the organization of human groups into large, centrally educated, culturally homogeneous units . . .'[60] A significant part of his sociohistorical explanation for the rise of nationalism is actually an account of the rise of statist nationalism. According to Gellner, modern, post-agrarian, industrial mass societies require cultural homogeneity[61] within units that are neither too small nor too large.[62] According to him, the need for such homogeneity brought about the rise of nationalism in the modern age. This is a sociohistorical explanation for the need for cultural homogenization and 'nation-building'. Significant parts of Gellner's book address this sort of nationalism.[63] However, in other parts of the book, he describes nationalism as the cultural and subsequent political awakening of ethnic groups that have yet not joined the process of integrating into the population of the state in which they live.[64] Such separatist groups first develop their own cultures and then aspire to lead their economic and political life within this culture.[65] Gellner is correct in that he does not base his explanations for the cultural and political awakening of these groups only on the need that industrialized societies might have for cultural homogeneity. If such a need were the sole underlying factor, the members of these groups would have assimilated into the culture of the population of the region and would not have awakened to their own culture. He explains their cultural awakening mainly by noting the fact that members of such groups have what he calls 'entropy-resistant

---

[60] Gellner, *Nations and Nationalism*, p. 35.   [61] *Ibid.*, p. 39.

[62] *Ibid.*, p. 35.   [63] *Ibid.*, pp. 19–52.

[64] *Ibid.*, pp. 19ff., mainly pp. 53–62, 88–109.

[65] Gellner calls the first stage *cultural nationalism* and the second *political nationalism*. By *cultural nationalism* he refers to just one stage in the development of national movements which, in my distinction, are movements of cultural nationalism, that is, the stage in which groups of intellectuals awaken the culture of their ethnic group. They develop its language, construct its museums, compose its poetry and symphonic music, initiate its archaeology, etc. With regard to *political nationalism*, Gellner means the stage where ethnic groups who have already awakened to their culture, start aspiring to a state. According to Gellner, this stage is necessary in order for movements to qualify as nationalist movements. As I suggested above, this stage is a possible but not necessary stage in the development of movements that are movements of cultural nationalism (in the sense I suggested), even if they aspire to a state.

attributes', genetic attributes such as skin colour, or psychological attributes such as cultural or historical or religious identity.[66] Gellner does not discuss the normative issues that pertain to elements of a group's identity. That is, he does not discuss the question of whether it is good that such attributes, as opposed to genetic attributes, are entropy-resistant.[67] He also refrains from explaining the fact that in some groups (e.g., the Catholics of Northern Ireland) such religious identity serves to block entropy and prevent assimilation, while this does not apply in the case of other groups (e.g., the Frisians in Holland).

In an article that refers extensively to Gellner's explanations, Charles Taylor attempts to answer the above question.[68] Like Gellner, he does not distinguish between statist and cultural nationalism. However, this distinction is implicit in his arguments. He says that homogeneity is a desideratum of the modern state and in this context quotes Gellner's thesis that this 'inescapable imperative eventually appears on the surface as nationalism'.[69] The nationalism in question is what I have termed *statist nationalism*, that is, nationalism in the sense of states aiming for the cultural homogeneity of their populations. However, Taylor later presents Gellner's account of the other nationalism, that is, the aspiration of people to preserve their own culture:

If a modern society has an 'official' language, in the fullest sense of the term – that is, a state-sponsored, -inculcated, and -defined language and culture, in which both economy and state function – then it is obviously an immense advantage to people if this language and culture are theirs. Speakers of other languages are at a distinct disadvantage. They must either go on functioning in what to them is a second language or get on an equal footing with speakers of the official language by assimilating. Or else, faced with this second distasteful prospect, they demand to redraw the boundaries of the state and set up shop in a new polity/economy where their own language will become official. The nationalist imperative is born.[70]

This explanation is clearly a sociological explanation of nationalism of the sort I have termed *cultural*, a nationalism of groups whose members are motivated by a desire to adhere to their own culture, to preserve it and to protect it politically.[71]

---

[66] Gellner, *Nations and Nationalism*, pp. 70–2.
[67] Though he does seem to demonstrate empathy towards such groups in one place, where he notes that 'changing one's culture is very frequently a most painful experience'. *Ibid.*, p. 40.
[68] Taylor, 'Nationalism and Modernity', pp. 31–55.   [69] *Ibid.*, p. 33.
[70] *Ibid.*, p. 34.
[71] In one place, Taylor comes close to making the distinction between statist and cultural nationalism: 'there is thus a sort of dialectic of state and nation. It is not just that nations strive to become states; it is also that modern states, in order to survive, strive to create national allegiances to their own measure.' *Ibid.*, p. 41.

According to Taylor, Gellner's account of cultural nationalism is unsatisfactory because, as noted above, it does not account for the fact that some groups assimilate while other groups fight in order to continue adhering to their culture.[72] Taylor therefore tries to provide such explanations himself, adducing the need people have for respect and recognition. However, regardless of whether or not Taylor's sociopsychological explanation is indeed adequate,[73] it must be noted that his discussion pertains to what I have called cultural nationalism, rather than to statist nationalism which was the main concern of Gellner's explanation.

Several contemporary advocates of what is called 'liberal nationalism', such as Yael Tamir and David Miller, also do not stress the distinction between cultural and statist nationalism.[74] Although they distinguish between liberal and non-liberal types of nationalism, they do not, in my opinion, pay sufficient attention to the distinction within liberal nationalism between its cultural and statist versions. They both seem to treat the arguments presented above as arguments supporting statist nationalism and those presented in support of cultural nationalism as arguments for one type of liberal nationalism. They thus seem to ignore the fact that these arguments actually support two distinct types of nationalism with distinct ideals that in reality often collide with one another.

Tamir does this in a less direct way than Miller. In the opening pages of the chapter on national self-determination in her book *Liberal Nationalism*, she notes that 'it is the cultural rather than the political version of nationalism that best accords with a liberal viewpoint'.[75] By this, she does not seem to mean that what I termed cultural nationalism (namely, the thesis that people have interests in adhering to their culture) accords with liberalism better than what I referred to as statist nationalism (namely, the thesis that states have an interest in the cultural homogeneity of their populations). Nor does she seem to mean that national cultures are not

---

[72] *Ibid.*, pp. 34, 43.
[73] Will Kymlicka rejects this explanation. He thinks, and I agree completely, that claims to recognition and for respect do not explain people's desire to adhere to their culture. According to him, the reverse is true. People's desire to adhere to their culture (because it is a component of their identity), explains why ignoring this desire offends people's dignity and respect. He says: 'It is true that nationalist movements involve a demand for recognition and employ the rhetoric of dignity. But the rhetoric of dignity is used to express a prior attachment to their language and culture; it is not an explanation of that attachment. To suggest, as Taylor seems to do, that people generate an attachment to their language and culture as a way of protecting their dignity seems deeply implausible to me' (Will Kymlicka, 'The Sources of Nationalism: Commentary on Taylor', in McKim and McMahan (eds.), *The Morality of Nationalism*, p. 62).
[74] They were recently followed in this respect by Margaret Moore's *The Ethics of Nationalism* (Oxford: Oxford University Press, 2001).
[75] Yael Tamir, *Liberal Nationalism* (Princeton University Press, 1993), p. 58.

entitled to political protection. She appears to mean only that the right to national self-determination need not necessarily be realized by means of independent statehood. That is, national self-determination could be realized as a more limited right within a state or a different sort of political organization that is not a nation-state.[76] Put in the terms I used above, she implies that a non-state-seeking form of nationalism is more compatible with the liberal point of view than a state-seeking form of nationalism. However, in a chapter called 'The Hidden Agenda', Tamir supports what she calls liberal nationalism by arguing that several significant practices that are current in liberal states can hardly be explained without the presupposition of certain nationalist tenets.[77] She observes that while liberalism celebrates personal choice, liberal states regard membership as a matter of birthright. She points out the fact that 'liberals believe that individuals owe political loyalty to their own government – as long as it acts in reasonably just ways – rather than to the government that is demonstrably the most just of all'.[78] Finally, she observes that 'the liberal welfare-state distributes goods among its own citizens, while it largely ignores the needs of nonmembers'.[79] According to Tamir, the only way to account for these practices is to ascribe a hidden agenda to liberalism. According to this hidden agenda, nationalism is an integral part of liberal political morality. Moreover, Tamir not only posits nationalist assumptions as the only possible explanation for actual practices of liberal states, but also seems to subscribe to these assumptions and to believe that they provide acceptable justifications for these practices. She notes that the liberal welfare state's conception of distributive justice 'is only meaningful in states that do not see themselves as voluntary associations but as ongoing and relatively closed communities whose members share a common fate'.[80] Similarly, she justifies the prevailing practices in liberal states regarding political obligation and membership. Even if all this is correct, which to a certain degree it probably is, can it lend support to the liberal nationalism on behalf of which Tamir has advocated a non-state-seeking form of nationalism rather than a state-seeking form? It seems that the answer to this question is negative because the realization of the non-state-seeking liberal nationalism would lead to the creation of states that would not consist of only one culturally homogeneous community. How would it be possible in such states to realize the welfare state's conception of distributive justice with regard to all their

---

[76] *Ibid.*, chaps. 3 and 7.
[77] *Ibid.*, chap. 6; Yael Tamir, 'Pro Patria Mori!: Death and the State', in McKim and McMahan (eds.), *The Morality of Nationalism*, pp. 227–41.
[78] Tamir, *Liberal Nationalism*, p. 117.
[79] *Ibid.*   [80] *Ibid.*

citizens? How would *all* the citizens of these states have political obligation towards their state? Tamir's arguments for the claim that liberal states
require the cultural homogeneity of their citizenries in order to account
for some of their major practices seem to express an idea typical of statist
nationalism. On the other hand, her claim that non-state-seeking nationalism better accords with liberalism than state-seeking nationalism makes
sense within the context of implementing the ideals of cultural nationalism in the present geodemographic conditions of the world. The latter
group of considerations rightfully lead Tamir to argue against a state-
seeking nationalism. However, the former considerations, which follow
from statist nationalism, commit her to the opposite position. Tamir does
not seem to have noticed this conflict.[81]

Another advocate of liberal nationalism who fails to distinguish between statist liberal nationalism and cultural liberal nationalism is David
Miller. Nationalism for him means a doctrine, one of the defining principles of which is the principle of self-determination, which he takes
to mean that political units (paradigmatically, states) coincide with national boundaries.[82] In the chapter in his *On Nationality* dedicated to
national self-determination, he supports this principle with arguments
which show how states could be instrumental for nations and arguments
which demonstrate how nations could be instrumental for states. Miller
recognizes the fact that in the geodemographic condition of the world
these two groups of arguments may in many cases lead to practical conflicts. He therefore proposes that these conflicts be reconciled in ways that
would make it possible to regard states as nation-states while simultaneously giving normative expression to the fact that they are multicultural.
For example, in any state where particular ethnic groups live within another group whose culture constitutes the dominant culture of this state,
he believes that a common cultural core should be created while allowing
the various communities within the state to preserve some components of
their respective cultural identities. I would concur with this suggestion as
long as it is intended to express the idea that the conflict between statist
nationalism and cultural nationalism – that is, between the interest states
have in the cultural homogeneity of their populations and the interests

---

[81] From all this it does not follow that what Tamir calls the hidden nationalist agenda
of liberal states does not provide some support to certain aspects of nationalism. The
fact that systems of distributive justice in liberal states discriminate in favour of their
members, and the fact that liberal states regard membership as a matter of birthright
rather than choice, weakens the objections which liberals could otherwise naturally make
against the particularistic and non-voluntary aspects of nationalism. However, this does
not mean that the particularism and non-voluntarism of liberal states necessarily coincide
with those of cultural nationalism.

[82] D. Miller, *On Nationality*, p. 82.

individuals have in adhering to their original culture – could ultimately be resolved as a compromise between the two positions rather than resulting in a victory of one and the defeat of the other. I shall return to this issue in further detail towards the end of Chapter 3. However, if one accepts that the arguments for cultural nationalism and the arguments for statist nationalism need to be reconciled by means of compromise, then one in effect presupposes that these arguments support distinct normative positions, and that these positions cannot always be fully realized simultaneously. Miller, however, seems to present these arguments as supporting one sort of nationalism.[83]

For example, one of Miller's arguments for ensuring that political units coincide with national boundaries pertains to the support that the state's machinery can lend to the determination and implementation of the particularistic duties of mutual concern which are assumed to exist among members of national communities.[84] Another argument for ensuring that political units coincide with national boundaries is that the particularistic obligations for mutual concern, which supposedly exist among members of one culture, may assist the state in fulfilling its duty to implement distributive justice among its citizens. Like J. S. Mill and Yael Tamir, he holds the presumably correct view that people are more prepared to assist one another, and perhaps sacrifice part of their income for one another, if they have some feeling of fraternity with one another. However, the hybrid multicultural nation-state that Miller envisages can achieve neither of these goals. On the one hand, it cannot assist many dispersed cultural groups that might exist at any particular moment in defining the specific meaning of their obligation of mutual concern. On the other hand, it cannot assist multicultural states in smoothly fulfilling their duty to apply distributive justice to their citizenries. Consider the Ukrainian ethnic minority living in Canada. As Ukrainians, they supposedly owe particularistic obligations of mutual concern to other ethnic Ukrainians all over the world, either in the Ukraine or outside it.[85] However, these particular

---

[83] See also: Chaim Gans, 'A review of David Miller's *On Nationality*', *European Journal of Philosophy* 5 (1997), 210–16; Brendan O'Leary, 'Insufficiently Liberal and Insufficiently Nationalist', in Brendan O'Leary (ed.), 'Symposium on David Miller's *On Nationality*', *Nations and Nationalism* 2/3 (1996), 444–51; Seymour, Couture and Nielsen, 'Ethnic/Civic Dichotomy', section 5.

[84] D. Miller, *On Nationality*, p. 83. This should be read with chap. 3 of *On Nationality* in mind which is devoted to arguing for the thesis that national communities constitute ethical communities, namely, communities whose members owe more extensive duties to each other than to other human beings in general.

[85] Anthony D. Smith calls the sociological epiphenomenon of the present normative phenomenon 'vicarious nationalism'. For the display of this phenomenon with regard to the Ukrainian minority in Canada and other similar cases see Smith, *The Ethnic Origins of Nations*, pp. 151–2.

obligations cannot assist the state of Canada in implementing distributive justice among its citizens, most of whom are not of Ukrainian descent. Nor can Canada's state machinery lend support to the determination and implementation of the particularistic duties of mutual concern that supposedly exist among members of the Ukrainian nation. Of course, Canada could do what statist nationalism has always done and initiate the creation of a new nation. It could do this by using the means characteristic of traditional statist nationalism, namely, 'building' a new nation by 'melting' the existing ones of which it consists into one entity. It could also use more refined means such as suggested by Miller, namely, creating a multicultural nation-state sharing a common cultural core.[86] The ethnic Ukrainians living in Canada could be part of this nation, as in fact they are. However, this nation is entirely irrelevant to their obligations of mutual concern as Ukrainians, and these obligations could hardly serve to support the Canadian government in implementing distributive justice among its citizens. In other words, the cultural nationalism of the Ukrainians would hardly be used by the state of Canada in fulfilling its duty to implement distributive justice among its citizens, and Canadian statist nationalism would hardly assist Ukrainians in the determination and implementation of their particularistic duties of mutual concern. A possible cultural nationalism of the Ukrainian ethnic minorities living in Canada and a possible statist nationalism of the state of Canada do not complement one another. They do not aim at the same goal and cannot form arguments for the same thesis. One of them must withdraw if the other is to win, or else a compromise between the two forms of nationalism is required. A compromise would in effect mean that each of the two forms of nationalism would give up the fulfilment of some of its aspirations.

But could they give up these aspirations? If the answer is affirmative, then to what extent and in what ways? In order to answer this question, it is important to investigate the origins of these aspirations and to see what human interests and values justify each of them. The discussion of cultural nationalism must be separated from the discussion of statist

---

[86] D. Miller is not unaware of the fact 'that citizenship is frequently extended to residents of the state who acknowledge a different nationality from the majority' (D. Miller, *On Nationality*, pp. 59, 72, 73). As noted above, he discusses ways to solve the problems such situations create for multicultural states. However, it should be noted that he does not discuss ways to solve the problems that such situations create for dispersed nations. In any case, the main point I wish to stress here is that despite his awareness of the fact of multiculturalism, D. Miller discusses nationalism, and especially the ideal of the nation-state, as if it were one ideal with two sorts of justifications. He does not regard it as a homonym for two different ideals that sometimes support each other but which usually collide.

nationalism. It is important not to blur the distinction between them and present them as if they were just two justifications for one thesis as Tamir, Miller and some other writers have done. That this must be done in order to attain a lucid and systematic understanding of nationalism can perhaps further be demonstrated by resorting to some elementary practical philosophy. Consider the following example of the principle that condemns lying. This principle could be presented as one principle supported by two sorts of justifications: justifications of self-interest and moral justifications. But surely our understanding of this principle would be enhanced if we investigated it separately as a moral principle and as a principle of self-interest. As a principle of self-interest, the principle against lying is only a rule of thumb. There are sometimes conclusive reasons of self-interest to lie that may conflict with moral reasons not to lie. We must thus enquire whether morality sometimes allows us to lie for reasons of self-interest. Otherwise, one cannot know if the moral principle against lying makes some allowances in those cases in which self-interest requires lying. It is therefore necessary to enquire separately into the principle of not lying as a moral principle. There are analogous reasons for separating the discussion of the principle that political units should coincide with national boundaries as a principle of cultural nationalism on the one hand, and as a principle of statist nationalism on the other. The reasons for separating the discussion of cultural nationalism generally from statist nationalism are even stronger. Even if, as Miller believes, cultural nationalism includes the principle of the coincidence of political units with national boundaries, it includes it only as a derivative principle and as one among a number of other principles. For statist nationalism it is, as implied earlier, the sole and defining principle.[87]

The purpose of this book is to discuss the possibility of advocating cultural nationalism within the framework of liberalism and not to discuss statist nationalism within liberalism. The fact that this is the book's purpose does not mean to imply a dismissal of the normative concerns which motivated liberal statist nationalism. The values for which it is important that states should be more than merely legal and administrative units, the values for which states need to enjoy also at least some degree of cultural unity, are far from unimportant. However, it is clear that in the geodemographic conditions of the world these values cannot be implemented

---

[87] The principle that political units should coincide with national boundaries forms a part of cultural nationalism only as one possible interpretation of a more abstract principle according to which the interests people have in living their lives within their culture and in sustaining this culture for generations should be protected politically. It forms a part of cultural nationalism as one among other principles such as the adherence thesis and historical thesis. For a detailed discussion see Chapter 2.

by providing a state for each and every cultural group which would consist of all and only the members of that group. As noted earlier, such a solution could simultaneously satisfy both cultural and statist nationalism. However, the moral as well as other costs required for implementing this solution (some of which will be discussed in the following chapters) would be unreasonable. In this state of affairs, both cultural nationalism and statist nationalism must make compromises regarding the optimal realization of their aspirations. Some of the aspirations implied by each of them must be relinquished. One of my main goals in the following chapters is to show that the maximum that cultural nationalism can expect to achieve in the current geodemographic conditions of the world could be considered as a sufficient minimum for a liberal version of this kind of nationalism. Such a minimum could be compatible with various solutions for the normative concerns of statist nationalism. I shall discuss these solutions briefly in Chapter 3.

2   The liberal foundations of cultural nationalism

According to cultural nationalism, members of groups sharing a common history and culture have a fundamental, morally significant interest in adhering to their culture and in sustaining it for generations. It further maintains that this interest should be protected by states. I shall examine three theses included in this statement. The first, the *adherence thesis*, asserts that people have a basic interest in adhering to their national culture. The second thesis is *historical*. It concerns the basic interest people have in recognizing and protecting the multigenerational dimension of their culture. The third thesis, a *political* one, holds that the interests people have in living their lives within their culture and in sustaining this culture for generations should be protected politically. Some contemporary writers who support a liberal version of cultural nationalism do so by arguing that people have an interest in culture mainly because it is a prerequisite for their freedom and also because it is a component of their identity.[1]

In the first part of this chapter I shall examine to what extent these arguments succeed in providing a foundation for the adherence thesis. Various critics have totally rejected the freedom-based argument as a possible basis for this thesis. After expressing some reservations concerning this total rejection of the freedom-based argument, I will discuss the identity-based argument at some length. I shall claim that this argument provides a basis for the adherence thesis independently of the freedom-based argument. However, the identity-based argument is more forceful as an argument for the adherence thesis in conjunction with the freedom-based argument.

Yet, neither the freedom-based argument nor the identity-based argument provides an adequate basis for the historical thesis. This will be shown in the second part of the chapter. I shall then offer a third argument that could serve to support the historical thesis. According to this

---

[1] Kymlicka, *Liberalism, Community and Culture*; Kymlicka, *Multicultural Citizenship*; Joseph Raz , *Ethics in the Public Domain: Essays in the Morality of Law and Politics*, revised edition (Oxford: Clarendon Press, 1994), chap. 8.

argument, people undertake projects, express the essence of their personalities and live their lives on the assumption that their lives have meaning and some impact on the world outside them which exists independently of their own existence. The world in which people's lives have meaning and where their endeavours leave their mark is for most people that of their own culture. For a great number of people living today, this culture is their national culture.

If it is true that the role of politics is to protect basic human interests, then the political thesis according to which people's interest in adhering to their national culture and in its existence for generations must be protected politically follows from the first two theses. Advocates of the liberal version of cultural nationalism believe that this third thesis must be realized by means of rights to self-government, representation rights, rights to cultural preservation and polyethnic rights. Rights of the first three types are intended mainly to enable members of a national group to govern themselves and live major parts of their lives (including major parts of their economic and political lives) within their culture. Multicultural or polyethnic rights enable groups of common national origin to express their original culture while integrating with another culture and living at least their political and economic lives within that other culture. In the third part of this chapter, after further clarifying these types of rights, I shall show that the very distinction between the first three types (namely, self-government, representation and cultural preservation rights) on the one hand, and the fourth type (namely, polyethnic rights) on the other, cannot be adequately justified by means of the freedom- and identity-based arguments. Such a distinction can only be justified if these two arguments are conjoined with the third endeavour-based argument.

The adherence thesis

The freedom-based argument

According to the first thesis of cultural nationalism, people have an interest in adhering to their own national culture. Certain advocates of this nationalism support the present thesis primarily by resorting to a freedom-based argument. This argument invokes the indisputable claim that in order to exercise freedom and shape their lives autonomously, people need materials of some sorts: ways of life and the elements which comprise them. Other than what they require for their very basic bodily needs, they need private and public institutions, occupations, etc. in order to fulfil their material and spiritual desires. Since all of these can only be provided by specific cultures, people do indeed have an interest in culture.[2] At least within liberalism, this interest must be considered fundamental, for it is a precondition for liberalism's most precious value, namely, freedom.

Many critics have pointed out that this argument cannot provide a plausible basis for cultural nationalism, because it rests on people's interest in having *some culture or other*.[3] According to these critics, this culture does not necessarily have to be their own national culture.[4] If this criticism is valid, it seems that the freedom-based argument falters at the very first hurdle confronting proponents of cultural nationalism. It fails to justify the first and rather modest thesis of this nationalism – the adherence thesis. However, the present criticism is only partially valid. People's freedom-based interest in some culture or another cannot in and of itself justify choosing their own national culture for the purpose of implementing this interest. However, people's freedom-based interest in a culture may retrospectively become an interest in their own national culture if there are valid independent reasons for choosing this culture.

Consider the right to private property. Like the interest in culture, one of its possible justifications revolves around its contribution to human freedom. Acknowledging a general right to private property on this basis, however, does not resolve issues concerning its concrete regulation. Since the world is full of potential objects to which one could claim property rights and since one can attain possession or control of them in a variety of ways, we must establish which ways of gaining possession or control would indeed link one to these objects through property rights. The resolution of these issues is not inherent in the freedom-based right to private property. Rather, they must be sought in other standards that are external to

---

[2] Kymlicka, *Liberalism, Community and Culture*; Kymlicka, *Multicultural Citizenship*; Raz, *Ethics in the Public Domain*.

[3] Avishai Margalit and Moshe Halbertal, 'Liberalism and the Right to Culture', *Social Research* 61 (1994), 504; Jeremy Waldron, 'Minority Cultures and the Cosmopolitan Alternative', *University of Michigan Journal of Legal Reform* 25 (1991–92), 751–93; John Danley, 'Liberalism, Aboriginal Rights and Cultural Minorities', *Philosophy and Public Affairs* 20 (1991), 172.

[4] Some have argued that the freedom-based interest people have in a culture should be implemented through the national culture of the majority in the state in which they live (Danley, 'Liberalism, Aboriginal Rights, Cultural Minorities'). Other commentators have argued that the freedom-based interest in culture should be concretized through a collage of fragments taken from many local cultures, a collage that each person should construct for himself (Waldron, 'Minority Cultures'). There could be other cosmopolitan alternatives, such as a homogeneous unified culture for all human beings, an invented culture or one of the existing cultures; perhaps a culture with which more people are already familiar to some degree, or a culture which in practice already exceeds any other culture in serving the needs of science, technology, transportation, international relations, etc. An example of such a culture would be one conducted in the English language.

freedom.[5] Economic efficiency may require first occupancy and then acquisition in accordance with existing legal rules. The value of equality may demand that a lottery be held every generation. If one of these standards is stronger than the other, then the particular objects people acquire by the method that this standard requires, become their private property. Once this happens, it would be correct to say that people's freedom-based interest in private property supports and lends force to their ownership over these particular objects.[6] I would thus agree with critics of the attempt to ground cultural nationalism in the freedom-based interest in culture since freedom, in and of itself, cannot initially serve as a basis for people's interest in their own specific national culture. However, if there are good reasons for implementing people's freedom-based interest in a culture specifically by means of their own national culture, then freedom retrospectively becomes one of the bases for people's interest in their own culture.

One reason for realizing people's freedom-based interest in culture specifically by means of their own national culture is that the fruits of people's endeavours are normally produced and continue to exist within their own national culture. I shall discuss this when dealing with the historical thesis. Another justification is that people's national culture forms a central component of their identity. Will Kymlicka, a prominent proponent of the freedom-based argument, presents a version of this justification. According to him, the empirical fact that most people are in

---

[5] Once there is a general justification for people's interest in property, first occupancy (and other forms of acquisition regulated by law) could serve as a key for assigning particular objects of property to particular persons. See Jeremy Waldron, *The Right to Private Property* (Oxford: Clarendon Press, 1988), pp. 284–6. It should also be noted that the rights to both property and culture could be justified in ways inherently containing answers to issues relating to their concretization, e.g., if we ground the right to private property on historical arguments, then the answer to the question 'What property belongs to whom?' is provided by the very justification of the general right to private property. The same holds with regard to cultural rights. If they are based on the interest people have in components of their identity, as I suggested earlier (and as I shall demonstrate below in greater detail), then the issue of their concretization is resolved by this justification itself. It does not require the formulation of principles of concretization as an external appendix. This is different in the case of the freedom-based right to culture. Here we need auxiliary principles of concretization.

[6] To illustrate the present point, consider an example from everyday life: I have an urgent desire to see a movie in order to relax. There are two possible movies showing, both of which I would probably find equally refreshing. However, one of them will also contribute something to some work I have to prepare for tomorrow. This fact explains why I ultimately choose to go to that film rather than the other. Yet from the moment I have made my choice, my reason for going to this particular film is no longer just because it will contribute something to my work, but also, perhaps primarily, in order to relax. Even though my desire to relax was not my reason for going to this film in particular, from the moment I have a reason to see that film rather than any other, my desire to relax turns into a reason for seeing it. It is perhaps the main reason I have for seeing it.

effect attached to their own culture can serve to link people's freedom-based interest in *any* culture, and the need to concretize this interest by means of their *own* national culture. However, apart from playing this auxiliary role within the freedom-based argument, identity can also serve as an independent basis for the adherence thesis. In contrast to Kymlicka, some authors do indeed regard it as such.[7] For reasons that will become apparent later, I will also present identity as an independent basis for the adherence thesis.

The identity-based argument

People have a fundamental interest in adhering to components of their identity. They have an interest in being respected for their identity and the components that comprise it, or at least in not suffering humiliation or alienation because of it. The normative claim that people have a fundamental interest in adhering to components of their identity pertains to those components *to which they want to adhere*. For example, a person who wants to convert to a different religion has no interest in adhering to his original religion. However, should he want to adhere to his old religion, his interest in doing so must be considered fundamental. It is important to stress this, because desires involving objects in which people have fundamental interests must be given special weight in determining the contours of the political order. In this respect such desires are very different from desires involving objects in which people do not have fundamental interests (for example, the wish to spend a vacation on one particular island as opposed to another island). The question of what makes interests fundamental is dependent on a philosophical theory of human nature. However, with regard to the interest under consideration here, namely, people's interest in adhering to components of their identity, the assumption that it is fundamental has ample support. It is supported by the fact that many people regard themselves as having this interest, especially in relation to their cultural identities.[8] I will therefore

---

[7] Kymlicka, in *Liberalism, Community and Culture*, appears to have justified cultural rights exclusively on the basis of freedom. However, in *Multicultural Citizenship* he also stresses the auxiliary role played by identity. Several of his critics (Charles Taylor 'The Politics of Recognition', in A. Gutmann (ed.), *Multiculturalism: Examining the Politics of Recognition* (Princeton University Press, 1994), pp. 40–1, Margalit and Halbertal, 'Liberalism and the Right to Culture') consider identity the exclusive basis for cultural rights. Others mention both values without clarifying the relationship between them. See, e.g., Joseph Raz and Avishai Margalit, 'National Self-Determination', in Raz, *Ethics in the Public Domain*, chap. 6; Raz, *Ethics in the Public Domain*, chap. 8; Tamir, *Liberal Nationalism*, pp. 35–6.

[8] See Kymlicka, *Multicultural Citizenship*, pp. 86–91 for a detailed account of the fact that many people are deeply attached to their cultural identities.

make this assumption without any further discussion of its philosophical background. My central concern here is not with the metaphysical complexities of the interest that people have in components of their identity, but rather with the limitations of this interest as a basis for cultural nationalism. It is such a basis because people's culture – just like their gender and sexual preference – is a component of their identity, and because the culture of most people living today is a national (or quasi-national)[9] culture. Most people living today therefore have an interest in adhering to their nationality.

According to this argument, the interest people have in their nationality is not a direct interest. It is mediated by the interest they have in components of their identity. The present identity-based interest in nationality need not necessarily be permanent. As many observers indeed maintain, it is possible that nationality will one day cease to be a central component of most people's identity. Even today, it is not an interest shared by all people. An increasing number of people are cosmopolitan; that is, their cultural identity is a collage of elements from more than one culture. The interest under discussion is therefore not only an indirect one, but may also be temporary. Furthermore, it is not universal. The above points could be regarded as drawbacks preventing the present argument from serving as a basis for cultural nationalism, or as justifications for dismissing cultural nationalism as a transient ideology. Proponents of this approach would claim that although people might have a fundamental interest in their culture as a component of their identity, it is not essential that they specifically have national cultures. The fact that the culture of most people living today is a national culture is merely accidental. It has applied to the majority of people only for the last hundred years, and will probably cease to be true for most of them within another hundred years. It does not form a part of human nature and thus should not affect the contours of the political order.

This approach to the limitations of the identity-based argument seems to me to be misconceived. The fact that people's identity-based interest in their nationality is not a direct interest, that it is not universal despite its prevalence, and that it may also be temporary, need not diminish the degree of seriousness with which it should be treated. People's interests in their national identities should be treated seriously even if it were true that such identities are undesirable and that it would have been better if most people's cultural identities were cosmopolitan rather than national.

---

[9] The concept I have in mind here is that of 'pervasive culture' in the sense used by Raz and Margalit (Raz and Margalit, 'National Self-Determination'). This includes not only national cultures but also ethno-religious (like Hinduism) or tribal, pervasive cultures.

Jeremy Waldron holds the latter view. According to him, national cultural identity is not merely a non-essential characteristic of human nature, but also undesirable.[10] He believes that it should be exchanged for cosmopolitan identities. He therefore concludes that nationalism should be totally rejected.

I will discuss Waldron's thesis in detail in Chapter 6. However, let me anticipate it and note at this point that to claim, as he does, that national identity need not be taken seriously since it is not an essential feature of human nature, is tantamount to claiming that because A's love for B is not an essential (but merely accidental) feature of A, it need not be taken seriously. Similarly, to claim as Waldron does, that because national identity is not a desirable component of identity, it need not be given any political weight, is tantamount to claiming that if A's love for B is undesirable, it need not be respected. However, if love is a fundamental and important human need, if it constitutes part of what makes life worthwhile, and if a person satisfies this need by loving a specific person, the proper way to respect this human need in this particular case is to respect the love he/she has for that specific person. Even if there were good reason to believe that it would have been preferable for him to love someone else, this would not automatically justify dismissing this love.[11] The same could be said with regard to identity. If people's interest in the components of their identity is a basic human interest, and if the concrete cultural identity of most people living today is national, then, even if it were the case that it would be preferable for people to be cosmopolitan, this cannot automatically justify the claim that the concrete cultural identity that most people in fact have, namely, national identity, need not be taken seriously. Moreover, to argue that the prominence of national cultures is transient because they are accidental and temporary components of identity is tantamount to making the same claim with regard to love. Most loves are in fact accidental, and many loves do indeed fade, and hence are temporary. Nevertheless, this cannot serve to justify the dismissive attitude implied in describing such loves as ephemeral.

Of course, interpreting the interest people have in adhering to their culture as analogous to their interest to be with their loved ones imposes

---

[10] Waldron, 'Minority Cultures'.

[11] Of course, there could be cases in which such a transition would be justified. However, such justification is not automatic. In other words, the fact that a particular love is undesirable is not *sufficient* reason not to respect it. However, love can be not simply undesirable, but destructive. In such a case one might possibly be justified in not respecting it. In order to justify disrespect for national identities because they are national, one must do more than simply say, as Waldron does, that cosmopolitan identities are better. One must also show that national identities are destructive as such; e.g., by arguing (in the Marxist vein), that national consciousness is a false consciousness.

certain limits on the demands that could be voiced in the name of this interest. For example, under this interpretation, cannibals could not use their interest in adhering to their culture in order to justify continuing with the acts that their cannibalism demands. Muslims could also not require adherence to the practice of issuing and carrying out *fatwas*, and Jews could not continue slaughter practices considered by many to be inhumane. Such demands could perhaps have been made on the basis of the adherence thesis if it were interpreted in terms of the romantic version of cultural nationalism. As noted earlier, according to the romantic version of nationalism, people are to their cultural group as animals are to their species. If bears cannot thrive unless they behave as demanded by their carnivorous nature, then perhaps cannibals cannot flourish without eating their fellow humans. However, it is doubtful whether it is desirable that such demands be voiced in the name of the adherence thesis. Attempts to resort to the adherence thesis in order to preserve customs such as cannibalism, executing heretics and the inhumane slaughtering of animals must be rejected. The above limited interpretation of the adherence thesis according to which the interest people have in their culture and its traditions is an interest based on the fact that for many people living today this culture is a significant component of their identity allows us to conceive of the adherence thesis as a principle which only produces a prima facie obligation to permit people to adhere to their cultural traditions and customs. Some traditions and customs (such as cannibalism and the execution of heretics) are *ab initio* not supported by this prima facie obligation, in the same way that murder and torture contracts are void *ab initio* and are not supported by the prima facie obligation to keep contracts. In other cases, the prima facie obligation to permit the adherence to customs and traditions conclusively supports allowing people to observe such customs, as, for example, in the case of Muslim women wearing the *hijab* in Western countries. In contrast, in some cases such as that of permitting immigrants to speak their original language when serving customers in their new country the adherence thesis does not provide such conclusive support. It is overridden by other obvious considerations.[12]

---

[12] Brian Barry has recently attempted to ridicule cultural nationalism and the adherence thesis by presenting them as entailing support for practices such as cannibalism and *fatwa*. Barry does this by creating the impression that the romantic version of cultural nationalism, according to which 'people can flourish *only* within their ancestral culture' (Barry, *Culture and Equality*, p. 263 – italics mine, C.G.) is the only existing version of cultural nationalism. He cites writers who seem to hold this view (Taylor and Tully, in Barry, *Culture and Equality*, pp. 282–3 and 261–3), and ignores writers who, like himself, believe that the adherence thesis (in his terminology, 'It is part of my culture') constitutes a basis only for a prima facie obligation to allow the preservation of cultural practices (e.g., Kymlicka, *Multicultural Citizenship*, pp. 35–44; Joseph H. Carens, *Culture,*

Cultures of origin versus *cultures of people's endeavours*

As noted above, the identity-based argument provides a basis for the adherence thesis *inter alia* because of the fact that the cultural identity of most or at least a great number of people living today is indeed national. However, the claim that the cultural identity of most people living today is national suffers from an ambiguity that contaminates the identity-based adherence thesis. In referring to people's national culture, one could in many cases mean more than one culture. This culture could be their culture of origin, but could also refer to the culture within which they have lived for a greater part of their lives, that is, where the major part of their endeavours have taken place. While for most people this is one and the same culture, for a great many people these may be two distinct cultures. Does the identity-based interest of the latter group in their culture refer to their culture of origin, or does it refer to the culture of their endeavours? This question is of practical significance at least for those who do not treat identity as an independent basis for the adherence thesis, but rather as the factor which serves to link people's freedom-based interest in *any* culture to their own national culture.

Although Kymlicka does view identity in this way, he fails to specify whether people's freedom-based interest in culture should be concretized by the culture in which their endeavours were undertaken or by their culture of origin.[13] This casts a shadow on the distinction he draws between self-government and polyethnic rights. From the viewpoint of the freedom-based argument, should people of particular national origin who spend the greater part of their active lives within another culture

---

Citizenship and Community: A Contextual Exploration of Justice as Evenhandedness (Oxford University Press, 2000), chap. 6). Moreover, Barry tries to create the impression that the adherence thesis can make a practical difference only if it is interpreted in terms of romantic nationalism (Barry, *Culture and Equality*, pp. 260–1). However, he implicitly seems to hold the more modest interpretation I have given here to this thesis. He smuggles this more limited interpretation into his arguments when defending the need to accommodate the practice of Pakistani women who wear *hijabs* when employed in department stores in London. According to him, this practice needs to be accommodated because it has a symbolic meaning for these women (Barry, *Culture and Equality*, p. 59). If the covering of heads by Pakistani women has a symbolic meaning, it must be a symbol of something, which is probably their commitment to their cultural identity. In expecting this commitment to be respected, Barry evidently presupposes that people have an interest in adhering to components of their identity. This presupposition, however, is not the assumption that 'people can flourish *only* within their ancestral culture', rather, it is the assumption that *part* of the well-being of people is tied up with their adherence to components of their identity, and the additional claim that for many people, their ancestral culture is in fact an important component of their identity.

[13] Kymlicka, *Multicultural Citizenship*, pp. 84–93. Some of Kymlicka's arguments (especially those relying on Rawls) support the culture of people's endeavour, but his conclusions seem to focus on their culture of origin.

be granted polyethnic rights? Their freedom-based interest in culture is actually materialized, *ex hypothesi*, by the culture within which they have been living. Thus, the freedom-based interest in culture cannot serve as a basis for any rights concerning their culture of origin. On the other hand, if people are entitled to concretize their freedom-based interest in culture through their original culture, why should they be granted only polyethnic rights, as argued by Kymlicka, rather than self-government rights? By their very definition, polyethnic rights cannot assist them in realizing their freedom, either fully or even to a substantial extent.

A complete justification of the distinction between polyethnic and self-government rights must wait until the historical thesis and people's interests in their endeavours are addressed in the next section. However, part of this justification is already pertinent at this point. It has to do with the fact that identity can serve as an independent basis for the adherence thesis, and not merely as a link between people's freedom-based interest in a culture and the need to concretize this interest by means of their own national culture. If identity serves as an independent basis for the adherence thesis, it explains how people who actually exercise their freedom outside their original culture do not need self-government rights within this culture, but nevertheless have interests concerning this culture which justify polyethnic rights. The fact that people have interests in adhering to components of their identity, and the fact that people's culture is such a component, explains why they are entitled to polyethnic rights in the first place, despite the fact that these rights have nothing to do with their freedom. The fact that they do not need their original culture for their freedom explains why they are entitled *only* to such rights, and not to self-government rights. In contrast, when people's original culture is not distinct from the culture of their endeavours, then their freedom-based interest in culture should be concretized by means of this culture. This is why they should then be granted rights to self-government and not just polyethnic rights. Hence, it seems that the ambiguity of the notion of 'people's national culture' does not preclude the possibility of basing the adherence thesis on identity. To the contrary, it serves to justify the distinction between the two routes for implementing this thesis, that of polyethnic rights on the one hand, and of self-government rights on the other.

I hope to have shown so far that the identity-based interest people have in their culture, and sometimes also the freedom-based interest people have in a culture, support the first thesis of cultural nationalism – the adherence thesis. Unlike Kymlicka, I have presented identity not merely as a link between people's freedom-based interest in a culture and the need to concretize this interest by their own national culture. Rather, I have presented identity as a basis for a separate argument which opens with a normative premise asserting the interest people have in adhering to components of their identities. On the other hand, and unlike some of Kymlicka's critics, I believe that the freedom-based argument can be used to support people's interest in adhering to their national culture. In conjunction with the identity-based argument it can sometimes provide a basis for people's interest in a more extensive adherence to their national culture, which would have to be protected not merely by polyethnic rights, but by self-government rights.

However, the fact that the identity-based argument, and in many cases also the freedom-based argument, support the adherence thesis does not render these two arguments sufficient foundations for cultural nationalism. In order to serve as bases for this type of nationalism, these arguments must also support the historical thesis, according to which people's interests in their national culture is not only in their own adherence to this culture but also in its continued existence. As I shall show in the following section, they do not succeed in doing this.

The historical thesis

Freedom, identity and the historical thesis

History is an inherent part of the essence of national groups and of nationalist ideologies. Nationalists attempt to secure not only the future existence of their nations but also their past.[14] When they have no such past, they invent one. This certainly applies to nationalist movements that have been politically active throughout the last two centuries. However, the historical dimension of national groups also forms an integral part of the normative theory under discussion here. As we shall see below, the political rights invoked by advocates of the liberal version of cultural nationalism in order to protect national groups are *inter alia* intended to protect their historical existence.

Can the freedom and identity-based interests people have in culture provide a basis for this historical dimension? It seems that the reply to this question is negative. As demonstrated earlier, the freedom-related

---

[14] As the opening lines of this chapter indicate, the notion of a national group relevant for the purposes of this chapter is a cultural notion. According to this interpretation, nations are the main cases of groups that Raz and Margalit (Raz and Margalit, 'National Self-Determination', p. 133) call 'encompassing groups', or groups sharing what Kymlicka calls 'a societal culture' (Kymlicka, *Multicultural Citizenship*, p. 76). This conception of a nation is different from an ethnic conception, according to which members of a nation must also share a common ancestry. However, it is not entirely unrelated to ethnicity, for, at least empirically, it so happens that ethnic groups usually share a societal culture so that many cultural nations are also ethnic groups or have such groups as their core. See also Chapter 1, note 9.

reasons failed to support the thesis that people have an interest in adhering to their own national culture. However, even if they did provide a basis for that thesis, they would have done so because such a culture is necessary in order to provide the members of a given culture with the materials to construct *their own* lives. Without these materials only *their own* freedom is hollow. This does not entail that their culture must be preserved over generations so that their grandchildren and great-grandchildren can also live their lives within it.[15] The same line of reasoning applies to the identity-based argument. People have an interest in adhering to their national culture because it is a component of their identity. However, the only conclusion that follows from this is that *they themselves* (i.e., the particular people involved) must be allowed to adhere to it. The fact that people's national culture constitutes their cultural identity does not mean that it also constitutes the cultural identity (as distinguished from the ethnic identity) of their descendants. This also applies to Kymlicka's version of the identity argument. His claim that it is a fact that people are attached to their culture does not explain why the freedom-based interest of their descendants in a culture should also be realized by this culture. At the time when people make claims under the historical thesis, their descendants (at least from the third generation onwards) are obviously not attached to any culture since they do not yet exist. When they are young, children's cultural identity may be shaped independently of their origins. They can be socialized within a culture other than that of their parents.[16]

I do not, of course, intend by this to suggest that children whose parents already live their lives within a given culture should be torn away from this culture. Raz elaborates this point: 'A policy which forcibly detaches children from the culture of their parents not only undermines the stability of society by undermining people's ability to sustain long-term intimate

---

[15] Taylor's criticism of Kymlicka's freedom-based argument oscillates between the present point and another criticism: 'Kymlicka's reasoning is valid (perhaps) for *existing* people who find themselves trapped within a culture under pressure, and can flourish within it or not at all. But it doesn't justify measures designed to ensure survival through indefinite future generations. For the populations concerned, however, that is what is at stake' (Taylor, 'The Politics of Recognition', p. 41). The first part of this quotation focuses on the fact that Kymlicka takes the weakness characteristic of North American minorities to be the reason for choosing their own culture and not the culture of the majority among which they live as the culture for concretizing their freedom-based interest in culture. However, the latter part of the criticism seems to refer to the fact that the freedom-based argument cannot justify measures intended to ensure the existence of groups into the future. It should be emphasized that this latter criticism is valid even if the rationale for actualizing people's freedom-based interest in culture by means of *their own and no other* culture derives not from their special weakness, but from their identity-based ties with that culture.

[16] D. Miller, *On Nationality*, pp. 141–3, believes that this is even desirable.

relations, it also threatens one of the deepest desires of most parents, the desire to understand their children, share their world, and remain close to them.'[17] I agree with this point, but I would like to emphasize that it cannot be helpful in providing a basis for the historical thesis. To fulfil the desire of parents to understand their children and to share their world, it is enough that their children live within the framework of their culture while they are also being acculturated within another culture. After they have been raised within this other culture, these children can, as they are growing up, fulfil their wish as parents to share in their own children's world, through that other culture. The desire of parents in each generation to share the world of their children can in this way be fulfilled. However, the fulfilment of this desire in this manner also implies the extinction of cultures every third or fourth generation and has little to do with the aspiration of cultures to endure historically.

As noted above, this aspiration is part and parcel of cultural nationalism, including its contemporary liberal versions. This is demonstrated by the political protection that the proponents of this nationalism require for it. First consider self-government rights. They are intended *inter alia* to facilitate the historical continuity of the national group and to enable the members of the present generation of a national group to determine the culture of that group's future generations. As we have just seen, people's freedom and identity-based interests in culture cannot justify granting them the power to determine their group's future. One might go even further with regard to freedom. Not only can it not serve as a basis for allowing people to determine what the culture of the future generations will be, but in many cases it can serve as an argument against allowing them to do just that. In the case of many national groups – those whose culture does not subscribe to pluralism as a value, or which have backward economies – allowing the members of the current generation to determine the culture of future generations means allowing them to impair the freedom and welfare of the members of those future generations. Bringing children up within that culture means constraining their upward mobility, that is, preventing them from attaining lifestyles that offer more cultural richness as well as material wealth. The freedom of members of the present generation, and the fact that their culture is a component of their identity, can in no way begin to justify such potential harm. This is so especially since this harm is neither required for securing the identity or for realizing the freedom of the members of the present generation. Therefore, in cases of this sort, present generations should not be allowed to prevent future generations from being educated in a manner that would

---

[17] Raz, *Ethics in the Public Domain*, p. 178.

facilitate their integration into other cultures. Yet, denying them that power means denying them one of the central components and expressions of self-government, namely, the right of a public to educate its younger generation.

All of the above applies even more forcefully to polyethnic rights. On the one hand, the liberal proponents of these rights do not regard them as temporary rights.[18] On the other hand, it is their intention that polyethnic rights enable members of groups sharing a common cultural origin to express their original culture in certain limited ways while mainly living their lives within a different culture. Members of such groups are expected to live in this way. This means that even the first generation – not merely the second and subsequent generations – is expected to integrate into the other culture. In any case, the cultural identity of the second and subsequent generations of such groups is not only that of their original nationality, but mainly the nationality of their surroundings. Why, then, should polyethnic rights be multigenerational? If plausible justifications for the historical dimensions of self-government and polyethnic rights could be found, perhaps they are to be found not in people's freedom and identity-based interests in culture but in a different interest.

People's interest in the meaningfulness of their endeavours

To a great extent, people do what they do under the assumption that it could have an impact in the world outside them. The hope for such an impact constitutes part of the meaningfulness of people's endeavours. The thesis that people engage in action in order for it to be significant and leave a mark in the world outside them has a long philosophical tradition. Various critics of psychological hedonism, from Samuel Butler to Robert Nozick, have given it much prominence.[19] In the name of this thesis, they reject the proposition that people do everything they do in order to experience pleasure and to avoid pain. According to this view, at least some of the acts that people perform and some of the projects they undertake are performed and undertaken in order to bring about certain results in the world.

---

[18] Kymlicka, *Multicultural Citizenship*, p. 31.

[19] See Henry Sidgewick, *The Methods of Ethics* (London: Macmillan, 1962), pp. 44–5, who refers also to Samuel Butler; Robert Nozick, *Anarchy, State and Utopia* (Oxford: Basil Blackwell, 1974), pp. 42–4. As I do below, Brian Barry takes this a step further, saying that '[if] it is reasonable to include in interests having certain things happen . . . while one is alive, it seems strange to draw the line at one's death' (Brian Barry, 'Self-Government Revisited', in David Miller and Larry Siedentop (eds.), *The Nature of Political Theory* (Oxford: Clarendon Press, 1983), p. 151).

Moreover, people strive to achieve ends or fulfil ideals not only in the world outside themselves, but also in the world beyond their own lifetimes. They want their existence and endeavours to have significance after their own death. This common aspiration was expressed by Plato in *The Symposium* and by Fichte in his *Addresses to the German Nation*.[20] This aspiration is not merely common but to a great extent follows from people's desire that their actions have significance in the world outside them. This is because the world in question must be a world whose existence is independent of their own existence. Any uncertainty as to whether that world will exist when they themselves no longer do can undermine their belief in their ability to undertake meaningful projects during their own lifetime. They naturally wish that the endurance of this world should somehow be secured.

Furthermore, people's ambition to undertake projects that will endure beyond their lifetimes also deserves moral support, at least from the standpoint of moral perfectionism. The hope that their projects or a memory of their endeavours will persist after they themselves have perished stimulates people to perform to the best of their ability. A state of affairs that does not allow people to harbour this hope hampers their creative capacity. It leaves them with a narrow spectrum of alternatives, comprising hedonism on the one hand, and despair on the other.

How can all the above serve as a basis for cultural nationalism and its historical dimension? The answer to this question derives from the fact that major parts of the lives and endeavours of many people living today mainly take place and have significance within their national cultures. A great many or perhaps most people living today live and act within the framework of national languages, practices, customs and memories tied with their national or quasi-national cultures. Cultural frameworks of these sorts do not only provide them with materials to construct their lives and concretize their freedom, and do not only give meaning to the options with which they provide people, as Kymlicka and others have emphasized,[21] but also form the sphere where the fruits of human

---

[20] Johann Gottlieb Fichte, *Addresses to the German Nation*, ed. George A. Kelly (New York: Harper Torchbooks, 1968), p. 113.

[21] Kymlicka seems to imply a right to cultural context. Cultures according to him (and also according to Raz) give meaning to the options with which they provide people. Giving these options meaning is what makes them options. Kymlicka (e.g., Kymlicka, *Multicultural Citizenship*, p. 83) and Raz (e.g., Raz, *Ethics in the Public Domain*, pp. 176–7) are very clear about this. However, they do not seem to emphasize the fact that, for many people, their cultures are the only frameworks within which their endeavours have a chance of leaving a mark, of benefiting others or of being continued and remembered by others. It is this component of the meaningfulness of human endeavour that I emphasize here as providing a basis for the historical thesis.

freedom take root, and where individuals' endeavours have a chance of leaving their mark. Such cultural frameworks offer the prospect that others might benefit from their endeavours or continue them.[22] People living their lives, expressing their personalities, or pursuing their projects within the frameworks of such cultures thus have a fundamental interest in the existence of such cultures and in their endurance, independently of their own existence.[23] The extinction of these cultures would mean not only the loss of their endeavours, the memory of these endeavours and whatever made them meaningful.[24] Such extinction casts a shadow on the value of their endeavours at the time they are undertaken and the meaningfulness of their lives when lived.

One could question the claim that many of the endeavours of a great many people living today are mainly meaningful within the frameworks of their national cultures. One would argue that many people act within extra-national, universal frameworks, such as science, technology, art or religion and many more act within sub-national frameworks. The latter act within practices such as traditional crafts, family businesses and similar specialized and localized enterprises. Their endeavours are meaningful within such frameworks and not within those of the national cultures within which they live. Therefore, if we protect the historical existence of the latter, then we must also protect the historical existence of the former. However, protecting the continued existence of practices such as goldsmithing, monastic orders, family farming or riverside laundering does not make sense. According to this line of argumentation, the same holds for the continued existence of national cultures.

There is some validity to this objection. It is true that many people's endeavours take place within specific practices and that many such practices do eventually die out. It is also true that sad as this might be, supporting the continued existence of such practices would be a mistake. However, all this does not entail that supporting pervasive or societal cultures is also a mistake. There are important differences between the two cases which

---

[22] For the distinction between projects undertaken in order to benefit future generations, and projects presupposing continuity along generations, see Lukas H. Meyer, 'More Than They Have a Right to: Future People and Our Future Oriented Projects', in Nick Fotion and Jan C. Heller (eds.), *Contingent Future Persons* (Dordrecht: Kluwer Academic Publishers, 1997), pp. 137–56.

[23] In his description of the nationalism of modern industrial societies, Ernest Gellner says of their members: 'The limits of the culture within which they were educated are also the limits of the world within which they can morally and professionally, breathe' (Gellner, *Nations and Nationalism*, p. 36). This description, which was of the industrial societies in the latter part of the nineteenth century and the first half of the twentieth, is also true with regard to many present societies and people.

[24] On the fear of the descent to oblivion as part of the explanation for nationalism, see also Benedict Anderson, *Imagined Communities*, p. 36; Smith, *National Identity*, pp. 160–1.

justify treating them differently. One such difference arises from the fact that many specific practices are components of societal cultures. Their disappearance, unlike the disappearance of the societal culture of which they are a part, does not necessarily mean the complete loss of the endeavours of those who engaged in them. Such endeavours are part of the overall cultural fabric to which the practice belonged and have meaning within it. Those who live within that societal culture benefit from it, since it contributed to a practice that was part of their culture.

Another, perhaps more important difference between societal cultures on the one hand, and specific practices on the other, is that many specific practices may become obsolete with changing social, technological or other circumstances. It is not very useful today to continue working on family farms or to do one's laundry in the river. The continued existence of specialized practices is conditional upon their usefulness. Societal cultures have no specific practical purpose and cannot be rendered obsolete by changing circumstances. The question of their continued existence is not at all subject to considerations of usefulness. Furthermore, the fact that unlike pervasive cultures, many specialized practices do have a practical purpose, means that if they are dying out due to obsolescence, this need not devalue the meaningfulness of the endeavours of those who participated in them earlier. Comfort of this sort is unavailable to those people whose endeavours lose their significance because the culture within which they were pursued has become extinct. Thus, unlike the case of specialized practices, it seems that in the case of pervasive cultures people's interest in the meaningfulness of their endeavours can be invoked to support the historical thesis.

Some additional points pertaining to the historical thesis

People's interest in the meaningfulness of their endeavours connects the historical thesis with the value of self-respect. One of the conditions for self-respect is that what people do can be done with the hope that it has some reasonable prospect of permanence. Insecurity with regard to the continued existence of their culture undermines the possibility of such hopes.[25] The present claim is not that people need to be assured that

---

[25] This is not the only way in which offence to one's culture can be an offence to one's self-respect. Offending someone's culture can be an offence to his/her person because culture is a component of one's identity, and offending one's identity means offending him/her. John Rawls says that people's confidence in their ability to realize their intentions is a condition for self-respect (John Rawls, *A Theory of Justice* (Cambridge, MA: Harvard University Press, 1973), p. 440). If people intend for their endeavours to exist independently of their own existence, and if many people's endeavours exists within

what they do will last forever. Rather, they need to be able to *hope* that what they do has some prospect of enduring and/or being remembered. A social order which treats people's culture dismissively and which provides them with no protection whatsoever can in many cases promise them the reverse, namely, that their own endeavours as well as those of their ancestors will amount to nothing. Most people know from their own experience and that of their acquaintances that most of what they and most other people accomplish will not endure or will be forgotten. Yet, this does not affect the claim that people need the hope that their accomplishments ultimately endure or be remembered in order to have a sense of self-respect and meaning in their lives. Love may again serve as an analogy. Most people know that most loves fade. Yet, this doesn't mean that the belief in its endurance and the intent that it should endure are not essential ingredients of love. Social institutions such as marriage exist, *inter alia*, in order to help people sustain their love, and to assert their belief in its endurance. Similarly, in order to sustain people's hope that their endeavours have some prospects of meaningfulness, social arrangements should be instituted to facilitate this hope and protect it.

To take the analogy further, just as the institution of marriage need not be interpreted as a prison for loves that have waned, especially when these loves have turned into enmity and hatred, the social arrangements which are constructed in order to protect cultures must also not be turned into prisons. They must not be used to lock in individuals who do not want to live their lives within them. They also must not be used to protect cultures that have degenerated to levels condemning their members to lives of misery. In other words, the grounds for the historical thesis for which I am arguing here, those arising from people's interest in the meaningfulness of their endeavours, constitute a reason for giving only limited protection to the preservation of national cultures. These grounds are certainly not reason for turning national cultures into fortresses and protecting them at any cost.

The grounds for protecting the historical existence of national cultures are defeasible in two senses. First, there might be cultures that should not endure either because of their content, or because they have become so stunted that there is no point in continuing to support them. Secondly, there are means such as prohibiting exit that should not be employed to protect cultures. However, the fact that the grounds for protecting the historical existence of cultures are defeasible does not mean that these grounds do not exist.

their national cultures, then the argument made here about the connection between the continued existence of national cultures and the value of self-respect follows from the present Rawlsian conception of self-respect.

People's interest in the meaningfulness of their endeavours explains why many people believe that they have moral reasons for cleaving to their culture. These reasons derive from the hopes of previous generations. People's interest in the meaningfulness of their endeavours also explains why many people believe that subsequent generations will have similar moral reasons for cleaving to their culture which would derive from the hopes of the current generation.[26] This point provides an explanation for the value that people ascribe to their original culture when it is distinct from the culture in which they are actually living. As we may recall, the freedom-based argument could not explain the value of people's original culture in these cases, because people can satisfy their freedom-based interest in culture by means of the culture of their endeavours. However, if the endeavour-based interest people have in their culture produces reasons for their descendants to adhere to their culture and preserve it, this may explain why people care about their culture of origin when it is distinct from the culture of their endeavour. They care about it because it is the culture of their ancestors' endeavours.[27] Yet, it should be stressed that the present point merely concerns a source of reasons for action rather than of duties and obligations, mainly because imposing such obligations might produce gross violations of individual freedom. In addition, individual disregard of the reasons arising from their ancestors' expectations would not necessarily cause significant harm to the interest in question, namely, the preservation of the culture.[28]

---

[26] The fact that we are dealing with the interests of existing people makes it clear why the present argument cannot serve as an argument for reviving extinct cultures.

[27] Kai Nielsen, 'Cultural Nationalism, Neither Ethnic Nor Civic', *The Philosophical Forum* 28 (1996–97), 42–52, argues that liberal cultural nationalism cannot be ethnic, because ethnic nationalism is necessarily racist. The endeavour-based argument explains the place which ethnicity may legitimately have within the liberal version of cultural nationalism. The endeavour-based argument shows both why cultural nations should not be ethnically exclusive, and why they may to some extent be ethnically inclusive. They should not be exclusive because if individuals have undertaken their endeavours within them, it is important for these individuals that they and their descendants belong to these cultures. Excluding them just because they themselves do not descend from individuals belonging to this culture makes their exclusion based only on biology. It is therefore racist. However, if an individual whose ancestors belong to a particular culture and who himself has not been a full-fledged member of this culture, wants to join because he wants to take part in preserving the framework within which his ancestors lived and worked, then he might claim to be acting on a moral reason, granting him some priority compared to others who want to join.

If descent has nothing to do with cultural nationalism, as Nielsen seems to believe, if attributing weight to descent is merely a form of racism, then people should not care about whether or not it is their descendants who form the future generations of their cultures. However, people do care about this matter. (For this point see Anthony K. Appiah, 'Identity, Authenticity, Survival: Multicultural Societies and Social Reproduction', in Gutmann (ed.), *Multiculturalism*, p. 157.)

[28] For a more detailed discussion of a similar point see Chapter 6, pp. 150–5.

The historical dimension of cultural nationalism does indeed produce obligations. However, these should not be personal obligations imposed on individual members of national groups, but rather public duties that apply to those who establish and uphold the political order (legislators, judges, and international and municipal executives). The duties in question are duties to forge practices and institutions which *do not force* individual members of national groups to act on the basis of reasons arising from their interest in their own endeavours as well as those of their ancestors, but nevertheless *allow* them to do so. As claimed above, this interest constitutes a possible justification for the historical thesis. It does what the freedom and identity-based interests people have in their culture could not do.[29] However, the interest people have in their endeavours does more than explain the historical dimension of nations. It also has a major role in justifying the interpretation accorded by the contemporary liberal advocates of cultural nationalism to its third thesis, namely, the political thesis.

The political thesis

Four types of cultural rights

According to the political thesis, people's interests in cleaving to their national culture and in the continued existence of this culture must be protected politically. The nationalist movements of the last two centuries usually demanded the implementation of the political thesis mainly in one way: self-determination within their own state. In contrast, the contemporary liberal advocates of cultural nationalism believe that the political thesis requires implementation through more than one type of rights. Will Kymlicka has distinguished between three types of cultural rights: rights to self-government, special representation rights and polyethnic rights.[30] However, his typology is incomplete, for there is a fourth type of cultural

---

[29] All three arguments are based on individual interests. However, this does not mean that they presuppose moral individualism or that such individualism is a defining tenet of liberalism. In other words, it is not assumed in this book that *only* individual interests can support liberal theses. It is assumed only that individual interests could be used to support liberal theses. This thesis is compatible with the possibility that non-individualist, collectivist, considerations could also support such theses, including considerations concerning the intrinsic value of cultures. Moreover, the individual interests on which the freedom, identity and endeavour arguments are based are interests the satisfaction of which depends on the existence of a collective good, namely, societal cultures. It depends also on the ascription of intrinsic value to such cultures (in the sense attributed to this term by Joseph Raz; see Joseph Raz, *The Morality of Freedom* (Oxford University Press, 1986), pp. 177–8).

[30] See Kymlicka, *Multicultural Citizenship*, pp. 26–33; Raz, *Ethics in the Public Domain*, chaps. 6 and 8.

rights, namely, rights to cultural preservation, which he himself and others
in fact acknowledge. Major examples of such rights are the collective language rights that were granted to the Francophone majority in Quebec,
the collective land rights of the native Fijians and the restrictions
imposed on non-aboriginal people in Indian reservations in Canada. The
Quebec language rights prohibit immigrants from educating their children in English, and mandates French as the language of education for immigrants. (Similar language arrangements exist in Belgium, Switzerland
and India.) According to the Fijian land ownership arrangements, the
native group collectively and inalienably owns the great majority of the
islands' land. The restrictions imposed on non-aboriginal people's residence and voting rights in Canadian reservations has resulted in an
almost exclusive aboriginal residence in these reservations. These rights
are very different from the polyethnic rights that Kymlicka distinguished
from self-government rights and representation rights in his well-known
typology of group rights.

Polyethnic rights are rights such as the provision of immigrant language
education in schools, the exemption of Jews and Muslims from Sunday
closing or animal slaughtering legislation, the exemption of Sikhs from
laws requiring motor-cycle helmets and the exemption of Muslim girls in
France from school dress codes so that they can wear the traditional head-
scarves (the *hijab*). Kymlicka characterizes these rights as rights that '. . .
are usually intended to promote integration into the larger society and not
self-government'.[31] The cultural preservation rights that constitute the
fourth group of rights listed above are intended to do the opposite, that is,
if they promote integration, they promote the integration of other groups
with the specific group that is entitled to these rights. They are mainly
intended to allow groups to sustain self-government within the framework of their culture and to preserve their status as distinct societies.
While Kymlicka's polyethnic rights are intended to allow the holders of
these rights to express their identity within a particular territory where the
public sphere and economic and political life are conducted mainly within
the framework of a different culture, rights to cultural preservation are intended to facilitate the centrality of the cultural group holding these rights
within a given territory. These rights are intended to make this culture
the culture of the public sphere of a given territory, within the framework
of which the major parts of the political and economic life take place.
Kymlicka's threefold distinction of cultural rights, which includes self-
government rights, representation and polyethnic rights, must therefore
become a fourfold distinction and also include rights to cultural preservation. Like special representation rights, the latter are needed in certain

[31] Kymlicka, *Multicultural Citizenship*, p. 31.

cases to complement self-government rights. Their role is to maintain the conditions that enable groups to be self-governing and members of these groups to continue living their lives within their culture for generations.

Self-government versus *polyethnic rights: best and second-best protection*

I have already tried to provide some explanation for the distinction between the cases in which rights to self-government and their complementary rights on the one hand, and polyethnic rights on the other hand, are justified. The latter rights are justified where people's interest in their nationality is based on identity only, while the former rights are justified where this interest is also based on freedom. However, this explanation is insufficient, since it fails to provide a criterion for determining the cases where people's interest in their nationality should be regarded as based on identity only, as opposed to those cases where this interest is based also on freedom. I shall try to show that this problem can be resolved by recourse to the endeavour-based interest.

Two strategies can be employed in order to distinguish cases for granting self-government rights from cases in which polyethnic rights are appropriate. First, it could be claimed that the interests present in cases of the former type are of a different nature than those present in the latter category and therefore require different treatment. Secondly, it could be claimed that although the interests involved in both types of cases might be of the same nature, cases to which polyethnic rights apply might also involve conflicting considerations. The presence of such considerations makes it practically impossible to provide what would be the optimal protection (i.e., self-government rights) for the interests in question, thus providing no recourse other than the lesser protection of polyethnic rights. Cultural nationalism that is justified only by the freedom- and identity-based interests people have in culture necessarily entails the second strategy. It must regard polyethnic rights as second best compared to self-government rights, since the latter provide the optimal protection for people's freedom and identity-based interests in their national culture. Giving up self-government rights for polyethnic rights may be justified, not because polyethnic rights provide adequate protection of these interests, but because there are other factors present that render the situation whereby lesser protection is provided inevitable. Those writers who have based cultural nationalism on freedom and identity in fact seem to have chosen this way to defend polyethnic rights. They view these rights as second best in relation to self-government rights, and justify this second best by appealing either to geodemographic factors, or to the fact that immigrants, by their very act of immigration, have forfeited their rights to self-government within their original culture. For instance, Joseph Raz believes that self-government rights should be granted to groups that are the majority within territories large enough for political independence. Groups not enjoying territorial concentration sufficient for political independence must be content with polyethnic rights.[32] Similarly, Will Kymlicka believes that self-government must be granted to national groups living in their homeland, while immigrants are entitled to polyethnic rights only, because their act of emigration implies consent to relinquish self-government under their original culture.[33]

I have already mentioned the difficulties inherent in this approach. If geodemographic considerations constitute sufficient reason to reduce self-government rights to polyethnic rights, namely, rights which do not allow people to realize their freedom fully through their own culture, why not also deny them their polyethnic rights for that same reason? This is especially applicable with regard to descendants of immigrants who find themselves in geodemographic conditions that are inappropriate for political independence. The connection of such people to their original culture is not as close as that of their immigrating ancestors, or at least does not have strong reason to be. It is certainly possible for these people to concretize their freedom-based interest in a culture by means of the dominant culture in their country of residence. The same could also apply to arguments of estoppel made by states in order to counter demands for self-rule made by immigrants. If the voluntary nature of immigration is a good enough reason to silence claims to self-government, why is it not sufficient grounds to also silence demands for polyethnic rights? In any case, such rights do not allow people to fully realize their freedom through their original culture. More importantly, descendants of immigrants can in fact easily concretize their freedom through the culture of the country in which they reside. Why grant them polyethnic rights when they do not really need such rights in order to realize their freedom-based interest in culture?

Self-government versus *polyethnic rights: protecting different interests*

The endeavour-based interest people have in their culture can provide us with a key for answering the above questions, because it provides a way to regard polyethnic rights not merely as second-best protection for the same interests protected by self-government rights but as protecting a different

---

[32] Raz, *Ethics in the Public Domain*, chaps. 6 and 8.
[33] Kymlicka, *Multicultural Citizenship*, p. 95.

combination of interests. In order to demonstrate this, let me begin by assuming that if the different interests people have in their nationality provide a prima facie justification for self-government rights in the case of one national group, then they provide a prima facie justification for granting such rights to all national groups. I will also assume that every national group could have sub-groups whose geodemographic conditions do not allow for the implementation of self-government rights. There are two different types of such sub-groups. One is of immigrants belonging to a national group which consists of other sub-groups at least one of which, typically the one living in the national homeland, enjoys self-government. The second type is either of immigrants or of members of indigenous groups that have no sub-groups living elsewhere under geodemographic conditions that would allow for self-government.

With regard to the first type, namely, immigrants belonging to nations whose core groups enjoy geodemographic conditions allowing for self-government, their first generation's freedom and endeavour-based interests in culture provide a prima facie case for granting them self-government rights. However, their nation already enjoys such rights, *ex hypothesi*, in its homeland. Because geodemographic reasons might make it practically impossible to grant sub-groups belonging to this nation such rights everywhere in the world, they must relinquish these rights almost everywhere. Polyethnic rights are justifiable in their case as a second-best choice both from the standpoint of their freedom-based interest in culture, and from the standpoint of their endeavour-based interest. Since they cannot cut themselves off from living at least partially within their original culture and since this culture is also, to a great extent, the culture of their endeavours, polyethnic rights are not the optimal instruments for serving their interests in this culture. However, they have voluntarily chosen this second best, presumably because their country of immigration better suits their other interests.

The situation of the second and subsequent generations of descendants of immigrants is different. As I noted earlier, it does not make sense in their case to argue that their freedom-based interest in culture must be concretized specifically through the culture from which they are descended. In many or probably most cases, it also does not make sense to argue that their endeavour-based interest in culture should be concretized through their original culture, since their endeavours usually take place within the dominant culture in the country they are currently living in and their interest in the meaningfulness of their endeavours is only linked to that culture. Nevertheless, they may still have an interest in their original culture, for they must be allowed to view themselves as having an interest to satisfy the expectations and hopes of their ancestors that their endeavours be carried on or remembered. If they do indeed view themselves as having such an interest, then they have two cultural identities. One is tied to their culture of origin while the other is linked to the culture within which they live. Polyethnic rights relating to their original culture, combined with self-government rights which they enjoy under the culture of their endeavours, do not constitute second-best protection for the combination of interests they have as a result of their double identity. On the contrary, the protection so provided is optimal. The fact that they are not granted self-government rights under their original culture is not due to any external constraints due to which they were required to surrender the best protection. Rather, their interests are complex and are therefore protected by complex means: self-government rights within their new culture, that is, the culture of their endeavours, and polyethnic rights *vis-à-vis* their original culture, which is the culture of their ancestors' endeavours.

The protection of their interests in the latter culture is even further enhanced, if, together with the polyethnic rights which allow them to retain their own ties with their original culture, other members of that original culture simultaneously have rights to self-government under it in the home country. In this event, the continued existence of the culture is protected not only through their partial connection to it under polyethnic rights, but also through the core group's total association with it under self-government rights. Furthermore, if the descendants of immigrants have certain privileges concerning their return to their original country, where the members of this culture hopefully enjoy self-government, then their interests in this original culture are fully protected. If they ascribe great importance to the hopes and expectations of their ancestors, they can act accordingly, if they so wish, and return to live within these ancestors' culture.[34]

National groups without potential for self-government

The third case we must address is of national groups that do not have sub-groups living under geodemographic conditions that would allow self-government. Such national groups can only enjoy polyethnic rights. From the standpoint of their freedom and endeavour-based interests in culture, their situation is no different from that of immigrant minorities enjoying only polyethnic rights. The freedom-based interest of the members of these minorities in culture is currently served by their integration into the dominant culture in the country they live in and their

---

[34] See also Chapter 5 below, on nationalism and immigration.

endeavour-based interest is also served by that dominant culture. However, their situation is different from the viewpoint of their interest to act in accordance with their forefathers' expectations and to continue the endeavours of their forefathers. Clearly, the prospects that these endeavours will benefit others and/or be continued by others are weaker in the present case than in cases of national groups that enjoy self-government. In cases of the kind under discussion, polyethnic rights do in fact provide only second-best protection compared to the protection provided by self-government rights. Yet, they do not provide second-best protection with respect to the freedom-based interest that members of a national minority have regarding their original culture, since they have no freedom-based interest in that culture. In the current case, the second-best protection provided by polyethnic rights is for the interest people might have in respecting their ancestors' expectations. The situation of diaspora groups that only have polyethnic rights is different if they belong to a nation whose core group enjoys self-government. Despite the fact that they do not benefit directly from these self-government rights, their original cultural group does. Thus, the ancestors' expectations concerning their endeavours are being respected.

All this can perhaps provide a key for answering questions concerning the justifiability of realizing people's freedom-based interest in culture specifically through their original culture, and of granting them self-government rights under this culture. The endeavour-based interest people have in their culture is a key for answering these questions, because self-government is the optimal way to serve this interest. Self-government enables people to treat their ancestors' endeavour as something they enjoy and continue in their daily lives, rather than as relics and rituals to be exhibited in museums, which is often the case when polyethnic rights protect this interest.[35] The constraints imposed by the geodemographic conditions of the world do not allow for all people to enjoy self-government rights under their original culture wherever they live. Yet, it does seem desirable to aspire, as far as this is geodemographically possible, for every nation to have one place in the world in which such optimal protection is provided to its members' interest in the meaningfulness of their endeavours. If this is done, then in that place, which should preferably be their national homeland, people's freedom-based interest in culture would be concretized through their original culture. This must be done not so

---

[35] See John Borrows, '"Landed" Citizenship: Narratives of Aboriginal Political Participation', in Will Kymlicka and Wayne Norman (eds.), *Citizenship in Diverse Societies* (Oxford University Press, 2000), pp. 332–3, where he says (among other things relevant to the present issue): 'Traditions can be the dead faith of living people, or living faith of dead people.'

much in order to serve their freedom-based interest in culture, but rather to protect their interest in the meaningfulness of their endeavours and the endeavours of their ancestors. In order to serve these interests, it is not necessary that all the members of a given culture enjoy self-government rights. It is sufficient that their core group enjoy such rights. This would also serve the interests of their diaspora members by allowing them to be content with polyethnic rights where they live. Knowing that their original culture is being enjoyed and continued by other members of this culture, polyethnic rights would enable them to demonstrate their membership in it and to show sufficient respect for their ancestral endeavour.

Conclusion

In this chapter I have tried to elucidate the various foundations for the liberal version of cultural nationalism. I first discussed the attempts to use freedom and identity as bases for the liberal version of cultural nationalism. After arguing that identity provides a basis for the adherence thesis and that freedom may in some cases strengthen this basis, I argued in the second section that neither could support the historical thesis, a thesis without which a political morality could hardly be considered nationalist. I then tried to use the interest people have in their endeavours as a possible source of justification for this thesis. As shown in the last section, this argument does not only provide a possible basis for the historical thesis; it could also be used to justify the particular interpretation given by contemporary liberal writers to the third thesis of cultural nationalism, namely, the political thesis. According to this interpretation, the protection of people's interest in their national culture must in some cases take the form of self-government rights, and in other cases the form of polyethnic rights. People's interest in the meaningfulness of their endeavours can explain the distinction between cases in which these two sorts of rights are justified. Cases in which the endeavour-based argument justifies self-government – usually cases of national groups living in their homeland – are also those in which the freedom-based interest people have in a culture should be concretized by their original culture. The freedom-based interest in culture does not constitute *a priori* justification of the right to self-government under one's original culture, but strengthens it in retrospect, if it is justified by the endeavour-based and identity-based considerations.

Compared to polyethnic rights, self-government rights provide better protection both for the realization of the adherence thesis and for the realization of the historical thesis. Whether the attempts to provide foundations for these theses succeed or not, it is a fact that these theses are widely accepted and that they are politically very powerful. In the name of these theses and in the name of some other aspects of their nationality, national groups make various practical demands which play a central role in the world's political agenda. The demands I have in mind are the demands made on the basis of the so-called 'historical rights', demands for language rights, for priorities in immigration, in land acquisition and the like. Whether the attempts to provide liberal foundations for the central normative theses of cultural nationalism succeed or not, it is worth examining whether and to what extent the practical demands of this type of nationalism are acceptable from the liberal point of view. In the following chapter I shall discuss the demand for national self-determination and self-government.

3 National self-determination

Self-determination and constitutional morality

Many national groups interpret their right to self-determination as a right to independent statehood, which they in turn interpret as a right to a state of their own, a state which 'belongs' to their people. Many nation-states view themselves as belonging to their predominant national group. Some nation-states, such as Israel and several of the new states that belonged to the former Yugoslavia, express this overtly in their constitution or by means of some other important laws.[1] Other nation-states have practices that support such an interpretation. For example, the Baltic states that seceded from the former USSR deny citizenship to their residents of Russian origin. Similarly, other nation-states, such as Germany and Japan, have made the process of naturalization very difficult for those residents who are not of German or Japanese origin. Most nation-states regard themselves as belonging to one particular people and express this through their names, languages, national anthems and the names of many of their main institutions.

I shall call the conception according to which the right to self-determination should be institutionalized by independent statehood *the statist conception*.[2] In terms of the distinctions made in Chapter 1, the

---

[1] Israel's Basic Law on Human Dignity and Freedom states in Article 1A: 'The purpose of this Basic Law is to protect human dignity and freedom, in order to lay down the ethical values of the State of Israel, as a Jewish and democratic state, in a Basic Law.' Article 2 of another Israeli Basic Law, the one concerning Freedom of Occupation, has a similar formulation. The constitution of Croatia states that the Republic of Croatia is 'established as the national state of the Croatian nation and the state of the members of other nations and minorities that live within it'. See Robert M. Hayden, 'Constitutional Nationalism in the Formerly Yugoslav Republics', *Slavic Review* 5 (1992), 657. The constitutions of several other republics of the former Yugoslavia contain similar articles. See Hayden, *ibid.*

[2] Certain authors incorporate the right to statehood in the very definition of a nation. For example, see Paul Gilbert, *The Philosophy of Nationalism* (Oxford: Westview Press, 1998), p. 16. Daniel Philpott and David Miller seem to hold the view that self-determination should as far as possible be protected in the form of independent statehood. See D. Miller, *On Nationality*, chap. 4; Daniel Philpott, 'In Defense of Self-Determination', *Ethics* 105 (1995), 359. See also Chapter 1 note 51.

nationalism subscribing to this conception is a state-seeking nationalism. In this chapter I shall argue for a thesis according to which the right of national groups to self-government should *almost always* be conceived of in sub-statist forms and institutionalized as such. In the case of groups that have diasporas, the right of these groups to self-government could also take an inter-statist form. National groups should almost never be entitled to conceive of the states within which they enjoy self-determination as states of their own, let alone as states which they own. The right of national groups to self-determination should be conceived of as a package of privileges to which each national group is entitled in its main geographic location, normally within the state that coincides with its homeland. This package of rights should mainly contain powers and liberties to practise their culture independently and to administer substantial parts of their lives within this culture, as well as rights to guarantee their fair share in the government and the symbols of the state.

This sub-statist conception of self-determination differs from the statist conception in mainly two matters: first, it represents the right to self-determination universally as a right within the state, never as a right to independent statehood. Secondly, according to this sub-statist conception, self-determination is not a right of majority nations within states *vis-à-vis* national minorities, but rather a right to which each national group in the world is entitled. This right must be realized at least in one place, usually the historic homeland of the national group enjoying it. Accordingly, the right is not one of majority nations as opposed to minority nations, but is rather that of homeland groups *vis-à-vis* non-homeland groups.

My discussion of the statist and sub-statist conceptions should mainly be viewed as concerning the frameworks for the constitutional interpretation of the relations between national groups and the states within which they enjoy self-determination and self-government. I shall not discuss them as questions concerning the rights of national groups to secede from existing states and establish new ones. Secession and the proper institutional framework for protecting the interest of national groups in self-government are two distinct issues. The view according to which the interest of national groups in self-government should be protected by a right to a state of their own necessarily entails their right to secede from existing states that are not their own. However, the opposite does not hold; acknowledging the right of national groups to secede does not necessarily entail that their interests in preservation and self-rule should be protected by a right to independent statehood. A right to secede may be justified on grounds such as the need of the seceding group to escape persecution, or the need to reinstitute old borders that were illegitimately violated. It may also be justified on grounds that pertain to the costs of intervention in unjustified acts of secession and for other reasons.[3] All this does not necessarily entail the recognition of the seceding group's right to independent statehood. This group might be conceived of as having only a right to a sub-statist self-rule within the new state it establishes.

The sub-statist interpretation will not make much of a practical difference compared to the statist interpretation in states where the population is culturally homogeneous. The national groups enjoying the rights included in the self-determination package within such states will not enjoy them as privileges which non-homeland groups do not enjoy, for *ex hypothesi*, there are no non-homeland groups in such states. They will also not have to share these privileges with other homeland groups, for again, there are no such groups in these states. Nevertheless, it would not be correct to conclude from the above that in culturally homogeneous states the sub-statist conception makes no practical difference whatsoever, compared to the statist conception. For example, it would make such difference in the case of immigration. According to the sub-statist conception, states in which the population consists of just one national group that enjoys self-determination in that particular state must not be viewed as belonging to that national group or as realizing independent statehood for that group. Such states are therefore not permitted to reject immigrants for the mere reason that they do not belong to the one national group exercising its self-determination within the state in question.[4]

I shall make four arguments against the statist conception, three of which will be presented in this chapter. These three arguments pertain to three types of injustice that are caused by applying the statist conception in the world's current geodemographic conditions. First, the application of this conception causes intra-statist, domestic injustice by creating two classes of citizens within most nation-states – citizens belonging to the national group which enjoys self-determination within the state, and citizens who do not belong to that group. Secondly, the application of this conception causes inter-national, global injustice by creating two classes of national groups. It creates a class of national groups that have independent statehood, and a second class of groups that have much less. Thirdly, the implementation of the statist conception causes intra-national injustice

[3] For a recent typology of normative philosophical theories of secession see Moore, *The Ethics of Nationalism*, pp. 145–6. Moore's typology perhaps exhausts the philosophical theories of secession discussed in the literature, but does not cover all the theories that could be suggested. For example, see note 6 below.

[4] For a detailed account of the implications of the statist and sub-statist conceptions of self-determination for immigration policies see Chapter 5, pp. 134–41 below.

for national groups that have a diaspora. Compared to those who live out-side the nation-state, unjust advantages are granted to the group members who live within the nation-state, with regard to decisions on matters that pertain to all the group's members. The fourth argument I shall make against the statist conception of self-determination is based not on the world's current geodemographic conditions, but rather on the geodemographic state of the world as envisioned by the statist conception. This vision is of a society of nation-states the citizenries of which include all the members and only the members of their nations. Such a vision is incompatible with the ideal of freedom of migration, and is not conducive to pluralism.

I shall present the first three arguments in the next few sections of this chapter where I shall also try to show that people's interests in the self-determination of their national group do not necessarily entail the statist conception of this right. The fourth argument will be discussed in detail in Chapter 5, which deals with nationalism and immigration. The sub- and inter-statist conception will be presented on pp. 89–91. I shall argue there that it provides a solution to the problems mentioned above and to some additional problems posed by the statist conception. I will end this chapter with a discussion of the problems of social cohesion that result from the fact that the sub-statist conception of self-determination entails that states that realize this conception be polyethnic and/or multinational (pp. 91–6).

The statist conception and domestic justice

According to the statist conception, the interest of national groups in collective self-rule should be protected by a right to independent state-hood, namely, by a right of national groups to a state of their own. As is well known, most of the populations inhabiting territories in which states could be formed do not enjoy national homogeneity. Under these circumstances, the implementation of the statist conception would in most cases involve either massive population transfers, or the creation of states for either the minority or the majority of their citizens. It goes without saying that the first possibility, namely, massive population transfers, must be rejected outright. The second possibility, that is, the creation of states for their minorities, is clearly anti-democratic. Thus, we are left with the third possibility. The only way to implement the statist conception on a large scale is to grant a right to independent statehood to national groups that constitute the majority in territories in which states could be formed.

Who exactly are the holders of this right? If we seek the answer in the rationale that underlies cultural nationalism, then the national group as a whole, including all its members, both those living in the territory and outside it, is the holder of this right. This answer best serves the interests national groups have in their self-preservation and in their self-rule. It is compatible with the fact that these could be the interests of all members of the national group, whether they live within the territory or outside it. However, the idea that the national group – comprising all its members – is the holder of the right to independent statehood seems to be diametrically opposed to democratic and liberal values. It means that states might belong not to their populations but rather to the national groups that constitute the majority of their populations. This would mean denying full membership to a part of the population, and granting at least partial membership to people who do not belong to the same population.

According to another interpretation, the holder of the right is not the national group as a whole, but only that part of the national group currently living in the relevant territories. This interpretation renders the conflict between the statist conception of self-determination on the one hand, and democracy on the other, less blatant, for it does not align states with people who are not part of their population. However, the conflict remains none the less, for under this interpretation full membership would be denied to some parts of the population of the state in question. For example, many Israelis believe their state belongs to all the members of the Jewish people. According to this view, the state belongs to non-resident Jews more than it belongs to resident non-Jews. However, even if one holds the view that Israel belongs only to its own Jewish population and not to the entire Jewish people, one must view non-Jewish Israelis (for example, Arabs who are Israeli citizens) as people living in a state which is not their own.

Supporters of the principle granting national groups which constitute majorities within territories a right to form their own states might perhaps argue that they support this principle not as a constitutional principle determining the relationships between national groups and the states within which they enjoy self-determination but rather as a principle determining the permissibility of secession. National groups constituting majorities have a right to secede and establish an independent state. However, once this has been done, the new state is not an expression of the independent statehood of these national majorities. Rather, it expresses the independent statehood that comprises the whole population including the minorities in this state. The principle that grants national majorities a right to statist self-determination is in fact formulated by many as a principle of secession rather than as a principle concerning the constitutional relations between national groups and states. One international jurist notes that '[a] people, if it so wills ... may establish a sovereign state in the territory in which it lives and where it constitutes a majority'.[5] However, the fact that this principle is formulated as a principle of secession does not exempt it from the drawbacks of the constitutional principle. Like the constitutional principle, it could also be interpreted as granting the right to secede to any given national group as a whole, comprising all its members, if there is a territory in which the national group in question or some of its members constitute a majority. In addition, it could also be interpreted as granting the right to secession to national sub-groups that constitute majorities within their territories. According to the former reading, the right to participate in the process of establishing a state is granted, on the one hand, to all individuals belonging to the national group that forms the majority, and not merely to those members of that national group who are currently living in the territory. On the other hand, this right is denied to all those people who are currently living in the territory who do not belong to the national majority. According to the latter reading, the right to participate in the process of establishing a state is granted only to those members of the national group who are currently living in the territory in which the state is to be established. This right is denied to all other residents of this territory.[6]

---

[5] Yoram Dinstein, 'Collective Human Rights of Peoples and Minorities', *International and Comparative Law Quarterly* 25 (1976), 102–200. It should be stressed that he refers to self-determination in the context of independence from foreign rule. However, it should be noted that international jurists hold different views regarding whether the right to secede and establish new states in international law is limited to colonial people and people under foreign rule, or whether it is a right of all peoples. See Hurst Hannum, *Autonomy, Sovereignty, and Self-Determination* (Philadelphia: University of Pennsylvania Press, 1990), p. 39; Christian Tomuschat, 'Self-Determination in a Post-Colonial World', in Christian Tomuschat (ed.), *Modern Law of Self-Determination* (Dordrecht: Martinus Nijhoff Publishers, 1993), pp. 2–3; Antonio Cassese, *Self-Determination of Peoples: A Legal Reappraisal* (Cambridge University Press, 1995), p. 319.

[6] It must be noted that the principle according to which 'A people, if it so wills . . . may establish a sovereign state in the territory in which it lives and where it constitutes a majority' may also be justified for reasons that derive from the rationale underlying *statist* nationalism. As explained in Chapter 1, the main idea embodied in this kind of nationalism is that it is desirable for states to share a common national culture (as opposed to the idea that it is desirable for nations to have states). According to this type of nationalism, the present principle of secession would provide a solution for the problem of how to divide the world into different states, that is, how to draw the borders between them. Since statist nationalism holds that states should share a common culture, then, other things being equal, the most efficient way to achieve this would be to establish states in places where the population already shares a national culture. Since the majority of populations that share cultures do not enjoy an exclusive presence in the territories that they inhabit, it would be necessary to compromise and establish states around cultural majorities. The cultural minorities would have to assimilate into the majority.

   Not only is the principle of secession under the present interpretation not based on the interests of people in adhering to their culture and preserving it for generations, but, given the geodemographic conditions of the world, it also implies a denial of the very existence

Granting the right to vote on secession not only to members of the national majority in the territory, but also to minorities, must not be used to obscure the fact that the right to secede is in fact granted only to the national majority, since the minorities do not really share this right. Allowing the members of the minorities to participate in the vote may even intensify the affront to these groups, because it could be regarded as an attempt to cover up the injustice by allowing them to participate in it. Consider the following putative principle: 'Whites, if they so desire, are entitled to deny blacks the use of the public educational system in the territory in which they live and constitute a majority.' Even if the vote on this proposition is open to both whites and blacks, a majority decision cannot validate it. In a sense, the opposite is true: if the substance of the proposition is offensive to certain people, allowing the same people to participate in the vote is tantamount to humiliating them twice.[7]

In any event, one must remember that the principle allowing national groups which constitute majorities in particular territories the right to secede is in fact interpreted as a principle granting them a state of their own which would be an expression of the continuing existence of their culture. This is regarded by many national groups and many nation-states as the rationale for making these states the nations-states of these groups. Many of the most common practices in states established around cultural groups that constitute the majority of their populations confirm this. As noted above, such states are usually named after the majority nation, their official language is the language of the majority group and their symbols, national anthems, political and civil institutions or at least their names derive from its national heritage. Some nation-states also grant the members of their predominant nation privileges in areas such as immigration and land acquisition, even if they are not citizens of the state in question. In all these matters there is, at the very least, some prima facie injustice towards the citizens of these states who are not members of the majority nation. Granting them minority rights does not remedy this injustice, for such rights firmly establish them as second-class citizens.

---

of these interests. This is so because if the reason for acknowledging the principle is that states should have their own nations, then individuals belonging to a national minority which shares a territory with another nationality would be required to renounce their own culture and assimilate into the majority. 'Nation-building' and 'melting pot' are the names of policies and processes that have, in fact, been used in the name of statist nationalism for achieving such assimilation.

[7] It does not follow, however, that those likely to be humiliated should not participate in the vote. If it is reasonable to assume that there are enough decent people among the white majority, the blacks would do well to participate in the vote, with the expectation that this peaceful method may nullify the implementation of the principle. However, none of this has anything to do with the democratic inappropriateness of the proposition.

This injustice becomes particularly acute when it applies to citizens who not only do not belong to the majority nation, but who also belong to a national minority that does not enjoy statist self-determination in any territory whatsoever. This brings me to considerations of global justice which are the second category of considerations militating against the statist conception.

The statist conception and global justice

Since many national groups do not enjoy an exclusive presence in their homelands, interpreting self-determination according to the statist conception means allowing domestic injustice to acquire global dimensions. It is necessary to distinguish this global scale of domestic injustice, resulting from the implementation of the statist conception, from an additional form of injustice resulting from the application of this conception. This additional injustice is not intra-statist but rather international. It takes place in the global arena due to the fact that some national groups have states of their own, while others do not. Unlike the intra-statist injustice, it does not merely result from the fact that the populations of most territories in which states could be formed are of mixed national origin, but rather from the fact that many national groups do not have exclusive or majority presence within a territory in which a state could be formed. Prima facie, it seems unjust to promote the right to self-determination by granting independent statehood and, consequently, international status with regard to some national groups while simultaneously condemning other national groups to an inferior normative status.

Some authors who are aware of the fact that many national groups do not have exclusive or majority presence within a territory in which a state could be formed ignore this problem completely by defining it mainly as a problem of stability and not one of justice. They seem to be concerned with what they call the 'Balkanization effect' which might result if the right to national self-determination is interpreted as a right to independent statehood. They conclude therefore that national self-determination, though it may sometimes have the form of independent statehood, need not always have this form. They seem to be unconcerned with the injustice inherent in this position.[8] None of these authors concludes that

---

[8] D. Miller, *On Nationality*, p. 111; Ernest Gellner, 'Do Nations Have Navels?', *Nations and Nationalism* 2/3 (1996), 369; Ronald S. Beiner, 'National Self-Determination: Some Cautionary Remarks Concerning the Rhetoric of Rights', in Moore (ed.), *National Self-Determination and Secession*, pp. 159–60. Yael Tamir is a clear exception. She says: 'Since not all nations can attain [statehood], and since restricting the implementation of this right only to nations able to establish one would lead to grave inequalities, other solutions must be sought.' See Tamir, *Liberal Nationalism*, p. 74.

at least in cases where acknowledging the right of national groups forming majorities in given territories to establish their own states condemns
other groups to inferior normative status, the self-determination of the
majority group should not be implemented by independent statehood.[9]

Those holding the position according to which some groups are entitled
to independent statehood while others are entitled to less could deny the
injustice inherent in this position in four possible ways. First, they might
try to deny the eligibility to statehood of some of the groups that do not
form majorities in territories where states could be formed by denying
their status as nations. This device was very common among writers on
nationalism in the nineteenth century. Many such writers attempted to
deny the rights of groups to their own states by distinguishing between
historical and ahistorical nations, or between nations and nationalities.[10]
There are some writers who use the same strategy today, though with different terminology. For example, Brian Barry and David Miller make use
of the distinction between national and ethnic groups, claiming that only
the former are eligible for statehood.[11] However, from the perspective
of the liberal version of cultural nationalism, this distinction is not very
helpful in reducing the number of groups eligible for self-determination.
Conceptually, one must indeed distinguish between national and ethnic
groups, since national groups do not necessarily share common ethnic
origins or a belief in such origins, whereas ethnic groups are not necessarily preoccupied with their common histories and/or cultural identities and
their preservation.[12] However, when they are preoccupied with their historical and cultural identities and the preservation of their culture, ethnic
groups can and do in fact become national groups and self-determination
is indeed important to such groups.

A second possible argument against the charge of global injustice could
be that in order for justice to be upheld, self-determination should be

---

[9] This also seems to apply to Tamir. As the quote in the previous note demonstrates, she is
sensitive to the problems of injustice that are created by the fact that only some nations
can attain states. However, her conclusion seems merely to be that this should not result
in the denial of any form of self-determination to other nations. It is not at all clear
that her position implies a total rejection of statist self-determination, though she clearly
sympathizes with non-statist solutions. See Tamir, *Liberal Nationalism*, pp. 150–1.

[10] Mazzini, Engels, Marx and many other nineteenth-century Polish, Hungarian and
German nationalists (prominent among them Friedrich List) used the present or
similar device. On this see Peter Alter, *Nationalism*, 2nd edition (London: Edward
Arnold, 1994), p. 20; Margaret Canovan, *Nationhood and Political Theory* (Cheltenham:
Edward Elgar, 1996), p. 8; Roman Szporluk, *Communism and Nationalism: Karl Marx
Versus Friedrich List* (New York: Oxford University Press, 1988), pp. 128, 155–6; Nimni,
Marxism and Nationalism, pp. 23–37.

[11] See Barry, 'Self-Government Revisited', pp. 133–41; D. Miller, *On Nationality*,
pp. 19–21.

[12] This formulation roughly follows that of Walker Connor, who follows Max Weber's
definition. See Connor, *Ethnonationalism*, pp. 102–3.

implemented differently in different cases. If a nation constitutes the majority or is the only nation in a given territory in which a state can be formed, it is appropriate to realize this nation's right to self-determination by means of statehood. In other cases self-determination could be manifested by means of minority rights. According to the present response, such inequality is not unjust but rather fulfils the different needs of different nations. Such a solution expresses equal concern more than an egalitarian solution would. According to this position, ethnic groups and small national groups that are not exclusive inhabitants in territories large enough to form states cannot realistically maintain themselves as an independent state. Therefore, the best way to serve their interests in self-determination is by granting them minority rights.

The claim that very small national groups, especially those that are not the exclusive inhabitants in a detached territory, cannot realistically maintain a separate state seems sound. However, it would be premature to infer that equal concern for these groups should be exercised by granting them autonomy and cultural rights within states belonging to other national groups. This conclusion ignores the possibility of serving the interests in self-determination that both large and small national groups may have by a solution that would provide less than statehood. The above conclusion ignores the possibility that a state that is not homogeneous in terms of the national affiliation of its citizens can belong to all of the national groups inhabiting it or at least to national groups whose self-determination has not been realized elsewhere or whose homelands are under the jurisdiction of the state in question. In this way, no national group would have an inferior normative status either domestically or globally. I shall discuss this possibility in detail below.

A third response to the accusation of global injustice could claim (a) that a state is indeed the optimal but not the only means of protecting self-determination; (b) that it is not because some groups are granted statehood, that others get less (i.e., just minority rights); and (c) that where important interests are at stake, the fact that only some of the groups receive better protection than others is not a good reason to deny the former this protection, as long as it is not granted to them at the expense of the others.

Unlike the arguments against the charge of global injustice presented earlier, it should be noted that this third argument is not based on the denial of the global injustice that results from the statist conception, but rather on a justification of this injustice. This response is based on the claim that there are circumstances in which it is permitted or perhaps even necessary to deviate from justice and from the principle of equal concern. This third response is satisfactory if the application of the statist conception to a majority in a territory in which a state could be formed, is not at the expense of other national groups living there. However, granting statehood to a national majority renders the national minorities who do not have a state of their own elsewhere normatively inferior, both domestically and globally. If the interests in self-determination were to be protected in all such cases by entities that are less than nation-states, there would be no differences in normative status between the majority and minority groups, either domestically or globally. For example, if the Russians' right to self-rule in Russia were interpreted as sub-statist self-rule, and if the national minorities in this country were also granted the right to a sub-statist form of self-determination, the normative status of these minorities would be equal to that of the Russians. However, if the Russian state is regarded as the manifestation of the independent statehood of the Russians, then all other national groups in this country, even if they enjoy minority rights to self-rule as opposed to independent statehood, are thus condemned to a lower normative status. Accordingly, it seems that, like the two responses presented above, this third attempt to clear the statist conception of self-determination of the charge of global injustice has failed.

A fourth possible response to the charge of global injustice could be that a state is necessary and not merely the optimal protection of people's interests in self-determination. Therefore, even if granting statehood to some groups is indeed the reason for not granting it to others, the infliction of injustice is in such cases unavoidable. Like the previous response, this argument does not deny the injustice, but rather attempts to provide a justification for it. The validity of such justification depends on the interpretation of the interests that justify national self-determination and on whether anything less than a state could protect them. If these interests are such that a state is necessary for their protection, then the fact that the territorial resources of the world cannot produce states for all nations is not a sufficient reason for not granting states at least to some nations. To provide any nation with less than a state would be tantamount to giving dying patients inefficacious medication merely because this particular medication is currently available, while there is a shortage of the medication which might save them. Just as there is no point in giving the available medication to patients just because it is available, there is no point in attempting to serve the interests of national groups in self-determination by anything less than independent statehood. Nationalist doctrines that regard nations as natural species whose members have a completely different character and needs might deem statehood to be a necessary means for protecting self-determination. According to such doctrines, the differences between various national groups and their members are far more important than what they have in common. Consequently, the institutions and the normative systems that are required for governing the various national groups must differ in their character. Attempts to place national groups under one institutional roof would therefore be unnatural and might severely impair the welfare of the members of these national groups.[13] According to the present doctrines, and given the conditions of global demography, humanity is doomed to a perpetual conflict between justice and nationalism. Yet, as I shall show in the section below, according to the liberal version of cultural nationalism, there seems to be no reason to believe that the nation-state is the only appropriate means for protecting the interests which people have in the self-determination of their national group.

The interests in national self-determination

The interests under consideration are mainly those that were discussed in Chapter 2 under the headings of the adherence thesis and the historic thesis – that is, the interests people have in adhering to their culture and their interest in recognizing and protecting the multigenerational dimension of this culture. People may wish to adhere to their culture and protect its multigenerational dimension while this culture and what they take to be the essence of their lives is of very limited scope and does not depend on extensive economic and human resources. On the other hand, people may wish to adhere to their culture and protect its multigenerational dimension and expect this culture and their own lives to prosper in as many spheres of human action as possible. In both these cases, there is no need for the group's self-government to be realized in a statist form. The important case is of course the latter of the two situations. With regard to the former situation, it is easy for people to adhere to their culture and sustain it for generations if their self-government applies only to a few areas such as family life, local community life and religious life, if adhering to their culture in these areas is not very expensive, and if they view these areas to be the essence of their lives. It is easy for people to adhere to their culture and sustain it for generations if what they mean by culture does not comprise many fields. They would thus not require a state of their own. To the contrary, such a state might force many of them to distance themselves from their culture, for it might force them to

---

[13] Herder, whose nationalist ideology, as noted in Chapter 2, could be interpreted as belonging to the present sort, detested the idea of mixing various nationalities under one rule. See Gilbert, *The Philosophy of Nationalism*, pp. 46, 94.

view as the essence of their lives matters which have nothing to do with religion, family and local community. Such limited cultures and their members also do not require a territorial dimension; all they need is self-government, the jurisdiction of which is personal and material, applying only in a few areas.

One could argue that such cases do not really constitute national cultures. Regardless of whether this is justified or not, such cases should not be the focal point of our discussion, since from the liberal point of view, people should be encouraged to live within cultures that comprise as many spheres of human action as possible. Secondly, these are not cases of the type that have caused nationalism and national self-determination to be at the centre of so many controversies and disputes. Controversies and disputes usually arise in cases in which cultural groups and their members aspire to thrive in many areas of human life (for example, literature, arts, science, technology, economics and politics). The experience of various groups shows that a state is not the only means to achieve this objective. A distinct language spoken within a given territory could also serve for this end.[14] The Flemish- and French-speaking populations in Belgium, the French- and German-speaking cantons in Switzerland, the Francophones of Quebec, and the Maharashtrans, Tamils and Bengalis of India, testify to this point.

David Miller seems to be the main contemporary speaker for the position according to which it is desirable to serve the interest that members of national groups have in the historical survival of their culture by granting them a state. Interestingly, however, he does not take this position because he believes that a state is *necessary* to satisfy these interests. Rather, Miller claims that there is a strong case for realizing the right to self-determination by means of statehood because there are empirical conditions that make states the *optimal* means for preserving national cultures.[15] He believes that states are optimal for the present purpose because '[w]here a state exercises its authority over two or more nationalities, the dominant group has a strong incentive to use that authority to impose its own culture on the weaker groups'.[16] In his opinion, although 'there are some noteworthy exceptions to this rule', even in such cases, multinational states provide less protection for each of the cultural entities than would be provided for each culture in a state of its own. In my

[14] See J. A. Laponce, *Languages and Their Territories*, trans. Anthony Martin-Sperry (University of Toronto Press, 1987) pp. 115, 159, 162.
[15] See D. Miller, *On Nationality*, p. 88. See also Daniel Kofman, 'Rights of Secession', *Society* 35 (1998), 32–6.
[16] D. Miller, *On Nationality*, p. 88.

opinion, this last claim is problematic. Miller's claim can be questioned simply because there are many variables which must be considered: among them, the strength of the cultural group (its size, its material wealth and/or its cultural strength, its ability to adapt to changing circumstances, the devotion of its members to it, and the like), the nature of the neighbouring national groups (whether they share the same state or an adjacent one), the nature of the sub-statist alternatives for protecting self-determination, and, finally, the values and norms of the international community and its ability to enforce the relevant policies and norms. However, even if Miller's claim is correct, it need not be decisive in the present context. Even if the statist conception of self-determination is the optimal one, it is so only in so far as individuals' interests in the continued existence of their culture are concerned. Yet, people have additional interests in their nationality – one such interest is that it be recognized and respected. Since, as stressed above, a statist interpretation of self-determination can be realized only for a limited number of national groups, this will create inequality among national groups on the global level, particularly for groups that do not have a state of their own. Stateless groups are not only affected by this basic inequality, but also by the consequences of this inequality, which is the denial of international status from some national groups, for such status is granted only to states and not to national groups as such.[17] A non-statist implementation of self-determination, or rather a sub-statist implementation such as I will suggest below (pp. 83–91), would enable states to serve as a link between the nations enjoying self-determination within them, and the international arena, and would prevent the state from becoming a source of inequality in the normative status of nations.

The statist conception: intra-national considerations

Above I presented two types of injustice that are inflicted by the statist conception on groups to which it is not applied. I will try to show that the statist conception could also be somewhat problematic for the groups to which it is indeed applied. According to the statist conception, the bearer of the right to self-determination is the national group or parts thereof who enjoy exclusive or majority presence in a given territory. This interpretation of national self-determination does not sufficiently emphasize the special status of homelands in defining the identities of most national

---

[17] Charles Taylor (Taylor, *Reconciling the Solitudes*, p. 53) articulates this point eloquently in describing the need that such groups have to be accepted by the international community as entities that 'count[s] for something, [have] something to say to the world, and [are] among those addressed by others – the need to exist as a people on the world stage'.

groups. More importantly, it leaves some interests which members of
national diaspora groups might have in their original nationality unpro-
tected.

The first problem can easily be resolved by revising the principle of
statist self-determination so as to emphasize that groups whose identity
is linked with their homeland should be entitled to independent statehood
mainly in their homeland or part of it, provided they constitute a majority
there. The second problem, namely, that the principle could lead to a disregard of the interests of those members of national groups currently not
residing in the territory in which their national group enjoys independent
statehood, is not so easily resolved. The specific interests which these national diaspora groups might have include their interest in their continued
membership in the national group, in participating in decisions concerning the identity of their national group, admitting new members into it,
returning to their homeland, etc. Admittedly, the fact that immigrants
and diaspora members usually live major parts of their lives outside their
original national culture makes their interest in their original nationality
much less powerful and extensive than those interests held by members
of the core group. However, their interest in their original nationality is
not negligible. The statist conception can serve many of these interests.
Nation-states can serve as sources for the cultural satisfaction of diaspora
members and could also serve as places of refuge. However, the statist
conception as it stands may potentially harm certain interests of national
diaspora groups.

A blatant example of a case in which the interests of a national diaspora
group were disregarded was recently provided by the Israeli Knesset. A
bill according to which conversions performed in Israel would be recognized only if performed by Orthodox rabbis and which would affect
membership in the Jewish people was passed in the first reading. Many
Jews both inside and outside of Israel consider Israel to be the realization
of Jewish self-determination. Accordingly, its parliament's decisions concerning Jewish identity and membership in the Jewish people are often regarded as having an effect throughout the Jewish world. Since many Jews
living outside Israel do not adhere to the Orthodox version of Judaism,
this particular Knesset decision offended many Jews who are not Israeli
citizens and who cannot participate in this debate or any other decisions
of this sort. If the issue were only related to Jewish life within Israel, and to
issues of identity resulting from the special status of homeland in national
identities, Jews living outside Israel might have had no case for complaint.
However, the decision in question is not of this type.

All this serves to illustrate the fact that the statist conception is problematic in two ways: first, it allows the national communities enjoying

statist self-determination to marginalize groups of people with whom they share a state but not a culture. Secondly, it also has the potential of allowing them to adopt a condescending stance towards groups of people with whom they share a culture but not a state. Thus, under the statist conception, national groups are not only granted more than they ought to be granted but also less. It grants them too much by placing them above national groups that do not enjoy statehood and it grants them too little because it ignores the unity of national groups and the interest in self-government that people belonging to a national diaspora might have.

All these problems could have been avoided even while adhering to the statist conception, if every national group had one state, comprising all its members and only its members, and every state was inhabited by only one nation, comprising all its members and only its members. This seems to have been the ideal of many prophets of nationalism in the late eighteenth century and in the nineteenth century.[18] One contemporary proponent of the statist conception also seems to believe that this is the ideal condition. 'The ideal group's ideal borders encompass all those who share its identity, and only those who share its identity.'[19] In Chapter 5 below, which deals with the issue of nationalism and immigration, I will argue that the statist conception of self-determination implies permitting nation-states to advance the ideal of the culturally homogeneous state by means of preventing the immigration of non-members or by demanding their assimilation. If the statist conception does imply permitting this, then its realization might significantly damage the liberal values of pluralism and freedom of movement. The statist conception should therefore be rejected not only because of problems arising from its realization in the geodemographic state of the world as it is today, but also because of the geodemographic state of the world to which it aspires. These reasons for rejecting the statist conception may be not as important as the considerations deriving from the injustice it brings about in the domestic and global spheres in the current state of the world, but they are nevertheless significant. If, as I argued earlier, the liberal considerations in support of self-determination do not require a statist interpretation, then

---

[18] Mazzini and quite a few German nationalists constitute major examples. It must be noted, however, that in conceiving of this ideal, they did not have in mind dispersed nations which do not enjoy exclusive presence in their respective homelands. Rather, they had in mind their own nations, which were fragmented into various principalities some of which were under foreign rule. See Joseph Mazzini, *The Duties of Man and Other Essays* (London: Dent, 1966), pp. 51–9; Alter, *Nationalism*, p. 68.

[19] See Philpott, 'In Defense of Self-Determination', 359. Other contemporary writers hold this view less explicitly. See Jules L. Coleman and Sarah K. Harding, 'Citizenship, the Demands of Justice, and the Moral Relevance of Political Borders', in Warren F. Schwartz (ed.), *Justice in Immigration* (Cambridge University Press, 1995), pp. 42–4.

it would seem that the above considerations regarding the adverse effect the statist conception would have in terms of discouraging pluralism and limiting freedom of movement might render its implementation questionable, even in those few cases in which it is not ruled out by considerations of justice. Those cases are the few existing cases where national groups are the only group in territories in which states could be formed (for example, the Icelanders, and perhaps the Portuguese, the Slovenes and the Czechs).[20]

It seems, therefore, that the statist conception should be rejected, at least as the normal way for implementing the right to national self-determination.[21] A state is not essential for the satisfaction of the interests in self-determination. Even if it did protect these interests in the best possible way, it would in most cases be ruled out by considerations of justice and in other cases by other considerations. As noted earlier, even if the statist conception of self-determination is optimal, it is so only in so far as individuals' interests in the continued existence of their culture are concerned. Even if these interests do have deep liberal roots, they are not the only interests that do so. It should also be remembered that arrangements that are not optimal are not necessarily inadequate. Non-statist arrangements for the protection of the interest in self-determination and for safeguarding it from any immediate or significant threat may be sufficient. It therefore seems that we would do well to try to interpret self-determination in non-statist terms.

A sub- and inter-statist conception of self-determination

I would like to argue that self-determination could and should be interpreted in sub- and inter-statist terms. According to such an interpretation, each national group and all those belonging to it should be granted a package of privileges normally within the state that coincides with their homeland. This package should include self-government rights, special representation rights and rights to cultural preservation. Self-government rights include powers and liberties that allow members of national groups

---

[20] There are also a few culturally homogeneous countries in Africa: Swaziland, Lesotho, Botswana and Somalia (see Cassese, *Self-Determination of Peoples*, p. 317). I did not mention them in the body of my argument because their economic and political condition is such that precludes any serious consideration of pluralism and freedom of movement.

[21] A particular national group may find itself in a situation within which an independent state is the only way it can protect its members' interests in adhering to their culture and preserving it for generations. It might also find itself in a situation in which even more basic interests of its members, namely, those in life, in bodily integrity and in self-respect are threatened and where the only way to protect them is by achieving independent statehood. However, this is not normally the case. See also Chapter 4 note 32.

to control their culture and substantial parts of their lives within its framework. Representation rights are rights guaranteeing the group a fair share in the government and in the symbols of the state. Cultural preservation rights are auxiliary rights and other means for protecting the ability of the group and its members to shape their culture independently and live their lives within it. Rights and means belonging to the latter category are such as will assist them in maintaining a majority in their territorial homeland (or parts of the territorial homeland which may decrease in size if their population decreases in numbers) and in maintaining their culture as the major culture of the public spheres of those territories.

This conception is sub-statist because the rights under discussion are rights *within* the framework of a state rather than rights *to* a state or to independent statehood. Therefore, they are rights that could be enjoyed by more than one national group within the framework of any one state. These rights are based on the interests that all members of a national group might have in their nationality, and not only on the interests of those who are in fact citizens of the state. This is part of what makes the present conception inter-statist. These rights may also reflect the different character of these interests for members of national groups living in their homeland, on the one hand, and for members living outside the homeland, on the other. For example, voting rights on matters concerning the homeland could be granted only or mainly to those living there. Voting rights on matters of national identity and membership that have little to do with life in the homeland, such as procedures for religious conversion (if, as in the example of Israel, religion is an important component of the group's identity) could be granted equally to all members of the national group.[22] Rights of return would naturally be granted only to members living outside the homeland. The latter two rights, among others that may evolve, stress the inter-statist dimension of the present conception.

All these rights must of course be subject to constraints deriving from the basic human rights to freedom, dignity and subsistence. Thus it goes without saying that these rights cannot, for example, permit national groups to limit the birthrate of non-members in the territories where they enjoy self-government. In order to preserve their majority status or to maintain their culture as the major culture of the public spheres, they may at most use means such as encouraging the integration of immigrants into their culture (but not necessarily requiring the full assimilation), or encouraging the return of members of their own diaspora to the homeland. This, in turn, must also be subject to conditions that follow from the requirements of demographic stability. These rights must reflect the

---

[22] See pp. 81–2 above.

geographic, demographic and historical conditions, needs and identities of the particular national groups enjoying them, as balanced against the conditions, needs and identities of the national groups living in proximity to them, because the latter will bear the brunt of the implementation of the rights of the former groups. Not only are these needs, constrictions and identities different with regard to different national groups, but they may also change from time to time with regard to any particular national group. Therefore, it would be pointless to try to work out the details of these rights in advance. Furthermore, the specific details of some of these rights cannot be determined in theory. In many cases, these rights must be the product of political negotiations and compromise among the relevant groups and must be decided on a case-by-case basis.[23] Some examples of the rights to cultural preservation have been mentioned already in Chapter 2: the collective language rights that were granted to the Francophone majority in Quebec, the collective land rights of the native Fijians and the restrictions imposed on non-aboriginal people in the reservations of Canada. Writers defending these rights emphasize the dependence of their details on circumstances and context.[24] The example

---

[23] With regard to rights concerning the symbols of the state, should the 700 Samaritans living in the town of Nablus be represented in the flag of a state in which 99.9 per cent of its population is Palestinian? Unlike cases in which national groups comprise 20 per cent or more of the population of the state in which they are entitled to self-determination, it is not clear whether the answer to this question should be affirmative. Nor is it clear, however, that it should be negative. On the theoretical level, there seem to be no clear definitive answers to questions of this kind. Political negotiations and compromise must therefore determine the answer. The same holds for more important questions concerning participation in government. Should this be implemented by techniques of consociation, or, to use Donald Horowitz's phrase, by 'making multi-ethnic participation at the centre of power rewarding to all the participants who espouse it'? See Donald L. Horowitz, 'Self-Determination: Politics, Philosophy and Law', in Moore (ed.), *National Self-Determination and Secession*, p. 196. Again, there is no definitive answer to this question.

[24] Thus, Kymlicka, who approves of the rights of the aboriginal minorities in Canada to almost exclusive residence in their reservations, says that '[i]n the reservations of southern Canada, where the population is high and land scarce, the stability of Indian communities is made possible by denying non-Indians the right to purchase or reside on Indian lands (unless given special permission)' (Kymlicka, *Liberalism, Community and Culture*, p. 146). In northern Canada, he says, the conditions are different (*ibid.*). Mainly for climatic reasons, the danger that non-aboriginal people would want to live there permanently is not a serious danger. Therefore, there is no need to absolutely ban immigration. It is enough to limit the voting rights of non-aboriginal people so that they acquire such rights only after three to ten years of residence (*ibid.*, pp. 146–7). Similarly, Joseph Carens, who approves of the constitutionally entrenched land ownership arrangements in Fiji, says that at the time in which they were first enacted (at the end of the nineteenth century) they were justified because they prevented flooding Fiji with European immigration. Similar to what happened to other aboriginal groups such as those of North America and Australia as a result of mass immigration, such immigration could have led to the marginalization of the indigenous Fiji culture and would also have been detrimental to the material

of the rights in question that I will elaborate on will be immigration. In Chapter 5 below I shall try to present general guidelines for nationalist immigration rights that embody the sub- and inter-statist dimensions of the present conception of self-determination. These guidelines and the other examples just mentioned might serve as a basis for arrangements in other areas where the interests that national groups might have in self-government deserve special protection.

At the moment, however, it is important to support the general idea that underlies the sub-statist conception of self-determination proposed here with regard to the relationship between national groups and individuals as members of these groups, and, on the other hand, states and individuals as their members on both the domestic and global levels. In previous sections I discussed the criticism directed against the statist conception regarding the domestic, global and intra-national injustices it creates. I also mentioned that it limits freedom of migration and hinders pluralism within states. Most of these criticisms clearly do not apply to the sub- and inter-statist conception. The sub-statist conception does not create inequality in normative status among national groups on a global scale. It does not have to deal with the problems arising from the world's limited territorial resources, its stability requirements, the size and population distribution of many national groups, and various objectives that states might have. The implementation of the sub-statist conception would not ascribe normative value to empirical inequalities that exist between national groups. It does not doom individuals around the world to inferiority merely because they belong to stateless national groups.

The sub- and inter-statist conception is also free of the intra-national shortcomings of the statist conception. Since it is overtly inter-statist, it makes various provisions for the interests that all members of the national group have in their nationality and not merely for those living in the homeland. First, the mere fact that the existence of the core national group in the homeland is protected is of importance for all members of the group, even those who are not part of this core. It guarantees the memory of their ancestors' endeavours. To some extent, it contributes to their own sense of personal safety, particularly if they belong to a national group with a history of persecution, and may provide a source of pride and honour because their identity is linked with it. Secondly, together with

well-being of indigenous Fijians (see Carens, *Culture, Citizenship and Community*, chap. 9). Today, however, he maintains that this justification does not specifically *require* this arrangement, since the threat which the Indo-Fijians constitute for the native Fijian culture may not be as serious as the threat constituted by European colonization at the end of the nineteenth century. However, since the threat is nevertheless serious, the above justification does constitute a basis for *permitting* inalienable ownership rights.

homeland members of the group, the non-homeland members may benefit from some of the rights included in the set of privileges related to self-determination, such as voting rights on matters of national identity which are not homeland-dependent. Thirdly, the non-homeland members may be the exclusive bearers of some rights associated with self-determination, such as individual rights of return.[25]

The shortcomings of the statist conception with regard to pluralism and freedom of emigration do not apply here either. The ideal of civil society implied by the sub- and inter-statist conception is a multicultural one. Such a society is one that is less homogeneous and less monolithic and more pluralistic than the ideal society implied by the notion of the nation-state. It is open to immigration without the encumbering requirements of cultural conversion. In this respect, it corresponds not only to an individual's interest in his/her nationality, but also to other interests, brought on by developments in technology and economics. It enables individuals to reside in one place while at the same time feeling a sense of belonging and loyalty to other places and people. It also provides alternatives for individuals with a cosmopolitan lifestyle who do not feel attached to any specific nationality or place. By facilitating a large degree of mobility among national groups and states that may be important to cosmopolitan individuals, it obviates the need for them to make certain peremptory decisions regarding their identities or lives.

However, regarding the most significant criticism directed against the statist conception, that is, the domestic injustice it causes, the sub- and inter-statist conception does seem, at least at first glance, to encounter grave difficulties. Even if the particular rights included in the package of the sub- and inter-statist conception of self-determination are satisfactory, and even if constraints imposed on this package by human rights considerations are adequate, there might be those who would argue that the whole conception should be rejected on the grounds that it overtly creates what the statist conception creates covertly, namely, two classes of citizens. According to the sub-statist conception, within each state there are citizens who belong to national groups that enjoy self-determination within that state, and, on the other hand, citizens who do not belong to such groups. Furthermore, according to the sub- and inter-statist conception, the state might serve the interest in self-determination of the members of the national group living elsewhere, who are not citizens,

---

[25] As noted above, p. 81, the statist interpretation of self-determination may also provide for the interests in nationality that non-homeland members of a national group may have. If it does so, it then becomes not only statist, but inter-statist as well. However, if in addition to being statist, it also becomes inter-statist, its problems of domestic and global justice will be intensified.

while at the same time failing to serve the identical interests of its own citizens who belong to national groups which enjoy self-determination elsewhere. It might be argued that, by so doing, the sub- and inter-statist conception commits the same wrong attributed to the statist conception, namely, that of domestic injustice. Moreover, in the case of the statist conception, this injustice is merely a by-product of the implementation of this conception in the unfortunate geodemographic reality of the world. It does not follow from the actual notion of the nation-state. The sub- and inter-statist conception, on the other hand, commits this wrong unabashedly and seems to take pride in it. The sub- and inter-statist conception does not aspire to a homogeneous nation-state. Rather, it is content with political arrangements that at least prima facie do not seem to be egalitarian, since they provide certain rights to certain citizens of the state that other citizens do not have. They protect the national culture of the former group and their right to regulate many possible aspects of their lives within its framework. At the same time, other citizens, those who do not enjoy self-determination within that state, do not enjoy similar protection.[26]

However, is this criticism valid? I believe not, because the inequality in citizenship sanctioned by the sub-statist conception can at least be justified as unavoidable, since self-determination is homeland-dependent, at least under the assumptions of cultural nationalism. It is linked with homelands because of the central role which homelands play in defining the identities of almost all national groups. These groups (except for the Roma and the Sinti and perhaps a few other groups) are not only non-nomadic, but their respective homelands constitute an integral part of their identities. Many national groups invoke this fact in order to make unreasonable territorial claims. They sometimes demand sovereignty over territories that are part of their historical homelands even in cases where their members do not inhabit these territories. Such sovereignty is demanded in the name of what they call 'historical rights'. I shall discuss this notion in Chapter 4 below and reject the demands for territorial sovereignty that are based on it. However, I will also argue that the fact that the ties between national groups and their historical

---

[26] Problems of the sort discussed here, which result in the creation of two classes of citizens, are implicit in similar suggestions made by writers dealing with the problems of diaspora groups of *Gastarbeiter* in Western and Northern Europe. See Tomas Hammar, *Democracy and the Nation-State: Aliens, Denizens and Citizens in a World of International Migration* (Aldershot: Avebury, 1990). For the possibility of differentiated citizenship see also Yasemin Nuhoglu Soysal, *Limits of Citizenship: Migrants and Postnational Membership in Europe* (University of Chicago Press, 1994). Also, Mark Tushnet, 'United States Citizenship Policy and Liberal Universalism', *Georgetown Immigration Law Journal* 12 (1998), 311– 22.

homelands cannot serve as a basis for their right to territorial sovereignty over these homelands does not entail that such historical ties are entirely void of normative import. I will argue that these ties are essential for determining the location where the right to national self-determination under its sub-statist conception should be realized. Since homelands are essential for this purpose, a state that does not include the homelands of a given national group can hardly satisfy the interests in self-determination for members of that group. Individuals who identify with a certain national group and yet do not live in its homeland can therefore hardly expect the state where they do live to protect their interest in national self-determination.

For this reason, it could perhaps be claimed that the inequality in citizenship sanctioned by the sub-statist conception is not only unavoidable, but also does not constitute an unjust inequality. Rather, it expresses the state's equal concern for the differences in the interest that its diverse citizens have in their nationality. This inequality differs from the inequality in citizenship resulting from the statist conception. The latter makes moral distinctions on the basis of majority/minority membership, which is irrelevant to people's interest in their nationality. In contrast, the sub- and inter-statist conception makes moral distinctions on the basis of homeland/non-homeland membership. This distinction is inherently relevant to people's interest in their cultural nationality.

These differences have important practical implications as well. The inequality in citizenship created by the statist conception could offend people regardless of where they choose to live their lives. It can marginalize and alienate people in their own homelands, just because they belong to minority groups. This cannot occur in the case of the sub- and inter-statist conception. Individuals belonging to minority groups in the state where their homeland is located enjoy a normative status that is equal to that of individuals belonging to majority groups. Individuals who do not enjoy equal citizenship rights because they have emigrated from their homelands are not necessarily destined to suffer from this inequality. If they regard this inequality as a disadvantage, they should be allowed either to fully assimilate into the national group in the midst of which they are currently living, or to enjoy certain privileges in immigration in their original homelands. As noted above, I will discuss the special privileges that should be accorded to members of a national group who wish to return to their homeland in Chapter 5.

From the viewpoint of the interest in self-determination as interpreted by the liberal version of cultural nationalism, these two options must constitute an integral part of the arrangements for self-determination. The sub-statist conception must be accompanied by arrangements which, in certain cases, ease people's return to their national homelands or, in others, enable them to assimilate into the national group in whose midst they live. These arrangements are necessary for people who waver between the two possibilities of realizing their freedom-based and identity-based interests in culture. Their decision will depend on a number of factors: Which of the two cultures has played a larger role in the formation of their identities? Within which of these cultures did most of their endeavours take place? With which of these cultures do they identify to a larger extent? In many cases, the answers are not clear and therefore the option of the complete integration into either culture must be protected. In cases where there are clear answers, the option of integration into the appropriate culture must be protected. If, as it should, self-determination includes the right to implement either of these options, inequality ceases to be the outcome of the normative arrangements. Rather, it is the result of the fact that people have different interests. Some of them have an interest in national self-determination outside the state in which they reside while others are not clear as to where their interests in self-determination lie.

Furthermore, many people often find it difficult to decide which nationality is closest to their hearts and choose to view themselves as cosmopolitan or as lacking any interest in nationality. At least in comparison to the statist position, the sub- and inter-statist conception of self-determination, which advocates at least a partial separation of state citizenship and cultural membership, does take such people into account. It reflects the ambiguities that such people feel regarding their national affiliation. The sub- and inter-statist conception does not force them to take a clear stand on issues on which they are undecided. It enables them to do what they really want to do, either oscillate between the two or more nationalities, choosing what they like from each (namely, being cosmopolitan), or ignoring them altogether. The statist conception of self-determination allows states to be intolerant of such people since it allows the state to coerce people into belonging to one national culture.

From the perspective of liberalism, another advantage of the sub-statist conception that has not been sufficiently stressed so far is that it places fewer burdens on individuals and more on the collective. Where the statist conception allows nation-states to force individual immigrants to join their nation, the sub- and inter-statist conception obliges the host state and the host national group to admit immigrants who wish to join them. In short, the sub-statist conception changes the balance of duties between individuals and the collective in favour of the former.

On the basis of the above, I would like to suggest that the sub- and inter-statist conception of self-determination not only does not suffer from any of the disadvantages of the statist conception, but also has distinct liberal advantages. Despite the fact that it creates some inequality among citizens, this inequality is not one that ignores their interests. On the contrary, it is a type of inequality that expresses equal concern for the different interests in nationality that different people may have. Under this interpretation, the principle of self-determination asserts that there should be a state for each national group. That state would normally be the one that coincides with its historic homeland. Within the framework of this state, each national group would be entitled to a set of privileges that protect its existence and self-rule. It is reasonable to assume that weaker national groups should have more privileges. These privileges would constitute a manifestation of justice since they express equal concern for all national groups and all human beings, whether they have a sense of national belonging or not. Moreover, these privileges would impose more obligations on states and national groups than on individuals.

The sub-statist conception and social cohesion – revisiting statist nationalism

Subscribing to the sub- and inter-statist conception would mean accepting and actively supporting the world's multicultural reality. Subscribing to the sub- and inter-statist conception would mean giving up the ideal that cultural groups should have states of their own which is what the idea of the nation-state means within the framework of cultural nationalism. It is important to note that because the sub- and inter-statist conception implies the acceptance of the world's multicultural reality, subscribing to this conception would also mean giving up the ideal of the nation-state in its traditional sense within the framework of statist nationalism. As explained in Chapter 1, according to this type of nationalism, this ideal means that sovereign political units should strive not only for legal but also for cultural unity. According to the liberal version of this nationalism, such unity facilitates the implementation of ideals such as democracy, distributive justice and economic welfare. The advocates of liberal statist nationalism believe that a common national culture that is shared by the entire population promotes mutual understanding and trust without which citizenries cannot bear the burdens and make the compromises required in order to execute societal decisions.

As noted in the previous section, by abandoning the ideal of the nation-state in its sense within cultural nationalism, the sub- and inter-statist conception has made a morally inevitable concession. However, the sub-statist conception has at most abandoned the optimal realization of the aspirations of cultural nationalism and also has not entirely given up these aspirations, since it strives to allow members of national groups to carry out a wide range of human activity within the framework of their culture. The sub- and inter-statist conception also maintains normative equality among national groups in this matter. The sub- and inter-statist conception has very similar implications with regard to the aspirations of statist nationalism. First, due to the constraints imposed by the world's geodemographic conditions, abandoning the aspirations to achieve social cohesion by means of forging one cultural identity for the entire state population must be considered morally imperative. Thus, in most of the world's territories, the institutionalization of multinational and multicultural frameworks is a moral necessity. Secondly, though the institutionalization of multicultural frameworks could be viewed as equivalent to abandoning the means necessary for social cohesion, this is not necessarily the case. As many have argued, accepting the multicultural vision of states need not necessarily result in abandoning the measure of social cohesion required for the realization of political values such as democracy, distributive justice and economic welfare.

Let me begin with the first issue, namely, that concerning the moral necessity of institutionalizing multicultural and multinational frameworks in most of the world's states. Jeremy Waldron has addressed this issue by invoking a principle which he attributes to Kant and which he calls 'the principle of proximity'. According to this principle, 'people have a natural duty to enter into political society with those with whom they find themselves in a condition of unavoidable co-existence'.[27] According to Waldron, 'Kant assumes that we are always likely to find ourselves, in the first instance, alongside others we don't trust, others with whom we share little in the way of culture, mores or religion, others who disagree with us about justice.'[28] However, '[e]ven if the explanation of our being side-by-side now is the existence of injustice in the past, still we have a duty to bring our present relationship under the auspices of right and legality, and that means we must form and sustain a political society among us – all of us – whether we like one another, or the circumstances under which we came into one another's company or not'.[29] This is because 'entering into political society with those with whom you were otherwise likely to be in conflict – was a matter of natural duty'.[30] Provided that a reasonable answer to the question of when it is appropriate to describe a situation as one in which people find themselves 'in a condition of unavoidable co-existence' can be found, Waldron's position seems inescapable.

[27] Jeremy Waldron, 'Redressing Historic Injustice', a paper presented in a colloquium on historical justice, Einstein Forum, Potsdam, 12–14 July 2001, p. 5.
[28] *Ibid.*, p. 9.   [29] *Ibid.*, p. 5.   [30] *Ibid.*, p. 6.

An argument against this position could perhaps be that, assuming that a common cultural identity is a necessary condition for the social cohesion required for the realization of the values of democracy and distributive justice, accepting the existence of political societies which do not enjoy a unified cultural identity would therefore mean abandoning political values that are no less important than the avoidance of violence and conflict. This brings us to the second issue mentioned above, namely, the measure of social cohesion required for the realization of political values such as democracy, distributive justice and economic welfare. This issue is mainly an empirical one. Cases such as Switzerland and Belgium refute the claim that the lack of one shared cultural identity means that it is entirely impossible to achieve the degree of social cohesion among a state citizenry necessary to realize the relevant values. An historical or geographic reality in which different groups live in a 'condition of unavoidable co-existence' and are therefore forced to create one political unit could create a sense of shared fate and social cohesion sufficient for the purpose of continuing the political co-operation between these groups. As indicated above, whether the historical and/or geographical circumstances which brought different groups into one political unit should be viewed as inevitable constraints forcing these groups to continue their political partnership and to view themselves as sharing one fate is a difficult question. The answer often depends on whether it is practically and morally feasible to leave the partnership and seek a separate and independent future. The lack of cohesion and the instability that often characterize states whose populations do not share one cultural identity seems to be due to the indeterminate character of these questions and the fact that they depend on what are often subjective evaluations which also change over time.[31]

However, if the sub- and inter-statist conception of national self-determination presented here is indeed just and is accepted as the appropriate way to interpret the constitutional relations between nations and states, it could weaken at least two factors which might jeopardize the social cohesion within multinational states and which could motivate national groups to establish new states and seek a separate future. One such factor is the inferior normative status that many groups have in the states where they coexist with other groups, since these states are conceived of as belonging to the other groups. The second factor is their hope to establish a state that belongs to them only and thus upgrade

---

[31] Compare the different circumstances within which the Scots had to decide whether to live in a united kingdom with the English at the beginning of the eighteenth century as opposed to the beginning of the nineteenth century and then again at the beginning of the twenty-first.

their normative status. The universal acceptance of the sub- and inter-statist conception as a way of interpreting the constitutional relationship between states and cultural groups enjoying self-determination within their framework would weaken both these factors. First, it would facilitate equal normative status for all national groups within the states in which they live. Secondly, it would undermine the hope of many national groups to upgrade their normative status by achieving statehood.

What forms of social cohesion should populations of states have in cases where such populations do not share one common cultural identity? Since my main goal in this study and in the present chapter was to outline the maximum degree of self-rule that cultural groups could expect to attain in the world's current geodemographic conditions and to examine the compatibility of this amount of self-rule with the liberal interpretation of cultural nationalism, I shall not answer the present question in the detail it deserves. However, it should be noted that short of full cultural unity, social cohesion could also develop on the basis of partial cultural unity or a historical partnership and a sense of common fate. What is necessary is that the various segments of the population are committed to the constitutional framework of their state and view it as just. In this context, I would like to refer to the republican conceptions of patriotism and love of one's country mentioned in Chapter 1 above. According to these conceptions, which were common throughout the seventeenth and eighteenth centuries and perhaps also in the ancient world, the concept of patriotism refers to the ties that members of a political community have with political ideals and principles rather than with a common culture and a common territory. As mentioned in Chapter 1, Habermas's notion of constitutional patriotism is an attempt to revive this idea. Habermas's notion seems to revolve around the possibility that the citizens of the state 'each identify with [its] institutions because they are subject to them and identify with the general principles which they embody'.[32] The traditional notion of republican patriotism could be understood as revolving around the possibility that the state's citizens 'identify with [its] institutions because they are subject to them and identify with the particular, historically situated way in which these institutions embody values such as liberty, justice, and democracy'.[33] Andrew Mason, who points out these possible interpretations of the notion of republican patriotism on the one hand, and Habermas's notion of constitutional patriotism on the other, suggests a third, even more minimalist, interpretation of the basis

[32] Andrew Mason, 'Political Community, Liberal-Nationalism, and the Ethics of Assimilation', *Ethics* 109 (1999), 279.
[33] *Ibid.*

required for states' social cohesion. In his view, social cohesion can be achieved even if citizens 'cannot be said genuinely to share principles'. What is needed is that they 'value the same institutions, and identify with them in a way that is sufficient to sustain them, but for very different reasons'.[34]

As mentioned in Chapter 1 above, republican patriotism proved to lack sufficient appeal in the nineteenth and twentieth centuries. It is even more likely that the models suggested by Habermas and Mason would have met a similar fate. The models that proved sufficient for cohesion in the nineteenth and twentieth centuries were those of statist nationalism. One such model was that of complete cultural homogeneity and one national identity for the population of any particular state. (This was achieved either by assimilating various territorial populations into one culture as in France, for example, or, as in Germany, by establishing a state around a population which had enjoyed such unity prior to the establishment of the state.) Another model was the more moderate one of creating a common nationality and a strong core of cultural unity while preserving some cultural differences and the nested nationalities of the groups sharing the common nationality (for example, England, Scotland and Wales in Britain). However, the fact that these models did indeed succeed in achieving cohesion does not constitute a sufficient reason to stick to the traditional notions of statist nationalism. The price paid for formation of states around existing national groups or by merging multicultural populations (especially indigenous populations) into one cultural identity has been very high in terms of human suffering. Attempts to repeat such strategies today are very unlikely to succeed. Models such as those suggested by Habermas and Mason might therefore be more appropriate in the present and in the future.

The sub- and inter-statist conception of self-determination as presented here is compatible with the various models for cohesion except for that of complete cultural homogeneity. All these models allow the different cultural groups in the state to adhere to their original culture and to preserve their sense of belonging to it. All these models are compatible with the sub-statist conception since all models could be realized while all of the world's national groups enjoy the privileges included in the sub-statist conception in their respective homelands. For example, Jews, Scots and Chinese people living in Britain could be 'constitutional patriots' there, while simultaneously adhering and belonging to their respective Jewish, Scottish and Chinese cultures. They could also be more than just 'constitutional patriots' in Britain by sharing its language, some

---

[34] *Ibid.*, 281.

of its traditions and acquiring a sense of *joining* its history (as in the case of many British Jews) or *belonging* to it from the start (as in the case of the Scots). They could do all this while partly adhering to their original cultures although those are more fully realized in their homelands. The sub-statist conception is compatible with these models of cohesion since it only requires relinquishing the idea that nations should enjoy independent statehood. According to the sub-statist conception, each nation should have a package of special privileges within its homeland. These privileges would allow its members to live their lives within their original culture as much as possible. In order to achieve this, there is no need to refrain from attempts to achieve some degree of cultural unity and create a cultural core in states with culturally mixed populations. What is important is that the main components that comprise this cultural core, namely, the language and various cultural institutions, remain the language and institutions of the homeland groups existing in these states.[35] For example, Switzerland maintains its four languages, its 'legacies of remembrances' and various institutions and constitutional arrangements as its cultural core even though there are other cultural groups living there, such as Turks and Yugoslavs. For each of these groups, there is a place somewhere else in the world where their respective language, traditions and institutions constitute the cultural core.

---

[35] By 'homeland groups' I mean groups that regard the territories of the state or a part thereof as important components of their identity. I do not mean groups that were the first (in relation to existing national groups) to occupy such territories. Thus, the Quebecois are no less a homeland group in Canada than the Inuit. The notion of homeland is dealt with more extensively in Chapter 4 below.

4   Historical rights and homelands

Introduction: two conceptions of historical rights

Rejecting the statist conception of national self-determination means, among other things, rejecting it as a basis for the right of national groups to territorial sovereignty. However, the right to self-determination is not the only principle to which national groups resort when demanding such sovereignty. Quite often they demand sovereignty in the name of what they call 'historical rights'. They usually make claims to historical rights independently of the question of whether they are already exercising their rights to self-determination elsewhere. In addition, national groups quite frequently apply such claims to territories that are not inhabited by members of their particular national group. When demanding sovereignty over such territories in the name of historical rights, they do so, of course, not so much in order to rule over those who are currently residing in the territory in question, but rather in order to acquire dominant demographic and cultural presence in this particular territory.

Territorial demands based on historical rights have a long history. Examples can be found in the writings of the ancient world's historians as well as on the front pages of daily newspapers today. Tacitus tells the story of the people of Sparta who submitted various petitions to Emperor Tiberius during the first few decades of the Common Era demanding the return of Messene to their possession. They had lost it to the Thebans some centuries earlier.[1] The Spartans regarded Messene as part of their fatherland. When they lost Messene, their crown prince Archidamus bewailed it, equating its loss with the loss of Sparta itself.[2] While this chapter was in progress, international newspapers reported the Serb

---

[1] See Tacitus, *The Annals of Imperial Rome*, Book IV, chap. 43.
[2] 'I should feel disgraced . . . if I did not strive with all the strength that is in me to prevent this territory, which our fathers left to us, from becoming the possession of our slaves. . . . To be sure, if we are in a mood not to defend our title to anything, not even if they demand that we abandon Sparta itself, it is idle to be concerned about Messene; but if not one of you would consent to live if torn from the fatherland, then you ought to be of the same

demand to retain Albanian-populated Kosovo, again, because they considered it an important part of their historical homeland. The history of the last two centuries provides many other examples, some of which I shall mention below. One of the purposes of the present chapter is to examine these claims. In Chapter 3, I rejected the claim that the right to national self-determination could justify a right to statehood. In this chapter, I shall reject the thesis that historical rights could justify territorial sovereignty for the same reasons. However, the main goal of this chapter is to clarify the connection between the sub- and inter-statist conception of self-determination presented in Chapter 3 and the concept of homeland. As we shall see, the most important meaning of claims to historical rights is associated with this concept. In this sense, such claims are not entirely void of normative significance. Historical rights could be a source for considerations on the basis of which the location of self-determination under its sub-statist conception should be determined.

When political philosophers refer to historical rights they have in mind such rights as A's right to a piece of land because he was first to occupy and cultivate it, or because he acquired it by means of a contract, or will or through matrimony.[3] These rights are different from such rights as the right to freedom of speech, the right to a minimum wage or the right to privacy. The latter can be said to be ahistorical. Their holders acquire them by virtue of belonging to general categories, such as being human or adult citizens, and not by virtue of particular events with which they are specifically associated. The rights of the former type are 'historical' because their holders acquire them by virtue of specific events that occurred at particular points in time.[4] In this very broad sense of the term, whatever takes place in time is 'historical'. Thus, every sneeze and hiccup could be considered historical. However, the term 'historical' is usually used in more narrow contexts. It does not denote each and every event occurring in time, but rather those events that we perceive as significant. For example, the assassination of the Austrian archduke in Sarajevo on a summer morning in 1914 is regarded as an event worthy of being called 'historical', in contrast, for example, to the fact that the archduke brushed his teeth the same morning.[5] The historical rights to

---

mind about that country; for in both cases we can advance the same justifications and the same reasons for our claim' (Isocrates, *Archidamus*). (I am grateful to Irad Malkin for pointing out this example to me).

[3] The tradition of calling such rights 'historical' has developed since Nozick's book *Anarchy, State and Utopia*.

[4] Compare with the analogous distinction between special and general rights, H. L. A. Hart, 'Are There Any Natural Rights?', in Jeremy Waldron (ed.), *Theories of Rights* (Oxford University Press, 1984), p. 84.

[5] Philosophers of history call this 'the problem of selection'. See William H. Dray, *Philosophy of History*, 2nd edition (Englewood Cliffs, NJ: Prentice Hall, 1993), pp. 37–8.

be discussed here – those that are used in nationalist disputes mainly in order to justify territorial claims – are 'historical' in this narrow sense; that is, they are historical by virtue of being acquired through significant events (or series of events). In public and academic political discourse, the notion of historical rights in this narrower sense oscillates between two conceptions. One conception focuses on the primacy of the national group in the history of the territory over which it demands sovereignty, while the other conception focuses on the primacy of that territory in the history of the national group demanding the sovereignty.

According to the first conception, the fact that a national group was first to occupy a disputed territory (at least in relation to existing national groups) is conceived within modern nationalist disputes (and perhaps not only modern disputes)[6] as a crucial link in the history of that territory for the purpose of determining sovereignty over it. On the basis of such a claim, Thomas Masaryk tried to convince the leaders of the countries that won World War I to include the Sudeten district, then mostly inhabited by Germans, within the Czechoslovakian republic. Masaryk referred to Czechoslovakia's right to sovereignty in the Sudeten district as a historical right, as it was the first in a succession of sovereigns in that area.[7] This conception of historical rights, a 'first occupancy conception', is also implicit in Iraq's demand for Kuwait and in that of the Iranians for some of the islands of Abu Musa from the United Arab Emirates.[8] The same conception figures in the Tamil–Sinhalese dispute over Sri Lanka, the Jewish–Palestinian dispute over Palestine, and the territorial demands which Native Americans, New Zealanders and Australians have made against the European populations of their countries.[9]

---

[6] Without taking sides in the dispute regarding whether or not, and to what extent nationalism is a modern phenomenon, it should be noted that territorial conflicts in which national or quasi-national groups invoke their primacy in the disputed territory are not entirely modern. The Spartans' complaint to Tiberius mentioned earlier is not the only example. A very similar story appears in the Talmud (Sanhedrin, 91: 1). It is about a dispute between the Israelites and Canaanites which was brought before Alexander the Great. The Canaanites argued that they had lived in Canaan before the Israelites and supported their claim with evidence from the Torah according to which the land of Canaan was promised to the Israelites. ('Command the children of Israel, and say unto them, When ye come into the land of Canaan (this is the land that shall fall unto you for an inheritance, even the land of Canaan according to the borders thereof).' (Numbers 34:1)). By calling it the land of Canaan, the Torah in fact admits that the Canaanites had indeed inhabited the land before the Jews. The Canaanites should therefore own it.

[7] Thomas G. Masaryk, *The Making of a State* (London: George Allen and Unwin, 1927), pp. 385–6.

[8] See Farhang Mehr, *A Colonial Legacy: The Dispute over the Islands of Abu Musa, and the Greater and Lesser Tumbs* (Lanham, MD: University Press of America, 1997).

[9] On the demands of the aboriginal peoples against the settlers' nations see for example: David Lyons, 'The New Indian Claims and Original Rights to Land', in Jeffrey Paul (ed.), *Reading Nozick: Essays on Anarchy, State, and Utopia* (Oxford: Basil Blackwell,

The great appeal of this argument in disputes between nations is sometimes demonstrated by the fact that the parties that seem to be the underdogs in these disputes do not try to deny the validity of this argument. What they do instead is construct a genealogy that supposedly demonstrates their kinship ties to extinct peoples who had occupied the disputed territories before their rivals. They thus win the argument by themselves becoming the first occupants. For example, among the peoples that exist today, the Hungarians were the first to maintain organized settlements in Transylvania. Romanians try to prove that they were the first by claiming to be descendants of the Romans who conquered Dacia (of which Transylvania is a part), in the second century AD.[10] Since among the peoples that exist today, the Jews were the first to maintain an organized settlement in Canaan, that is, Eretz Yisrael or Palestine, the Palestinians have tried to prove they were the first occupants by claiming to have descended from the Canaanites, who had occupied the land before the ancient Hebrews.[11]

According to the second conception, the fact that the disputed territory is of primary importance in forming the historical identity of the group, is considered as strong enough reason for the purposes of determining sovereignty over it. Israel's declaration of independence clearly expresses this conception. It states that it was in Eretz Yisrael that 'the Jewish people came into being', and that it was there that 'the people's spiritual, religious and political image was forged', where 'it lived a life of sovereign independence, in which it created national and universal cultural treasures'. 'Bearing this historical tie', the declaration goes on to say, 'the Jews of every generation have striven to return and re-embrace their ancient homeland.' These passages express a view according to which the experiences which the Jews underwent in Palestine were formative in their becoming a nation. This is why they strive now to return to Palestine. As

---

1982), pp. 355–79; J. Waldron, 'Superseding Historic Injustice', *Ethics* 103 (1992), 4–28; John A. Simmons, 'Historical Rights and Fair Shares', *Law and Philosophy* 14 (1995), 149–84; Margaret Moore, 'The Territorial Dimension of Self-Determination', in Moore (ed.), *National Self-Determination and Secession*, pp. 134–57; Andrew Sharp, *Justice and the Māori: The Philosophy and Practice of Māori Claims in New Zealand Since the 1970s*, 2nd edition (Auckland: Oxford University Press, 1997); Ross Poole, *Nation and Identity* (London and New York: Routledge, 1999), chap. 4; Paul Haveman (ed.), *Indigenous Peoples' Rights in Australia, Canada & New Zealand* (Auckland: Oxford University Press, 1999); Duncan Ivison, Paul Patton and Will Sanders (eds.), *Political Theory and the Rights of Indigenous Peoples* (Cambridge University Press, 2000).

[10] See Nicolae Stoicescu, *The Continuity of the Romanian People* (Bucharest: Editura Stiintifica si Enciclopedica, 1983).

[11] An Israeli daily recently published a news item with the following title: 'Palestinian Archeologists: We have uncovered Canaanite buildings from 3000 B.C., which confirms our historical right to Palestine' (Ha'aretz, 4 August 1998.)

implied here, the Jews have an historical right to Eretz Yisrael, not because they were the first among contemporary peoples to occupy it, but
rather because it was of primary importance in forming their identity as
an historical entity.

The second conception of historical rights shifts the emphasis from
a people's primacy in a given territory to the primacy of this territory
for a given people. One result of this shift is that the primacy considered relevant is mainly value-based rather than chronological. Moreover,
according to the first occupancy conception, the normative importance
of the entitling fact is based upon its chronological primacy, while within
the second conception which could be called 'the formative territories
conception', the chronological primacy is based on the normative importance of the territory. Because the territory is of primary importance in
the formation of the group, it is also the first territory in the chronological
sense in which the group as such ever existed.

Both conceptions of historical rights, namely, that of 'first occupancy'
and that of the 'right to formative territories', involve problems that pertain to the criteria to be used in order to apply each of their key concepts.
That is, with regard to first occupancy, when can a people be said to
'occupy' a territory? Can a people occupy a territory that lies beyond
the area actually inhabited by its members?[12] Similar problems are raised
by the notion of historical rights as rights to formative territories. When
can a territory or an object justly be said to be 'of formative value' to
the historical identity of a given people? Should we adopt objective and
uniform criteria for answering the above questions? Or should we ascribe
some importance to the subjective feelings of the people whose right is
in question, provided that there is documentation of these feelings?

I believe these difficulties can somehow be resolved, but do not wish to
elaborate on them here. The more significant problems concerning historical rights do not pertain to how the conceptions of occupancy and formativeness should be applied, but rather to the normative status of these
conceptions. Does the fact that a given people were the first to occupy
a certain territory, or that the territory is of formative value for a given
people indeed justify granting this people sovereignty over this territory
and/or the right to demographic and cultural presence there?[13] In answering this question, the significance of claiming a right to sovereignty must

[12] With regard to this point, Rousseau scoffed at the practice of fifteenth and sixteenth-
century European discoverers to stake a claim to the places they reached by sounding
declarations in ceremonies held for this purpose. See Jean Jacques Rousseau, *The Social
Contract*, book I, chap. 9.

[13] Answering these normative questions is my main concern in this chapter. However, this
should not conceal the fact that national movements invoke claims of historical rights as
mobilizing tools and that their efficiency as such deserves a separate discussion. It should

be borne in mind. A right to sovereignty over a given territory means a power to subject the whole world to the right-holder's decisions regarding life within this territory and to his or her decisions regarding the use and enjoyment of this territory and the resources which it contains.[14] To sustain such significant consequences, a claim to such a right must be backed by powerful considerations.

In what follows I will examine what considerations regarding vital needs and interests of the people concerned could be linked to first occupancy and formativeness respectively. However, my discussion requires two further distinctions. The first distinction pertains to whether first occupancy and formativeness could justify *acquisition of territorial rights within the framework of distributive justice*, as opposed to whether they could justify *restitution of territorial rights within the framework of corrective justice*. When national groups nowadays invoke historical rights in order to justify territorial claims they usually do so in order to demand the restitution of territorial rights. However, it must be noted that such demands for restitution are inconceivable if the historical rights under consideration did not also justify rights of acquisition in the first place. If the demand to restore the sovereignty of a given nation in a given territory is based either on first occupancy or on a formative tie, then it necessarily presupposes that this occupancy and formative tie were also grounds for its sovereignty over the territory in question before the physical tie with that territory was lost. Only if this presupposition is indeed valid, that is, only if the historical rights under discussion here constitute primary rights of acquisition within distributive justice, can the loss of the physical tie with the territory be considered a wrong which must be rectified by returning the territory to the possession and sovereignty of the group that has lost it.

The distinction between the role of historical rights as grounds for acquisition within distributive justice, and the role of historical rights as grounds for restitution within corrective justice is important in practice not only because their validity as rights of distributive justice is a necessary condition for their ability to play a role within corrective justice, but also because this validity is *merely* a necessary condition. As we shall see below, historical rights as grounds for acquisition do not constitute a

---

be noted that such claims usually sustain popular participation in national movements only to the extent that they are supported by expectations of concrete gains or losses. Moreover, it also should be noted that claims to sovereignty over territories have more often been recognized not as a result of acknowledging their moral justifiability, but rather because of victory in war or international treaties that support a particular balance of power.

[14] Thus, territorial sovereignty seems to be more than ownership. On the need to distinguish between the two see Lea Brilmayer, 'Consent, Contract and Territory', *Minnesota Law Review* 74 (1989), 15.

sufficient condition for restitution. Especially for reasons associated with limitation, prescription and adverse possession, the fact that historical rights may play a certain role within the context of distributive justice does not automatically justify granting them a similar role within the context of corrective justice, especially not for purposes of restitution.[15]

The second distinction that my discussion requires is between *the right to territorial sovereignty* and, on the other hand, how *the location of territorial sovereignty* is to be determined. The need to make this distinction stems from the fact that peoples' right to territorial sovereignty could be based on ahistorical considerations such as their right to self-determination and independent statehood. National groups could be entitled to independent statehood and therefore to territorial sovereignty simply by virtue of being national groups and not by virtue of particular events with which they may specifically be associated. If national groups have a right to territorial sovereignty then, in order to exercise it, questions concerning the location of the territories to be under their sovereignty must first be resolved. First occupancy and formativeness could serve as bases for resolving the issue of location even if they cannot serve as bases for the very right to territorial sovereignty. However, it must be noted that considerations for determining the location of sovereignty do not necessarily apply to the scope of this sovereignty. The scope of this sovereignty could perhaps be determined by the size of the groups, their lifestyles and other factors. Thus, it could be the case that the territorial sovereignty of a given national group (the specific location of which is determined either by first occupancy or formativeness) would extend only over *part of the territory* which was first occupied by that group or with which this group has formative ties. It need not necessarily extend over the *entire territory*. Hence the practical importance of the present distinction.

---

[15] It must be stressed that the existence of corrective/remedial rights in the realms of sovereignty and property, though they are necessarily historical (for people have them by virtue of events with which they are specifically connected), does not entail the existence of distributive/primary historical rights. John Simmons seems to believe otherwise. According to him, since our moral and legal practices take historical rights of rectification very seriously, we need also take historical rights in acquisition seriously (see Simmons, 'Historical Rights and Fair Shares', 156). However, it seems to me that this conclusion is misconceived. One may take rectification rights seriously, as legal and moral practices in fact do. Yet this does not entail that the primary rights themselves are historical. It is possible for a person to have been the owner of a piece of property not necessarily because he was the first to occupy it or because he had a formative tie with it, but because, like everyone else, he is entitled to a piece of property for one reason or another. If one believes that X ought to compensate Y for a piece of land of which he dispossessed him, one need not necessarily believe that Y's original title to this piece was based necessarily on Y's first occupancy of it, or his formative tie with it. On the relationship between distributive and corrective historical rights see also note 35 below.

In the second part of this chapter, I shall discuss the possibility that historical rights in their first conception – that of first occupancy – could form a basis for the right to territorial sovereignty. In the third part of this chapter, I shall discuss the possibility that historical rights in their second conception – that of formative ties – could form such a basis. The first conception (first occupancy) has been discussed extensively in the legal and philosophical literature dealing with the right to private property. Within this literature, first occupancy has been a dead horse for a long time. This issue should perhaps be invoked again in the context of national disputes because it is frequently used by nationalists. In any case, it might help clarify the role played by historical rights in national disputes when they are conceived as rights to formative territories. In the next section, after rejecting first occupancy as a basis for the very right to territorial sovereignty, I shall argue that it can serve as a basis for the right to determine the site of sovereignty for purposes of acquisition, but not for purposes of restitution. Later in this chapter (pp. 109–23) I shall argue that formative ties also could not serve as a basis for the very right to sovereignty. However, formative ties could serve as a basis for determining the site of national self-determination, sometimes not only with regard to the original acquisition and preservation of that site, but also in order to restitute physical ties with it.

First occupancy

First occupancy as grounds for sovereignty

According to Raz, to have a right means to have an interest that justifies imposing a duty or duties on others.[16] If we accept this definition, then it follows that a nation's first occupancy of a given territory justifies its sovereignty over it if it has interests in it (due to the fact that it was its first occupant) that justify imposing the duties that correspond to sovereignty rights on the whole world. It is clear that neither the interest that national groups have in their own continuous survival, nor their interests in self-determination (such as the interest in cultural preservation, or the interest in determining their own destiny), necessarily require their sovereignty over the territories in which they were the first occupants. With regard to the interest in continuous survival, national groups could also survive without any sovereignty rights. This, in fact, has been the case for many national groups. The survival of national groups certainly does not depend on gaining sovereignty over the specific territories that they were

---

[16] See J. Raz, *The Morality of Freedom* (Oxford University Press, 1986), chap. 7.

first to occupy. As for the interests in self-determination, it is widely believed that the fulfilment of these interests usually requires territorial sovereignty. I shall argue below that self-determination is, indeed, typically connected with the specific territories that have acquired primacy in the nation's history. However, it is not clear why self-determination has anything to do with first occupancy in any specific territory. The interests which national groups have in self-determination do not seem to derive from the fact that they were first to occupy a given territory. Nor does it seem that the satisfaction of these interests depends on the territories that they were first to occupy.

If first occupancy plays any special role whatsoever, that is, if it constitutes a source of any human interest, then this interest must in some way be related to the expectations held by the first occupants with regard to the territories they occupied. David Hume was of the opinion that first occupants of a territory would eventually develop expectations to continue occupying this territory for a prolonged period.[17] Perhaps first occupants may develop such expectations because they did not evict anyone from the territories in which they were first occupants. However, most nations existing today, including those who resort to historical rights, cannot seriously claim that they are first occupants in this sense (except, perhaps, for some of the aboriginal peoples of North America, Australia and New Zealand).[18] At most they can claim that they are first relative to all other nations that exist today.[19] They therefore expect that none of the latter should object to their occupation for reasons related to a common past. However, could such expectations serve as a basis for sovereignty rights? It seems that the answer to this question must be negative not only with regard to occupants whose occupancy is first relative to all other nations

[17] See Hume, *A Treatise on Human Nature*, book III, chap. 2, sec. 3. See also Jeremy Bentham, 'Principles of the Civil Code', in Charles K. Ogden (ed.), *Jeremy Bentham: The Theory of Legislation* (London: Routledge and Kegan Paul, 1931), pp. 158–98; Waldron, *The Right to Private Property*, p. 286.

[18] It is likely that only some of these groups could claim absolute primacy in these territories. See Kymlicka, *Multicultural Citizenship*, p. 220. Ross Poole argues that the Australian aborigines have lived there for 60,000 years. 'In terms of any conceivable human experience of time, the Aborigines have been in Australia forever' (Poole, *Nation and Identity*, p. 129). See also Moore, 'The Territorial Dimension', p. 143.

[19] According to the Talmudic source cited in note 6 above, the Jews who presented their dispute with the Canaanites to Alexander acknowledged the fact that they were not really the first occupants in Canaan. To overcome this difficulty, they quoted the biblical curse according to which the Canaanites were doomed to be slaves ('Cursed be Canaan; A servant of servants shall he be unto his brethren' (*Genesis* 9, 25)). They then argued that slaves could not own property. Again, this is similar to the Spartan–Messenian case. The Spartans acknowledged the fact that they were not the first occupants of Messene, but claimed sovereignty over it since they regarded its original occupants to be their slaves. This is explicitly stated by Archidamus quoted in note 2 above.

that exist today, but also with regard to occupants whose primacy is absolute. If absolute first occupants still occupy the territories in which they were the first occupants, then they could at most assume that it is *prima facie* undesirable to push them out of these territories by resorting to violent or fraudulent means. Those who are first occupants only in the relative sense could assume, *ex hypothesis*, that no existing nation could resort to grievances pertaining to a common past in order to justify evicting them. However, this does not justify sovereignty rights, since sovereignty means a right to govern the territory even if others are currently occupying it.[20] The duties corresponding to this right involve the risk of losing sources of livelihood as well as the conditions necessary for freedom. It seems unlikely that the expectations of absolute first occupants, and especially the expectations of those whose occupancy is first only relative to other existing nations, could be important enough to justify endangering such urgent interests. Rousseau stated this point clearly. 'How can one man or a whole people take possession of vast territories, thereby excluding the rest of the world from their enjoyment, save by an act of criminal usurpation, since, as the result of such an act, the rest of humanity is deprived of the amenities for dwelling and subsistence which nature has provided for their common enjoyment?'[21]

The above quote from Rousseau contains two points. One pertains to the intensity of the sacrifice entailed by the duties corresponding to sovereignty rights. The other concerns the inequality resulting from the imposition of these duties. Rousseau deals with the possibility of obtaining sovereignty by virtue of first occupancy, without specifying the interest which is to be protected by granting sovereignty to first occupants. However, it seems safe to believe that his arguments and conclusion apply if the interest in question is the first occupant's interest that his expectations be respected. People develop various sorts of expectations and might have an interest that their expectations be respected. However, whether these expectations could serve as a basis for rights depends on the price others would have to pay for respecting these rights. In our case it seems quite obvious that first occupancy cannot serve as a basis for acquiring sovereignty.

Many of those who use the historical rights argument in the first occupancy sense tend to speak of first occupancy without adding elements which play a central role in what is held to be the best philosophical version of the original acquisition argument for private property, namely, that

---

[20] These points are similar to those cited by Waldron from Kant and others with regard to first occupancy as a basis for the right to private property. See Waldron, *The Right to Private Property*, pp. 267–8.

[21] Rousseau, *The Social Contract*, book I, chap. 9.

proposed by John Locke. Locke insisted not merely on first occupancy, but on first cultivation of what beforehand had been common property. One might want to believe that the first occupancy argument for sovereignty could be rescued if it were stated in terms of Locke's original acquisition argument for private property. However, this would not save the argument. Rousseau's objections against first occupancy regarding the magnitude of the burdens imposed by acknowledging first occupancy as grounds for sovereignty, and the inequality entailed by such recognition, also apply to original acquisition by labour and cultivation.[22]

The purpose of the above arguments is to deny the possibility of granting sovereignty to first occupants who still occupy the territories over which they claim sovereignty. According to these arguments, first occupancy cannot be a basis for acquiring and preserving sovereignty within the framework of distributive justice. However, as noted above, the national groups that usually resort to arguments based on historical rights are national groups that lost their occupancy many generations ago and wish to restore it. They do not demand the preservation of the status quo, but rather the restitution of a previous state of affairs. If the wisdom inherent in Rousseau's dictum is sufficient for denying sovereignty to first occupants who still occupy the territory in question, then, *a fortiori*, it must be sufficient for denying sovereignty to first occupants who have lost their occupancy. From this it does not follow that a possession fraudulently or violently usurped in recent times need not be returned to its former possessor. However, what the perpetrator could grant the victim is that the victim repossess the property. If the arguments which claim that first occupancy in a territory cannot justify sovereignty over it in the first place are sound, then first occupancy cannot justify sovereignty merely because the occupant had been dispossessed and was later reinstated.

Grounds for determining the location of a people's self-determination

Thus, first occupancy cannot serve as grounds for territorial sovereignty. However, if a general right of nations to territorial sovereignty could be justified by ahistorical considerations such as their interests in self-determination, should first occupancy serve as the basis for resolving the

---

[22] Jeremy Waldron has convincingly shown this in detail with regard to private property and with regard to all possible sorts of unilateral acquisition, not only with regard to first occupancy. He formulated Rousseau's arguments in terms of contractarian political morality. Waldron also has demonstrated how the standard method by which adherents of original acquisition theories of property attempt to avoid the present criticism, namely, modifying it by a Lockean Proviso, is bound to fail. See Waldron, *The Right to Private Property*, chap. 7.

issue of determining the site of this sovereignty? I would like to argue that it could in principle serve as such a basis, since merely determining the location of a given people's sovereignty does not involve imposing on others the type of concessions that derive from the duties and liabilities corresponding to sovereignty rights. Given the scarcity of resources and space in the world, grounding sovereignty rights on first occupancy may, as shown above, endanger the livelihood and autonomy of many people. However, no such danger is involved if first occupancy only serves as grounds for determining the location of sovereignty. People will only have to pay the price of being excluded from specific areas. These areas would not be any larger than those from which they would in any case be excluded, if the territorial rights accompanying self-determination were justly distributed among national groups.

Furthermore, unlike the expectations of first occupants that they be granted sovereignty, their expectation that first occupancy should serve to determine the site where their territorial rights are to be realized is justifiable. This is so since the issue of the site for the realization of such rights, as opposed to, for example, the issue of the scope of these territories, can only be resolved by methods of pure procedural justice such as flipping a coin.[23] There are no independent substantive criteria for determining this issue.[24] Since chance is involved here, why not resort to historical chance, that is, to the fact that certain peoples happened to occupy certain regions before others did? Why is flipping a coin any better for that purpose than historical chance? In order to see that this is indeed the situation, it is sufficient to imagine a kind of original position with a Rawlsian veil of ignorance. What people know is that they belong to a certain people and that this people is located in a certain territory. However, they don't know which people they belong to and which territory it occupies. Would they opt for flipping a coin or for staying put? The risk of moving to worse places due to flipping the coin is equal to the risk of being in a bad spot due to staying put. Consequently, they are likely to choose the latter. Moreover, the criterion of first occupancy provides the simplest, most convenient and most economical procedure for solving the problem of determining the site of the territorial sovereignty (or lesser territorial rights accompanying self-determination) of various peoples. Any other procedure would entail the relocation of peoples, which would be costly and would involve extreme discomfort. The expectation of the first occupants of a territory that their occupancy should

---

[23] On the concept of pure procedural justice see Rawls, *A Theory of Justice*, p. 86.

[24] Such substantive criteria could, for example, be different peoples' taking turns in occupying given territories. However, this of course is impractical.

serve as grounds for locating their territorial rights are thus sound, and can serve as grounds for determining the site of these rights.

All this, however, if it indeed proves to be correct, applies only when the first occupant is also the present occupant. First occupancy could serve as a basis for determining the site of sovereignty for the purpose of acquiring and preserving it. If a certain people was the first occupant of a given territory but lost its physical tie with it, then considerations of convenience and economy can no longer be invoked to justify the location of this people's self-determination in that particular territory. To the contrary, these considerations now favour determining the territory in question as the site for the current occupants' self-determination. Of course, this is subject to the condition that the later occupant did not attain occupancy through morally objectionable means. If this occupancy was attained through such means then, first, it would not be supported by one of the reasons cited above as supporting the current occupancy as grounds for determining the location of sovereignty, that is, historical coincidence as preferable to flipping a coin, for the occupancy is not a result of a morally neutral coincidence. Secondly, there would be reasons for not allowing the present occupant to enjoy the occupancy since it was attained through violence. However, if the later occupancies are not associated with such moral wrongs, or if they are associated with ancient wrongs that are subject to prescription, then these later occupancies rather than the first occupancy are supported by the reasons presented above as favouring first occupancy.

Hence, in cases of restoring a previous state of affairs, first occupancy does not only fail to provide a basis for territorial sovereignty, but also fails to justify a more limited potential right, namely, a right to determine the site of territorial sovereignty. This is significant in view of the fact that historical rights are most often employed to demand the restitution of old regimes, not the preservation of existing ones. As we shall see below, the alternative construal of historical rights as rights to formative territories may constitute a better basis for the restitution of sites for sovereignty, a basis which may be of practical significance in at least some cases.

The right to formative territories

Grounds for territorial sovereignty

Unlike the above interpretation of historical rights, if historical rights are interpreted as rights to formative territories, it is not difficult to identify interests that these rights are meant to protect. Attempts to identify such interests are far less unnatural than my above efforts to extricate a particular interest that is to be protected by historical rights in their first occupancy conception. If the events thought to have formed the historical identity of a national group took place in specific territories, it seems likely that these territories would be perceived by the members of that group as bearing deep and significant ties to their national identity. A natural analogy which would explain the ties between peoples and their formative territories is that of the ties between individuals and their parents. Many languages have a term for the concept of 'fatherland'.[25] This concept represents an abstraction of territories common in many cultures, and is consistent with the above analogy.[26] If we appeal to this analogy, then the claim that national groups possess some important interests in their formative territories is in need of no elaborate proof. Providing evidence for the existence of such an interest is much like attempting to prove that the tie between children and their parents forms a source of special interests. The existence of such interests would seem to be clear and self-evident, requiring no proof. However, while no evidence is necessary for the existence of these interests, the normative implications that they entail do require some elaboration.

The interest in formative territories which the parental ties analogy represents is the desire to be in close physical proximity to one's loved ones, that is, not to be separated from them or to spend one's life in a state of pining. The crucial question is whether the force of these interests renders them solid grounds for sovereignty rights, which, as noted above, imply the power to subject the whole world to the right-holder's decisions regarding the regulation of life within the territory over which he/she is the sovereign and to his/her decisions regarding the use and enjoyment of this territory. In order to answer this question I would like to resort here to a case in which historical rights were invoked in order to justify not a territorial entitlement but a different sort of entitlement. The case is that of Melina Mercury, Greece's Minister of Culture in the 1970s, who demanded the return of the Acropolis treasures from the British Museum. A comparison between this case and historical rights as grounds

---

[25] See the quote from Archidamus in note 2, above. The notion of fatherland was common not only in ancient European civilization (on this see, for example, Viroli, *For Love of Country*, p. 18), but also in the pre-European American world. 'In 1761', says Tully, 'the Chippewa leader Minivavana enlightened the English trader Alexander Harvey at Michilimackinace in the following typical manner: "Englishman, although you have conquered the French, you have not yet conquered us. We are not your slaves. These lakes, these woods and mountains, were left to us by our ancestors. They are our inheritances: and we will part with them to none"' (Tully, *Strange Multiplicity*, p. 119).

[26] On this abstraction see Smith, 'States and Homelands', 196–7. See also Smith, *National Identity*; Ladis K.D. Kristof, 'The State-Idea, the National Idea and the Image of the Fatherland', *Orbis* 11 (1967), 249–55.

for territorial sovereignty may serve to provide a comparative perspective. The interest that the British have in the prestige of their museums would seem to constitute a rather weak rival to the historical interest that the Greeks have in the treasures of the Acropolis. It would seem that the latter could rather easily override the former. However, can the interest national groups have in their formative territories also easily override its rivals, namely, people's interests in their livelihood and freedom? The interest in formative territories is certainly a much more serious candidate for overriding the interests in livelihood and freedom than the interests underlying first occupancy claims. This is so not only because it is a more real and powerful interest, but also because acknowledging it as a basis for sovereignty does not endanger the interests that others might have 'in dwelling and subsistence' to the same extent that acknowledging first occupancy does. The reason for this is that the process in which formative relations are formed between a territory and a national group is a relatively slow and long process whereas first occupancy can be acquired instantly. The danger of the sort to which Rousseau was referring, namely, the danger of depriving people of the 'amenities for dwelling and subsistence', seems much less threatening when one acknowledges formative links between nations and territories as a basis for sovereignty, than when one recognizes first occupancy as such a basis. However, dangers smaller than other dangers could nevertheless be serious. Since national entities are dynamic in their nature, since new ones are continually formed and old ones expand or shrink, the danger under consideration is far from negligible. It therefore seems to me that it is dangerous to acknowledge the interest national groups have in their formative territories as a basis for territorial sovereignty. The last two centuries provide ample examples as to why this is so.

We must here discern various types of cases. The first type consists of national groups whose sovereignty actually extends over their formative territories. However, some of those territories are vacant and could serve the basic needs of some other community. The second type consists of national groups whose sovereignty actually extends over their formative territories. Yet, some of these territories are actually inhabited by another group and serve its members' basic needs. The third type includes groups whose sovereignty actually extends over their formative territories, while the population of some of those territories is not homogeneous in its nationality. Cases of national groups who have no sovereignty whatsoever but have formative ties with vacant territories which are under the sovereignty of others form the fourth type. The fifth category comprises national groups that have no sovereignty, but have formative ties with territories that are inhabited and ruled by others. Most of these are of course abstractions from concrete examples, some of which I mentioned earlier. Should the Serbs hold on to their sovereignty over Kosovo with which they claim to have formative ties, despite the fact that its population is mostly Albanian? Should Transylvania be under Hungarian or Romanian sovereignty? Should the fact that the native minorities of North America do not enjoy sovereignty in any way determine whether their formative ties to territories there could serve as a basis for sovereignty rights over some of these territories, at least those which are vacant? Should the fact that the Jewish people did not enjoy sovereignty determine whether its formative ties to Eretz Yisrael could serve as a basis for sovereignty rights in those territories, even if those territories were populated?

These cases demonstrate that, given the world's scarce territorial resources, the question of the territorial sovereignty of particular national groups can hardly ever be determined only on the basis of their formative ties with certain territories. The first two types of cases show that a formative tie can probably not be the basis for sovereignty even from the point of view of distributive justice and for the purposes of acquiring sovereignty and retaining it. The first case is of the type in which a group has sovereignty over its formative territories some of which are vacant. These vacant territories are required in order to satisfy the basic needs of other populations which do not actually reside there. Recognizing a formative tie as the basis for sovereignty in cases like this means, in the name of this tie, allowing one group to ignore the most urgent material interests of another group, namely, their interests in 'amenities for dwelling and subsistence'. This is so because sovereignty over a territory includes the authority to refuse any sort of use by other parties. (This does not, of course, entail the conclusion that in every case in which one party's sovereignty allows it to ignore the basic needs of another, the sovereignty of the former party is nullified. All that is claimed here is that formative ties cannot be sufficient grounds in and of themselves for justifying the creation of such situations.) The second case is that of groups exercising sovereignty over their formative territories, some of which are inhabited by other groups. To regard the formative tie as a basis for sovereignty in such cases would in effect mean to deny the interests of the other groups in self-government, since sovereignty over a territory also includes political rule over its population. Some typical contenders for historical rights in cases of the present type try to circumvent the fact that their position implies the denial of other peoples' rights to self-government by expressing a willingness to grant certain limited governance prerogatives to the populations of the territories over which they continue to assert their dominance. The Serbs are currently being forced to make such an offer to the Albanians of Kosovo. In the last decade, Israel has been under pressure to make such an offer to the Arabs living in the West Bank. (Israel still refuses to grant the same rights to the Arabs living in East Jerusalem.) We must bear in mind that this sort of attempt at circumvention cannot succeed, because what is offered are limited governance rights that would perpetuate the political inferiority of the populations in question. It should be noted that it is not logically possible to offer more than such limited governance rights while simultaneously endorsing the position that the formative ties form a sufficient basis for sovereignty rights. To offer the other group more in effect means to offer it either sovereignty or joint sovereignty. In either case, the first group's sovereignty or at least it's exclusive sovereignty is forfeited.

Cases where historical rights are used to justify demands to restore a prior state of affairs are, of course, more problematic, at least with regard to demands by national groups to return and resume their sovereignty over currently inhabited territories as well as their presence in these territories. There are three reasons why this is more problematic. The most significant of these reasons is the danger of uprooting the territory's present inhabitants and turning them into refugees. How substantial this danger may be depends, of course, on the density of the population of this territory, the size of the returning population, the relations that develop between them, the relative political and military strength of these groups as well as other factors. Despite the fact that such dangers may not actually be realized, we may deduce from history that these dangers may indeed be significant. The second reason for rejecting formative ties as grounds for restoring former sovereignties over populated territories is that doing so means denying the rights of the current populations of these territories to self-government. I clarified this point earlier when discussing the possibility of viewing historical rights as grounds for acquiring and/or perpetuating sovereignties over territories populated by other national groups. The third argument against recognizing formative ties as grounds for restoring old sovereignties over populated territories is that such recognition sometimes entails ignoring the formative ties that the present inhabitants have with the territory. It should be remembered that specific territories could play a formative role in the historical identity of more than one national group.[27] Take, for example, the Māori and Pākehā in Aotearoa/New Zealand, or the Jews and Palestinians in Eretz Yisrael/Palestine. To acknowledge only the formative role of Aotearoa in the Māori identity means to ignore the formative role New Zealand plays in the Pākehā identity. To acknowledge only the formative role that

---

[27] Cf. Onora O'Neill, 'Justice and Boundaries', in Chris Brown (ed.), *Political Restructuring in Europe: Ethical Perspectives* (London and New York: Routledge, 1994), p. 77.

Eretz Yisrael has in Jewish identity means to ignore the formative role of Palestine in the Palestinian identity.

Incidentally, it should be noted that this fact, namely, that specific territories do sometimes play a formative role in the historical identity of more than one national group, is the major disadvantage of historical rights arguments when understood under the formative territories conception, compared to the first occupancy conception. Unlike the latter conception, the formative territories conception of historical rights does not imply that the right in question is necessarily an exclusive one. This point should be emphasized as it reveals the elusive ambiguity of the notion of historical rights. If a territorial right is historical due to the primacy of the people in the history of the territory, then this people is the exclusive possessor of this right. This is so because (notwithstanding the difficulties concerning the individuation of territories), it is unlikely that more than one people was the first in the history of a given territory.[28] Conversely, if the right is historical due to the primacy of the territory in the history of the people, this does not necessarily mean that the people in question is the exclusive possessor of such a right. A single territory could obviously be primary in the history of more than one people. In addition to the aforementioned examples of Palestine/Eretz Yisrael for the Palestinians and the Jews, and New Zealand/Aotearoa for the Pākehā and Māori, one might also cite Transylvania for Romanians and Hungarians, Sri Lanka for the Tamil and Sinhalese, Kosovo for the Serbs and Albanians, as well as many other cases. All this makes the ambiguity of the notion of historical rights a potential source for political self-deception or malicious manipulation. Those who most frequently resort to historical rights in order to claim sovereignty prefer (even if inadvertently) to oscillate between its two meanings, thus enjoying the best of both worlds. On the one hand, they seek the exclusivity attached to historical rights in the first occupancy conception. On the other hand, they wish to take advantage of the considerable normative power of historical rights when construed as rights to formative possessions. However, if historical rights are first occupancy rights, then they do indeed belong exclusively to one group but they are also, as shown earlier, normatively void for purposes of corrective justice and restitution. On the other hand, if historical rights are rights to formative possessions, then they do have a certain normative

---

[28] The proviso concerning problems of individuating territories is important, for a people can claim to be the first occupant of a territory which it conceives as one individuated territory, while another people can claim to be first occupant on part of that territory, and regard this specific part as a separate territory. For example, the Sinhalese claim to be the first occupants of Sri Lanka, while the Tamil claim to be the first occupants of the northern part of the island.

weight but they are not necessarily exclusive. The formative ties of the nation occupying the territory compete with the formative ties of the nation demanding restitution. Allowing restitution would mean ignoring the ties of the occupying nation.

Let me return to the main discussion. As I noted earlier, questions of territorial sovereignty must be decided mainly by considering interests more urgent than people's interest in not being cut off from the territories from which their national groups originated. Such interests are, first, their interest in 'amenities for dwelling and subsistence' and then their interest in self-government. Given the limited territorial resources of the world, as well as its demographics, these interests do not allow much leeway for people's interests in their formative territories to serve as grounds for sovereignty rights. But does this imply that the fact that certain territories constitute formative territories for a given nation is normatively meaningless? I will now try to answer this question negatively. I will try to show that *if* considerations of self-determination can indeed serve as justification for granting territorial rights to national groups, then historical rights as rights to formative territories *ought to play a role in determining the location of these rights*. This would pertain to the acquisition of such rights, the preservation of such rights as well as, in some cases, for purposes of restitution.

Grounds for determining the site of self-determination

The distinction between justifying territorial rights and determining their site was explained in my earlier discussion of historical rights as first occupancy rights. I shall adhere to the assumption I made there, namely, that peoples have territorial rights and that these are derivatives of the right to national self-determination. This justification for territorial rights does not address the question of determining the location where these rights should be realized. I would like to argue that if first occupancy can sometimes serve as grounds for resolving the issue of location for purposes of acquiring territorial rights, then, *a fortiori*, the formative links that a given people might have to a particular territory could also serve as such grounds.

As noted above, the fact that a given group was the first to occupy a particular territory can serve as grounds for determining the location of this group's self-determination in that territory. This is so because the burdens that this will impose on others do not involve the type of sacrifices required by the duties corresponding to the actual right to territorial sovereignty. Determining the site of self-determination, even under its statist conception which implies a right to territorial sovereignty, does not necessarily entail that that sovereignty applies to all of the historical territories. Consequently, the burdens involved do not include the possibility that people may have to risk their interests in 'amenities for dwelling and subsistence'. They only involve the risk that people will have to abstain from realizing these interests in certain territories, that is, in the territories where others have attained realization of their own right to sovereignty. (However, they will have to abstain not from areas any larger than those from which they would in any case be excluded, if sovereignty rights are justly distributed among national groups.)

If these sacrifices are considered acceptable in relation to first occupancy, then it is all the more acceptable in relation to the interest of peoples and their members in their formative territories. For peoples and nationally conscious individuals, the interest in not being severed from their formative territories touches on emotions that are inextricably intertwined with their conception of their identities. The expectations and emotions that accompany this matter concern a much deeper human level than the expectations and emotions stirred in first occupants. As we have seen, the expectations of the latter type, if indeed sound, are sound by virtue of considerations of objective rationality which, from a personal point of view, are totally neutral. Just the opposite is true of the emotions and expectations regarding the interest in formative possessions. These are interests tied to some of the deepest layers of identity, both in their origin (the perception of selfhood) and in the consequences which result from the deprivation of these needs (feelings of alienation and longing).

Perhaps there is more to it than that. Given the centrality of historical territories in the formation of national identities, there seems to be an inherent link between these territories and the right to national self-determination. Unlike the case of first occupancy, the territories in question are not only *suitable* for determining the location of this right. They are territories that are *essential* for determining this location.

This inherent link is implied in the considerations used by certain contemporary writers to account for the distinction that was discussed in Chapter 2 above between rights to self-government and polyethnic rights. According to these writers, self-government rights, which enable members of a national group to live their lives as fully as possible within their national culture, apply to national groups living in their homeland.[29] Moreover, multicultural or polyethnic rights, according to which groups of common national origin may express their original culture while mainly

---

[29] See Kymlicka, *Multicultural Citizenship*, mainly at pp. 26–31. Raz, *Ethics in the Public Domain*, chaps. 6 and 8, distinguishes between these two sorts of rights without resorting to homelands.

living their lives outside that culture, apply in cases of national groups not living in their homeland. If living in the homeland may indeed be considered a criterion for the distinction between the cases in which self-government rights apply, and those in which polyethnic rights are warranted, then this presupposes that historical territories under their present conception are essential for the realization of self-determination. If living in the homeland were not a condition for exercising the right to self-determination, why would it then be improper to grant self-government rights in places where national groups have no formative ties, and to grant polyethnic rights in places where they do have such ties? The claim that formative territories are not merely suitable but also essential for the implementation of the right to self-determination also enjoys certain empirical support. History has shown that the chances of successfully implementing this right in territories to which national groups have no historical ties are very slim indeed. Experiments in this field are of course very rare. The only one known to me is the case of the Jewish people. The attempts to realize its right to self-determination outside its formative territories were failures; Britain's plan in East Africa (the 'Uganda Plan'), and Stalin's attempt to establish Jewish autonomy in Birobidzhan. In contrast, the attempt to implement Jewish self-determination in territories to which Jews had historical connections did succeed.[30]

The force with which the interest in formative territories provides grounds for determining the location of self-determination is not its only advantage over the grounds that first occupancy provides for this purpose. It has additional advantages. One of them is that the formative tie is not dependent on whether the group demanding to realize its sovereignty at that particular site was really the first occupant in this territory. As noted earlier, most national groups cannot seriously make territorial claims on the basis of historical rights if they mean to claim that they were first to appropriate and live in the territories in question. As stressed above, most groups demanding territories in the name of historical rights were first occupants only relative to other groups that exist today. Their occupancy was usually acquired by means of crimes committed by them against the previous occupants of the territories in question and by bringing about the physical or at least cultural and political destruction of the latter. Thus, it is not clear why this justifies sovereignty rights, or even rights to determine the location of sovereignty. The interpretation of historical rights as based not on the primacy of given national groups in the history of given territories but rather on the primacy of these territories in the

---

[30] See also A. D. Smith, *Myths and Memories of the Nation* (Oxford University Press, 1999), pp. 219–20.

histories of the groups in question does not involve this moral entanglement. It is not dependent on the question of whether the group invoking historical rights was really the first group to inhabit the territory, or on the means by which it became first relative to other groups that exist today.

However, the main advantage of historical rights as rights to formative territories is that they are a serious candidate for determining the location of self-determination not only for purposes of acquisition and perpetuating existing states of affairs, but also for purposes of restoring former states of affairs. As explained earlier, first occupancy cannot do this. It can provide grounds for determining the location of self-determination only for the purpose of acquiring this site within the framework of distributive justice. Some of the reasons due to which first occupancy can serve as grounds for determining the location of self-determination, that is, reasons of economy, convenience and simplicity, lose their force when the first occupant ceases to occupy the territory in question. In contrast, the interest in formative territories is not tainted by this disadvantage. A national group's interest not to be cut off from its formative territories remains in force regardless of whether or not the group and its members are currently occupying these territories. This applies when members of the national group have sustained this tie despite physical separation. In this sense the physical separation between members of a national group and their formative territories is not dissimilar to the physical separation between people and their respective family members. Both constitute ties that can continue to be a part of one's being and identity even when they are not physically manifest. Hence, unlike the reasons supporting a national group's expectations as first occupants, a national group's interest in occupying their formative territories does not necessarily disappear with the loss of the physical connection to these territories.[31]

Nevertheless, does the fact that formative ties do not lose their force with the loss of the physical connection constitute a *sufficient* reason for determining the location of national self-determination in cases where restoring former states of affairs is in question? Or does it merely constitute support in favour of this solution? Given the geodemographic conditions of the world and given its history, it is likely that the cases in which national groups resort to their formative ties to territories as grounds for returning to these territories, will be cases where *all* the relevant territories are inhabited by members of other national groups in a way which does not allow exclusive or even dominant presence of the claimant group without placing at least some of the current residents of these territories in danger of being uprooted. From the normative standpoint, groups

---

[31] Cf. Waldron, 'Superseding Historic Injustice', 17, note 13.

that aspire to have their sovereignty in sites located within their historical territories would find themselves in a situation very similar to the position they would have been in if they had resorted to their histories as grounds for their very right to sovereignty. They would be placing the current residents of these territories in danger of being uprooted, and in any case would be denying them their right to self-rule. It must be noted that these geodemographic problems cast a shadow not only on the possibility that the historical tie would have some practical impact on determining the location of the right to territorial sovereignty for purposes of restitution, but also require further qualification of my earlier comments about the possibility of viewing formative ties as grounds for locating national sovereignty for the purpose of perpetuating the status quo. In cases in which the historical territories of certain national groups cease to be solely or mainly populated by these groups (following migration, or war, or population transfers), doubts arise as to whether such territories can be subject to the territorial sovereignty of those groups. In fact, it is because of problems of this type that I earlier rejected the statist conception of the right to national self-determination and consequently the possibility that this right could ever be a basis for the right of national groups to territorial sovereignty.

However, it must be noted that rejecting this possibility does not entail denying any normative value whatsoever to historical ties as formative ties. Such ties could still serve as a basis for establishing the location of self-determination under its sub-statist conception, both for purposes of acquisition and for purposes of restitution. Such self-determination does not involve sovereignty of the national group over the territory in which it exercises self-determination. It merely involves demographic and cultural presence that could be exclusive only if the historical territories of the group include vacant territories. This would not be possible if no such vacant territories existed. Accordingly, the formative ties of the Jewish people to Eretz Yisrael could have justified its choice of that particular place in order to realize its national self-determination. However, since Eretz Yisrael was not a vacant territory, not even at the inception of Zionism, the Jews were not justified in interpreting their right to self-determination there as a right to statist and territorial sovereignty. The ordinary justifications of the right to self-determination certainly could not justify the right of the Jewish people to statist and territorial sovereignty. As noted above, the historical rights of a given nation to a given territory, when understood as referring to the primacy of the territory in the history of that nation, are not always the exclusive rights of the claimant nation. The case of the Jewish people and Eretz Yisrael is a paradigmatic case of this sort. As noted above, the territory in question is Palestine for the Palestinians. In my view, the only way in which the Jewish people could have exercised its right to self-determination in Eretz Yisrael/Palestine is under the sub- and inter-statist conception of self-determination, which allows both Jews and Palestinians to realize their self-determination there.[32]

If what I said in relation to the Jewish example is correct, then historical rights as rights to formative territories are valid for purposes of restitution regardless of whether the national group that presently occupies the territory is the group that dispossessed the group demanding restitution. If nations have an equal right to sub-statist self-determination, and if it is correct that such a right is essentially linked with the concept of homeland, then the question of whether the nation which presently occupies the territory is the nation which caused the dispossession of the claimant nation does not make much difference in terms of the applicability of this right. The restoration of the group to its homeland thus seems to be a realization of a type of justice which is partly corrective and partly distributive. It is corrective because it revolves around restoring previous states of affairs, and it is distributive because the party which is required to make the concession is required to do so not because it wronged the other party, but because the present distribution of the right to self-determination among national groups demands this concession.

If historical rights as rights to formative territories have practical significance in cases where the current occupants of the territories have not wronged those demanding to return to the territory in question, then historical rights are certainly of practical significance if a wrong has been committed. There may be doubts concerning the right of the Jewish people to realize its self-determination in Palestine because the Palestinians did not originally wrong them. However, such doubts could not apply to the right of the aboriginal peoples of North America, Australia and New Zealand to restore their self-determination in territories from which they were dispossessed by the European settler nations. The latter are the ones who dispossessed the former from these territories. Even if the first

---

[32] This must be qualified with one reservation. During the 1930s and 1940s in Europe, the Jews' need for political independence was not only a consequence of the usual interests justifying self-determination. For many of them, this need was also motivated by the most basic human interests, namely, those in life, in bodily integrity, in self-respect and in 'amenities for dwelling and subsistence'. These interests were violated in the most brutal manner. In this particular period it seems to have been justifiable or at least excusable for the Jewish people to try to achieve independent statehood. Its formative historical connection with Eretz Yisrael was good reason for this attempt to be located there rather than elsewhere. However, this could not justify all the means which were used by the Jewish community in Palestine for this purpose. It certainly cannot justify Israel's current attempts at territorial expansion in the name of Jewish historical rights.

occupancy and the formative tie of the aboriginal peoples did not justify the realization of their self-determination in all the territories which they in fact occupied and from which they were dispossessed by the settler nations, they surely justified their self-determination in some of these territories proportional to their size (and perhaps also their lifestyles) at different times. If, as a result of the dispossession, the aboriginal nations lost their physical ties with lands in which their self-determination should have been realized, the dispossessing nations must return some of these territories to their possession, either for their exclusive presence, or for their joint presence (demographic and cultural).[33] They need not return all these territories, first because it is not certain that they all should have been under the aboriginal peoples' self-determination at the time of dispossession, and mainly because in the centuries that have passed since the original dispossession, the settler nations have themselves forged formative ties with some of these territories. Moreover, members of the dispossessing nations have their lives established there.[34] The questions of what proportion of these territories ought to be restored to the native nations' possession, in what proportion of these territories should the groups reside side by side, and what proportion of these territories should be allocated to each group separately, are matters to be resolved by complex calculations which cannot be very accurate.[35] My main concern in this chapter was, first, to distinguish historical rights as rights to formative territories from historical rights as rights of first occupancy or original acquisition. Secondly, I attempted to show that historical rights as rights to formative territories are valid not only within the context of distributive justice and for purposes of acquiring and preserving certain territorial rights, but also for purposes of restitution. The purpose of all

---

[33] On the possibility of participatory presence see also Marcia Langton, 'Estate of Mind: The Growing Cooperation between Indigenous and Mainstream Managers of Northern Australian Landscapes and the Challenge for Educators and Researchers', in Haveman (ed.), *Indigenous Peoples' Rights*, p. 73.

[34] See, e.g., Haveman (ed.), *Indigenous Peoples' Rights*, p. 4.

[35] These calculations must be based on principles of distributive and corrective justice. With regard to distributive justice, the present size of the groups, their lifestyles, and how deeply they identify with different parts of the territories in question must be considered. With regard to corrective justice, the damages suffered by the dispossessed group from the time of the dispossession must be considered. On the other hand, the fact that the present members and institutions of the dispossessing group are not personally responsible for the dispossession must be considered. However, it must be noted that the wrongs committed by their ancestors form a part of their collective identity. They might therefore feel responsible for the rectification of these wrongs. Each of these points requires a detailed and complex discussion that is beyond the scope of the present study. On this matter see Waldron, 'Superseding Historic Injustice'; Simmons, 'Historical Rights and Fair Shares'; George Sher, *Approximate Justice: Studies in Non-Ideal Theory* (Lanham, MD: Rowman & Littlefield, 1997), chap. 1; Lyons, 'The New Indian Claims', pp. 355–79.

the above was mainly to emphasize the concept of the homeland in the context of national self-determination.[36] Recent judicial decisions made in Australia and Canada are compatible with this approach that stresses the notion of homeland. In view of this emphasis on this notion, the aboriginal peoples are entitled to demographic and cultural presence in certain territories because of the identity relationship that they have with these territories.[37] At least in some of these territories, they have to live with the settler nations because the latter also have identity relations and material needs which justify this.[38]

In sum, what I have salvaged of the historical rights argument is much less than what most proponents of historical rights could wish. The proponents of historical rights vacillate between their national groups' precedence in the histories of the territories over which they claim sovereignty, and the primacy of these territories in the histories of their national groups. They use historical rights as justification for the very right of sovereignty, and in general as grounds for claims to territorial expansion. I rejected the possibility that claims to historical rights in these two senses could serve as grounds for the very right to sovereignty. If my arguments on this matter have been persuasive, then historical rights cannot be grounds for the claims of national groups who enjoy self-determination and sovereignty to expand their sovereignty to additional territories. Among all the claims to a historical right, I have tried to salvage

---

[36] On the importance of homelands in national identities and for national self-determination see also D. Miller, 'Secession and the Principle of Nationality', in Moore (ed.), *National Self-Determination and Secession*, p. 68; Moore, *The Ethics of Nationalism*, pp. 167, 176, 191.

[37] On the importance of traditional lands for the identities of aboriginal peoples see Borrows, ' "Landed" Citizenship', pp. 326–42; James Tully, *An Approach to Political Philosophy: Locke in Contexts* (Cambridge University Press, 1993), pp. 153–4; Poole, *Nation and Identity*, p. 131.

Richard H. Bartlett, 'Native Title in Australia: Denial, Recognition, and Dispossession', in Haveman (ed.), *Indigenous Peoples' Rights*, pp. 417–18, emphasizes the historical and traditional identity links of the Australian aborigines to their lands as the central reason for the change that the *Mabo no. 2* case (*Mabo v. Queensland (no. 2)* (1992) 175 CLR1) brought about with regard to their title in their traditional lands. He emphasized the centrality of their lands in their identities, and not their primacy in these lands relative to the European settlers, as the reason for acknowledging their title. Other writers (such as Jeremy Webber, 'Beyond Regret: Mabo's Implications for Australian Constitutionalism', in Ivison, Patton and Sanders (eds.), *Rights of Indigenous Peoples*, pp. 72–4) emphasize the constitutional significance of the *Mabo no. 2* case and similar recent decisions (*Delgamuukw v. British Columbia* (1997) 153 DLR (4th) 193 (SCC)). They argue that these decisions do not only pertain to property law but also to the constitutional issues of self-determination. Self-determination is linked with the formative role that the traditional lands have in the identities of the aboriginal nations. The present writers also emphasize that for these reasons the settler nations must share sovereignty with the native nations.

[38] See also Poole, *Nation and Identity*, p. 138.

a consideration for determining the location of peoples' territorial rights. If used for the purpose of perpetuating an existing state of affairs, both the right of first occupancy and the right to formative territories could serve as grounds for determining the location of the territorial rights of national groups. If used for the purpose of restoring the *status quo ante*, it is only the right to formative territories that may be used as a consideration for determining the location of groups' territorial rights. This consideration determines the location of such rights if they follow from the right to self-determination.

5   Nationalism and immigration

In Chapter 4 I argued that historical rights as rights to formative territories could serve as a basis for determining the location of national self-determination for the purpose of restoring past states of affairs, if there are empty territories within which this could be done. If this claim is correct, then the state that has jurisdiction over these territories should allow some or all the members of the national group in question to immigrate to these territories. However, such cases are very rare, and thus do not require further discussion of the issues of nationalism and immigration. Another more central issue, due to which further elaboration is urgently required, is the right to national self-determination, which is the subject of Chapter 3. If one acknowledges the right to national self-determination, whether it is interpreted under its statist conception or under its sub- and inter-statist conception, then one is in effect subscribing to a view that raises questions concerning the immigration rights of members of national groups to the state within which their group enjoys self-determination. This is so because if people's freedom, identity and endeavour-based interests in their culture justify their nation's right to self-determination, it seems that, at least prima facie, these interests could also justify attributing some weight to people's culturally based desires to immigrate to the state in which this right is implemented.

Despite all this, many people, including some who support the right to national self-determination, reject the idea of granting priority regarding immigration on a national basis. In Israel, one of the country's most fundamental laws is the Law of Return, which grants every Jew a right to immigrate to Israel. Many Israeli liberals believe that this law verges on racism. At most, they are willing to tolerate a law of this type as a form of affirmative action intended to compensate Jews for their loss of the right to self-determination and other national rights during the two millennia of exile. In the first part of this chapter I shall examine and reject this view. I shall try to show that those who acknowledge the legitimacy of the right to national self-determination cannot consistently classify as affirmative action those nationality-based priorities in immigration intended to compensate for breaches of this right. Nor can they possibly subscribe to a position according to which nationality-based priorities in immigration are necessarily racist.

However, the fact that granting special priorities in immigration on the basis of nationality may not necessarily be racist does not mean that such priorities are just. Although racism does constitute a gross form of injustice, it is not the sole form of injustice that could be inflicted on people. Later in this chapter (pp. 130–4), I shall argue that the nationality-based priorities in immigration that the statist conception of self-determination allows may in many cases lead to consequences that are both unjust and inconsistent with liberal values. Israel's Law of Return is an example of nationality-based priorities regarding immigration that are facilitated by a statist conception of self-determination. The principal injustice perpetrated by this law does not stem from the very fact that it grants priorities regarding immigration on a nationalist basis, but rather from the fact that it grants unlimited advantages to one national group while completely denying these advantages to another national group. Later in the chapter (pp. 134–41), I shall propose principles for nationality-based priorities in immigration that do not result in this injustice. I shall then try to clarify and justify these principles by comparing their implications to those of a law of return similar to the Israeli one (pp. 141–4). I shall end the chapter with a discussion of some possible objections to the nationality-based principles of immigration (pp. 144–7).

Nationality-based immigration and racism

The United Nations International Convention on the Elimination of All Forms of Racial Discrimination states (in Article 1) that the term 'racial discrimination' applies to 'any distinction, exclusion, restriction or preference based on race, colour, descent, or national or ethnic origin which has the purpose or effect of nullifying or impairing the recognition, enjoyment or exercise, on an equal footing, of human rights and fundamental freedoms in the political, economic, social, cultural or any other field of public life'. In his discussion of this issue, a prominent Israeli writer, Asa Kasher, presents a justification which he later rejects for making citizenship and naturalization laws an exception to the prohibitions imposed by the UN treaty.[1] According to this explanation, the scope of the principles of justice is limited in that they apply to the individuals who are members of the particular community adopting these principles and do not apply

---

[1] Asa Kasher, 'Justice and Affirmative Action: Naturalization and the Law of Return', *Israeli Yearbook of Human Rights* 15 (1985), 101–12.

to non-members. Since immigration and naturalization policies apply to individuals who are not yet the members of the community adopting these policies, such policies are not subject to the principles of justice.

Kasher rightly rejects this explanation and presents two main reasons for doing so. First, he believes that principles of justice apply not only within the community adopting them, but express the moral point of view that pertains to humans as such without discriminating between citizens and non-citizens.[2] Secondly, even if the scope of justice were only local, it would apply to immigration laws because different immigration policies affect the welfare of different parts of the domestic population in different ways.[3] The justice of these immigration policies can be judged by the impact they have on various domestic groups. For instance, a state that prefers its potential immigrants to be doctors rather than engineers is in effect discriminating in favour of its citizens in need of medical treatment as opposed to those citizens in need of engineering services. If this discrimination is unjust, then it follows that the immigration priorities that caused it are also unjust. In the same manner, adopting nationality-based priorities with regard to immigration means increasing the number of members of one cultural group within the population *vis-à-vis* other groups. This may for example result in a higher standard of living for members of the former group than for members of other groups. For instance, items connected to the culture of the immigrants would cost less since immigration has led to an increase in the number of consumers for these items. Moreover, most people conceive of their cultural membership as a central part of their identity. Therefore, discriminating against them because of their national affiliation is not merely an instance of inequality, but may offend also their sense of worth and their self-respect.[4] Nationality constitutes a component of one's identity that is not chosen but is usually acquired by birth or upbringing. This is what renders nationality-based priorities in immigration not merely unjust but also suspect of racism.

Kasher tries to rescue the Law of Return from the charge of racism by interpreting the nationality-based priority created by this law as a case of affirmative action. He believes that if a national group has been deprived of the conditions that would have allowed it to realize its self-determination, it ought now be permitted to become a majority in a given territory, thus attaining the condition necessary for self-determination. He therefore argues for a principle that he calls 'the case of the founding fathers' and which, he believes, is derived from the right to national

---

[2] *Ibid.*, 103.   [3] *Ibid.*, 103–6.

[4] Kasher believes that nationality-based discrimination can constitute an offence to self-respect for different reasons. See *ibid.*, 105–6.

self-determination. This principle asserts the right of individuals belonging to a national group to immigrate into a territory in numbers sufficient for the realization of their right to self-determination, that is (according to him), to become a majority in that territory. Despite the fact that this priority is nationality-based, it is not racist because it is a case of affirmative action. Affirmative action justifies this priority in the same way that it permits the discrimination in favour of African-Americans and/or women in university or employment quotas, despite the fact that this preferential treatment is actually based on race and/or gender. The latter bias is considered to be justified as a temporary means that serves to rectify the consequences of the injustice suffered by African-Americans and women. Similarly, the nationality-based priorities created by 'the case of the founding fathers' are also claimed to be temporarily justified, until the injustice suffered by the Jews with regard to their right to self-determination is rectified, that is, until they constitute a majority in their country.[5]

One obvious reason for objecting to nationality-based priorities in immigration as a kind of affirmative action, at least in the case of the Jews in Israel, is that those who are required to pay the price are the Palestinians, who are not at all responsible for Jewish suffering in the past. This is in contrast to the cases of African-Americans and women in the United States, who are currently favoured at the expense of whites and men who discriminated against them in the past. However, there are more fundamental considerations in view of which the priorities established by the Law of Return cannot be interpreted as a case of affirmative action rectifying earlier wrongs. Affirmative action pertains to the rectification of racist evils. However, not every rectification of racist evils constitutes affirmative action. For example, if blacks are imprisoned just because they are blacks, they must be released and be compensated for their false arrest. Yet releasing and compensating them in this case is not affirmative action. It is simply a case of rectifying a wrong committed earlier.

Affirmative action pertains only to advantages that are granted to members of groups where their membership in these particular groups is in principle irrelevant to the particular matters for which the advantages are being granted. Those who advocate affirmative action for African-Americans and women in education in the United States, also believe that race and gender should in principle not affect a person's educational opportunities. The interests African-Americans and women have in education, and the reasons they have for wishing to be educated have nothing to do with their skin colour or gender. This point makes it impossible to classify the nationality-based priorities created by the Law of Return (including the priority created under Kasher's 'founding

---

[5] *Ibid.*, 112.

fathers' interpretation) as affirmative action. Compensating members of the Jewish people for the deprivation they suffered with regard to their interest in self-determination pertains to a matter to which their Jewishness is relevant. If they deserve compensation in this matter, then this compensation cannot be classified as affirmative action. In other words, those who acknowledge the legitimacy of the interest people have in the self-determination of their national group necessarily hold a position according to which nationality-based priorities are not necessarily racist and therefore nationality-based priorities in immigration intended to serve this interest are not necessarily racist.

Distinctions between groups are racist if and only if they satisfy the following two conditions. First, they apply to people by virtue of their membership in the groups to which they belong by birth or upbringing. Secondly, the priorities are invoked for purposes in relation to which this group membership is considered irrelevant. Discriminating against doctors and in favour of lawyers in determining their income tax even in cases where their income is equal is not racist because it does not satisfy the first condition. That is, it does not apply to people by virtue of their membership in groups to which they belong due to birth or upbringing. Similarly, discriminating in favour of blacks as potential candidates for the role of Othello, or in favour of tall people when choosing candidates for a basketball team, or in favour of handicapped people in distributing parking spaces, is not racist because it does not satisfy the second condition. This form of discrimination is based on involuntary membership in groups but is relevant to the legitimate purposes for which it is invoked. For the same reason, those who acknowledge the legitimacy of the right to national self-determination would not consider those nationality-based priorities in immigration invoked for the purpose of implementing the right to self-determination as necessarily racist.

As indicated above, rejecting Israel's Law of Return as a case of affirmative action does not preclude the possibility of justifying it on ordinary grounds of corrective justice. The possibility that a group could be entitled to return to its homeland as part of an attempt to compensate it for the deprivation it suffered for having to leave was mentioned in Chapter 4. If one accepts my earlier arguments, it follows that a principle of the sort that Kasher calls 'the case of the founding fathers' might be justified under the conditions discussed in Chapter 4 not as a matter of affirmative action, but of ordinary corrective justice. However, if there are cases in which nationality-based priorities could be justified on grounds of corrective justice, then it is almost certain that they could be justified on grounds of distributive justice. Rights that are based on considerations of corrective justice are remedial rights. They presuppose the existence of primary rights based on considerations of distributive justice, the violation of which they are intended to rectify. If a wrong that a national group has suffered with regard to its self-determination can be rectified by granting nationality-based preferences in immigration, then self-determination and the justifications for it could perhaps also serve as justification for primary immigration rights that do not depend on a history of wrongdoing.

Without undermining the possible importance of remedial considerations in establishing national immigration rights, my main concern in what follows are nationality-based priorities in immigration as a matter of distributive justice rather than corrective justice. Unlike priorities based on considerations of corrective justice, priorities based on considerations of distributive justice are not temporary. At first glance, the possibility of justifying nationality-based priorities in immigration on considerations of distributive justice seems quite solid. This at least is the case for those who hold the position according to which people's interests in their freedom, in the components of their identities and in their endeavours justify their interests in their culture, and that all this justifies a right to national self-determination. As indicated at the beginning of this chapter, if the interests people have in adhering to their culture and preserving it for generations justify measures that to a great extent determine world order, then it would seem that these considerations could also justify certain nationality-based priorities in immigration. The right to self-determination, either in its statist conception or in its sub-statist conception places significant responsibilities and duties on individuals, states and the international community. These responsibilities and duties are towards national groups and individuals as members of national groups. If people's interests in their nationality justify such responsibilities, and if these interests constitute part of the basis for normative and institutional arrangements both on the municipal and global level, it seems that they must also play a role in shaping immigration policies. It seems to me that the important question is not whether they ought to play such a role, but what their specific role should be. The statist and the sub-statist conceptions of self-determination imply different answers to this question. The statist conception, as I shall show below (pp. 130–4), makes it possible for states to adopt immigration policies that are purely nationalist. As I shall show later (on pp. 134–41), the sub-statist conception implies much more balanced immigration policies. I shall argue that the immigration policies that follow from the statist conception ought to be rejected while those that follow from the sub-statist conception ought to be accepted.

Nationality-based immigration – the statist conception

The realization of the statist conception of self-determination in the geodemographic conditions of the world would cause various types of injustice. In Chapter 3 above I noted that all these forms of injustice could be prevented if every national group had a state consisting of all its members and only its members, and if every state had a citizenry including all and only the members of one national group. It goes without saying that no liberal would want to promote the ideal of the homogeneous nation-state by measures such as forced population transfers. These constitute crimes against humanity and therefore are categorically forbidden. But it is not evident that liberals could totally reject the possibility of promoting the present ideal by making nationalist considerations the sole considerations in determining the immigration policies of nation-states. Closing states to all potential immigrants who are not members of their national group, and allowing the entrance only of immigrants who are members of this group or who are prepared to undergo conversion and join it is not categorically forbidden from the moral point of view. Such arrangements do not uproot people from their surroundings or cause major disruptions to their lives, and in accordance with my argument in the first part of this chapter, they do not discriminate against potential immigrants for racist reasons. (This is in contrast to, for example, the exclusion not of all those who do not belong to the group to which the state belongs, but of those who belong to a particular national group or race.) Several states – Germany, Japan, Israel and even the Nordic countries – have, or have until recently, practised immigration policies which realize this option or an option close to it, by rarely permitting the immigration and/or naturalization of people who do not belong to their group, and by making it very easy for people belonging to their groups to enter (the country).[6] Are such policies worthy of support?

It seems to me that the answer to this question must be negative. Both of the above dimensions of pure nationality-based immigration policies are problematic. Permitting the immigration of all the members of the nation to its state could cause demographic instability and threaten the fundamental interests of those who are already living in that state, or perhaps even of those living in close proximity to the state in question. Such a danger applies to groups that have large diasporas and small states. The Jewish and the Palestinian peoples may be the only examples of such national groups. However, these examples are sufficient to demonstrate

---

[6] Coleman and Harding, 'Citizenship, Justice, Political Borders', pp. 21–2.

the dangers of the inclusive dimension of pure nationality-based immigration policies. The purpose of both the inclusive and the exclusive dimensions, that is, allowing all immigrants who are members, and not allowing the immigration of non-members or of those who are not willing to assimilate into the national group, is to make states nationally homogeneous. This ideal is not consistent with four prominent liberal ideals, namely, pluralism, freedom of movement, individual well-being and equality. Preserving a state's national homogeneity is not a particularly successful guarantee for the value of pluralism with regard to different ways of life and creates difficulties on several levels. It limits the availability of diverse lifestyles for individuals within the borders of the state and bars them from adopting ways of living common outside their own states. It undermines the possibility of pursuing a cosmopolitan way of life, or even prevents such a way of life from developing.[7] Secondly, it drastically restricts freedom of movement and migration in the world. Only those who wish to migrate back to the state of their original nationality, or those who are willing to assimilate into a new nationality are permitted such freedom of movement. Imposing considerable restrictions on immigration seems to contradict the liberal value of freedom of movement. Stipulating that immigration is permissible only if one is willing to convert from one national identity to another is also problematic. People who wish to enjoy one value – freedom of movement – must pay a heavy price in terms of another value, namely, the preservation of their identity.[8] Thirdly, preventing the immigration of non-nationals to nation-states also means eliminating a significant channel for achieving more efficient production of wealth and for a more equal distribution of the world's wealth. Immigration of the members of the poorest and most backward nations to the states where the richest and most advanced nations live could assist in advancing these aims and could help reduce the gaps between the rich and the poor.[9] It

---

[7] See also Tully, *Strange Multiplicity*, p. 207.

[8] In stating that freedom of movement (migration) is one of liberalism's central values, I do not mean to say that people have an absolute right to immigrate to the states to which they wish to immigrate. The implementation of many liberal values by most states will quite often require the imposition of many restrictions on immigration. It therefore does not make sense to speak of a general right to immigrate. However, this does not mean that freedom of movement is not a very important value within liberalism. On liberalism and migration see Brian Barry and Robert Goodin (eds.), *Free Movement* (Philadelphia: Pennsylvania State University Press, 1992), especially pp. 23–84; Veit Bader 'Citizenship and Exclusion', *Political Theory* 23 (1995), 211–46; Schwartz (ed.), *Justice in Immigration*.

[9] Barry and Goodin (eds.), *Free Movement*, p. 8; Joseph Carens, 'Migration and morality: A liberal egalitarian perspective', in Barry and Goodin (eds.), *Free Movement*, p. 35; Bader, 'Citizenship and Exclusion', 211; Jean Hampton, 'Immigration, identity, and justice', in Schwartz (ed.), *Justice in Immigration*, pp. 82–3.

could do so both by improving the standard of living of the individual immigrants, and by making them a bridge for improving the conditions in their countries of origin.

It might be argued that the way in which I have described the immigration policies that the statist conception of self-determination allows is too severe. Nation-states could at least be more flexible in accepting potential immigrants who are not members of their national groups. David Miller seems to hold such a view. He argues against the proposal made by some British Conservatives to repatriate members of the West Indian and the Indian communities who had already been naturalized in Britain. The Conservatives demanded this (voluntary) repatriation because they thought that these communities 'embody values that are antipathetic to the British sense of nationality'.[10] Miller argues that this Conservative position is based on a mistaken conception according to which national identities are frozen and unchangeable. He says that 'national identities are not cast in stone... they are above all "imagined" identities, where the content of the imagining changes with time'.[11] He therefore believes that immigrants should not be thought of as posing a threat to national identities but rather as partners to a dialogue concerning the nature of possible changes in such identities.

Yet, Miller's claim that 'national identities are not cast in stone' is only partially true. First, it applies only to the content of identity, or, to use Kymlicka's expression, to its character.[12] It does not apply to whether or not a given national identity is separate from another national identity. It is important to distinguish between these two points. The fact that the Jewish identities that prevailed in Eastern Europe and in North Africa were different in content, and that both these identities are different in content from Jewish identity that has developed in Israel, does not alter the fact that this is an identity that is commonly regarded as one continuous national identity which is distinct from other national identities. The same holds with regard to the British identity in the colonial and post-colonial eras. Although these identities differ from each other in content, historically they constitute one identity, or at least are conceived as such. At least from the viewpoint of cultural nationalism, as opposed to statist nationalism, this point is of considerable importance. From the viewpoint of cultural nationalism and the justifications for it, the fact that the state's population shares common cultural materials is less important than the continued existence of the cultural group as a separate historical identity. From the viewpoint of cultural nationalism, if nation-states can

---

[10] See D. Miller, *On Nationality*, p. 126.   [11] *Ibid.*, p. 127.
[12] See Kymlicka, *Multicultural Citizenship*, pp. 184–5.

afford to accept immigrants who are not members of their nations and perhaps even be open to their cultural influence, they can do so on the condition that these immigrants assimilate into the historical identity of the state's nation. Such openness is possible only if the immigrants do not exist as a separate historical entity or regard themselves as belonging to such an entity, and provided that they are not a threat to the historical existence of their hosts. Secondly, the claim that 'national identities are not cast in stone' is also only partially true from the viewpoint of the content of national identities. As Miller himself recognizes, such identities have constitutive components or at least what a given national group regards as its constitutive components at any particular point in time. Miller argues that such components could be incompatible with the constitutive components of other national identities to a degree that justifies separation between the two groups. Although he makes this argument when discussing secession,[13] there is no reason why it should not also apply in the context of immigration. Miller's discussion of immigration seems to lead to the same conclusion, albeit inexplicitly. He mentions two types of situations in which immigration poses a problem to the nation-state. One is the case 'where the immigrant group is strong and cohesive enough to constitute itself as an independent nation'. In such cases, he says, 'the receiving nation may have good reason to guard itself against being turned into a bi-national society'.[14] However, if the fear of being turned into a bi-national society justifies the prevention of immigration, why are not what could be considered less significant fears, such as the fear of becoming a multicultural society, not good reasons for preventing it? It must be remembered that fears that may be less significant than other fears are not necessarily insignificant.

Thirdly, it must also be noted that the very notion of national self-determination means granting the national group the authority to decide which fears it takes to be significant. National self-determination means that it is the national group itself that determines its identity, and this includes decisions on issues such as which components of their identity are constitutive and which are not. Moreover, there could be cases in which the members of a national group wish their identity to remain the same and not to change even with regard to non-constitutive components of their identity. Granting them self-determination means allowing them to take this position, even if it is not necessary for the sake of preserving a separate identity. In light of all this, it seems that the claim that immigrants need not be seen as a threat to national identities is somewhat imprecise, for it seems that there could be many cases in which accepting

---

[13] See D. Miller, *On Nationality*, p. 113.   [14] *Ibid.*, p. 129.

immigrants might indeed be threatening. These are cases where the constitutive components of the identity of the receiving national group are not compatible with the components that comprise the identity of the potential immigrants, or where the members of the national group want to preserve their identity as it is and not allow it to change. Even if the difference between the identities is not a great one, those states which conceive of themselves as belonging to particular national groups will hesitate to take any risks with their identities. Of course, states that belong to national groups whose identity is very flexible and especially national groups whose identity includes the notion of immigration as part of their national ethos would be more generous in admitting immigrants. However, this is not because the statist conception of self-determination encourages this, but rather because of the particular nature of their national identity.

Moreover, it is important to note that the crucial question is not whether the statist conception can allow non-nationalist immigration, but whether it allows the opposite, namely, the banning of non-nationalist-based immigration. The answer to this question is affirmative. That is, the statist conception of self-determination permits states to exclude immigrants who do not belong to their national group. This is of great practical importance in light of the fact that the identities of many national groups are perceived by their members as not allowing a great degree of flexibility, and in light of the fact that many nation-states actually adopt immigration policies that are very ungenerous towards potential immigrants that do not belong to their nations. The purpose of these policies is to preserve their cultural homogeneity.[15]

Nationality-based immigration – the sub-statist conception

In what follows I shall propose three principles that ascribe special weight to nationalist considerations in determining immigration policies. As I will immediately show, these principles follow from the liberal justifications for cultural nationalism and from the right to self-determination. They constitute guidelines for balancing between the nationalist needs of members of groups enjoying self-determination within a given state, and non-nationalist needs of both potential immigrants and the citizens of these states. National groups have the right for the state within which they enjoy self-determination to be guided by these principles. Such a right should be included in the package of rights that comprise

---

[15] See Coleman and Harding, 'Citizenship, justice, political borders', pp. 21–2.

self-determination, according to the sub- and inter-statist conception proposed in Chapter 3 above. This particular right is a manifestation of the sub- and inter-statist conception in the area of immigration. The three principles are as follows: (1) The national needs of potential immigrants must have considerable weight within the overall considerations which ought to determine immigration policies. States must allot a portion of their immigration quotas to those immigrants who, for nationalist reasons, wish to live where their nation enjoys self-determination. (2) National groups may allow into their homelands the number of members that is required in order to maintain their self-determination. (3) States have a duty to take in refugees and persecuted members of specific national groups that have a right to self-determination within the specific states, and also to grant priority to members of these groups within all the other categories that make up their immigration quotas.

The first principle, according to which states must take the desire of potential immigrants to realize their national identity into consideration when determining their immigration policies, is implied by the right to national self-determination. This right is based on the freedom-, identity- and endeavour-based interests that individuals have in their culture. The geodemographic conditions of the world, together with the link that usually exists between national groups and their homelands, means that these interests only have a chance of being fully met in one place, usually the national homeland. As mentioned above, the right to self-determination, even under its sub-statist conception, places significant responsibilities and duties on individuals, states and the international community in relation to national groups and to individuals as members of such groups. If people's interests in their culture justify such responsibilities, and if these interests constitute part of the basis for international and municipal normative and institutional orders, it seems that they must also play a role in the determination of immigration policies. After all, giving considerable weight to the interests of potential immigrants in their culture does not involve burdens to the extent that acknowledging the right to self-determination does.

The issue under discussion here is granting priorities on an individual basis to members of national diasporas because of their wish to participate in the self-determination of their nation. It must be stressed that the priorities in question do not amount to full-fledged immigration rights of the sort Israel has granted diaspora Jews, that is, a right the correlative duty of which is the state's obligation to accept them. Rather, the priorities in question are much more modest and mean only taking the interests that potential immigrants might have in their national identity into consideration and perhaps ascribing special weight to these interests. As I have already emphasized, states should also determine their immigration policies on the basis of other considerations, such as the economic needs of potential immigrants who do not belong to the same national group but wish to alleviate their own poverty, or the demand for manual workers in the state. The question of whether the importance ascribed to the national needs of potential immigrants is critical depends on the relative weight of other considerations. The immigration priorities granted to diaspora members of national groups should not amount to a full-fledged immigration right since the nationalist interests of diaspora members in their culture are not usually urgent, unless they are persecuted in their current place of residence. Members of national diasporas do not usually conduct most of their lives within the framework of their original culture. They usually form their lives out of the materials provided by the culture within which they are currently living and undertake most of their endeavours within this culture.[16] The interest they have in preserving their endeavours is therefore also not tied to their original culture. Moreover, even if the members of national diasporas did conduct a substantial part of their lives within the framework of their original culture, it could still be argued that their presence in their nation's centre is not necessary in order to satisfy their freedom-based interests in this culture and the interests they have in it in order to preserve their endeavours. It could be claimed that the very existence of such a centre already satisfies these interests and that there is therefore no need for their own physical presence in that centre. As far as the identity-based interests of the diaspora members in their nationality is concerned, they should in any case be able to preserve that identity within the state in which they are living, even if this is not the state in which their group enjoys self-determination. The sub-statist conception of self-determination ensures this. Unlike the statist conception, the sub-statist conception implies that the state within which the diaspora members live and in which other groups enjoy self-determination, cannot require their full integration in its culture since this would mean that they would have to surrender their separate historical identity.

Thus, two aspects of the sub-statist conception show that the interests of diaspora members in immigrating to the state where their cultural group enjoys self-determination need not be protected by a full-fledged right to immigrate to that state. First, according to the sub-statist conception, the state in which a national group enjoys self-determination does not *belong* to that group. This state must ascribe weight to the national needs of the members of this group. However, the needs of others must

---

[16] Cf. Stephen R. Perry, 'Immigration, justice and culture', in Schwartz (ed.), *Justice in Immigration*, pp. 94–135, for a similar point.

also be recognized. Secondly, according to the sub-statist conception, it is not only the state where a national group enjoys self-determination that ought to care about the interests people might have in adhering to their culture. Unlike the statist conception, the sub-statist conception requires that these interests be sufficiently respected by all states.

If the above holds, not only could it be claimed that diaspora members should not be granted a full-fledged right to immigrate to their homeland but one could also argue that their desire to do so should play no role in the state's immigration policies. If people are also allowed to preserve their identities in the states where their national group does not enjoy self-determination, why should any weight be ascribed to their culture when the immigration policies of the state where their group does enjoy self-determination are determined? There are two replies to this question. First, people might want to move from passive adherence to their original culture to a more active membership in it. They could perhaps do this better in the place where their group enjoys self-determination. Secondly, and perhaps more importantly, people who do not live within their original culture may be able to preserve their original identity while living in a different culture, but might have good reason to believe that their children might ultimately be fully assimilated into the other culture and would thus lose all ties to their cultural heritage. As clarified in Chapter 2, the importance of intergenerational relationships within cultural nationalism explains why people's desire for their children to preserve their cultural identity could be a good reason for ascribing weight to their wish to immigrate to the state where their national group enjoys self-determination. The chance that their children might lose their original identity in this state is smaller, for their daily endeavours would be conducted within this culture.

The second principle regulating nationalist priorities in immigration posits the right of national groups to take in the number of members that is required to maintain their self-determination. The duties corresponding to this right are mainly the state's duties to allow, and perhaps even to actively support, the smooth integration of those immigrating on the basis of this right. This right is an example of the third group of rights which comprise the sub- and inter-statist conception of self-determination. It is also an example of rights to cultural preservation, which form the fourth type of cultural rights listed in Chapter 2. This right is an auxiliary right deriving from the right to self-determination. If national groups have the right to self-determination, they must also have the right to take in the number of members required to sustain that self-determination. If they have a right to self-determination, they must also have rights to use the appropriate means for sustaining their self-determination. In many circumstances, the absorption of members of the national group could be such a means. A presumption in favour of this right therefore applies in such cases.

It should be noted that there might be circumstances in which the argument under discussion might justify not only a nation's right to encourage immigration and to take in members in the territories where it enjoys self-determination, but also to exclude non-members from these territories. One of the examples of the rights to cultural preservation mentioned in Chapter 2 is very close to being a right to exclude non-members. This is the right that native minorities in Canada have to restrict the residence and/or voting rights of non-aboriginal people in their reservations. The possibility of such rights does not contradict my earlier argument against the total exclusion of non-members with regard to immigration. My arguments against exclusion are valid with regard to states that have a secure cultural identity and conceive of themselves as belonging to one nation and do not hold with regard to nations whose culture is in danger of extinction.

Unlike the first principle, which benefits *individuals* who for nationalist reasons wish to immigrate to their nation's centre, the second principle expresses a *group* right. This right is not intended to serve the interests of the potential immigrants in living in their nation's centre but rather to serve the interests of all the members of the national group in the continued existence of the group and in its self-determination. Immigration based on this right could therefore include members of the national group who wish to immigrate for economic, religious or other reasons, and not necessarily for nationalist reasons.

The principle under discussion must be conceived of as allowing immigration only in order to maintain a situation in which a particular group's right to self-determination can be actualized. In other words, it is meant to assist national groups in whose homeland the population is declining to try and rectify this problem by allowing the immigration of their diaspora members. The principle under discussion, namely, that national groups should be allowed to absorb in their homelands the number of members required in order to sustain their self-determination, must not be interpreted as a principle establishing the right of national groups to create a core group in their homeland, if such a group does not already exist there. A principle allowing the creation of such a core seems to be expressed by Kasher's 'founding fathers' principle mentioned earlier. According to him (and to many other Israeli liberals) Israel's Law of Return should be interpreted as intended to enable the Jews to create a demographic core in Israel in order to realize their right to self-determination. Kasher seems to believe that if a national group is indeed entitled to self-determination, it must constitute the majority in a given territory.[17] Without fulfilling the conditions specified in Chapter 4, namely, without an empty territory to which the members of a given national group can return in order to realize their self-determination, supporting 'the case of the founding fathers' in effect means that one is in favour of initiating demographic upheavals that could cause great injustice to those already living in the territories to which the 'founding fathers' immigrate. Zionism inflicted such injustices on the Arabs living in Palestine when the principle manifested in Israel's Law of Return was invoked to create a Jewish majority in Israel. As clarified in Chapter 4 and contrary to the view held by many people affiliated with the Israeli Left, the fact that these were injustices is not, in my opinion, their only moral feature. Nevertheless, it is one of their salient moral features that should not be ignored. Accordingly, I do not think that supporting immigration laws that permit such deeds is morally desirable. In the spirit of Kasher's terminology, the principle I propose here could be called 'the case of the continuing sons'. That is, national groups who enjoy self-determination should be allowed to encourage the immigration of their diaspora members in order to prevent the core group from decreasing in size. This principle involves no danger of creating demographic upheavals, instability and related injustices. Contrary to the prevailing view among Israeli liberals, it seems to me that now that the Jews constitute a majority in the state of Israel, the moral problem presented by the Law of Return in the past no longer exists, provided it is interpreted as the principle of 'the continuing sons' rather than of 'the founding fathers'.

The third principle asserts that states have an obligation to take in the refugees and persecuted members of the national groups that enjoy self-determination within these states, and also to grant priority to members of these particular groups when considering the admission of immigrants under any other criteria that they might have for filling their immigration quotas. The obligation to absorb refugees and persecuted members (mainly those who are persecuted for their nationality) is based first and foremost on one of the justifications for the right to national self-determination. This right is meant to enable not only the continued existence of the national group, but also to contribute to the dignity of its individual members. However, there are two additional considerations in support of the third principle. One straightforward consideration is that of efficiency. Since the absorption of immigrants who share the same

---

[17] See Kasher, 'Justice and Affirmative Action', who also supports another principle of return, which asserts the right of national groups to absorb their persecuted members and refugees. As evident below in the body of this chapter, I fully agree with this principle.

national identity as those who absorb them stands a greater chance of success than absorption by those who do not share such identity, it seems appropriate to prefer the former. The second consideration is based on particularistic prerogatives and obligations that exist between national groups and their members and which allow and require them to prefer their own members over others.[18] The legitimacy and possible justifications of such prerogatives and obligations will be discussed in the first part of Chapter 6. If particularistic obligations are indeed legitimate, then they provide an additional and solid foundation for the immigration principle under consideration. They justify preferring the members of national groups enjoying self-determination within a state over potential immigrants who are not such members.

However, such a preference can be justified only within the categories included in the immigration quotas. For instance, if, due to the needs of its own population, a state decides to include a certain number of doctors or manual workers in its immigration quotas, or if, due to considerations of global justice, it decides also to include a certain number of poor people from the Third World in its immigration quotas, then it is also permitted to grant priority to members of its own national group within the quotas of doctors, manual workers or poor people from the Third World. The principle under discussion is not intended to grant priority to members of the national group over all other potential immigrants. If it did, all non-nationalist considerations for determining immigration policies would become meaningless.

Unlike the first principle, according to which the nationalist needs of potential immigrants must have considerable weight compared to the other considerations determining immigration policies, the third principle is not based on the same justifications of the right to self-determination. Unlike the second immigration principle, according to which national groups are allowed to absorb in their homelands the number of members required for maintaining their self-determination, the right granted by the third principle does not derive from instrumental considerations. Rather, acting according to the present principle is one among many *expressions* of national self-determination. It enables core groups of nations, who have the main claim to the right to self-determination, to demonstrate their solidarity and realize their responsibilities towards their diaspora members. Furthermore, unlike the first

---

[18] Perry uses these two considerations in order to explain why refugees belonging to national groups should be admitted by countries where these groups live. But he refuses to apply these considerations in cases of non-refugee potential immigrants and provides no argument in support of this position. See Perry, 'Immigration, justice and culture', pp. 123–4.

principle, which grants advantages on an individual basis to members of national groups who wish to immigrate to their homeland for nationalist reasons, the present principle grants a collective advantage to the national group by allowing the group to favour its members. It is the group, not its individual members, who can claim the benefits granted by this principle. Unlike the members who may benefit from the first principle, the members who are the potential beneficiaries of such a claim need not be motivated by nationalist considerations. In this respect, and with respect to the collective nature of the benefit, the present principle – according to which states have a duty to take in refugees and persecuted members of specific national groups that have a right to self-determination within the specific states, and also to grant priority to members of these groups within all the other categories that make up their immigration quotas – is similar to the second principle. The second principle also grants a collective right to the group. It grants it a collective right to take in immigrants in order to maintain its self-determination. Accordingly, these potential immigrants need not be nationally motivated.

Israel's Law of Return

In order to further elucidate the three principles and in order to expose some of their implications, I shall compare them with Israel's Law of Return and its naturalization laws. These laws grant every Jew the right to immigrate to Israel and become a citizen. One salient difference between them stems from the fact that the Law of Return presupposes the statist conception of self-determination and that the State of Israel constitutes the implementation of this conception with regard to Jewish people. The principles proposed above were based on the sub-statist conception of self-determination. They allow for the possibility that self-determination could be enjoyed by more than one nation within the framework of any one state. Such a possibility must be realized in cases of states comprising the homelands of more than one national group. There is no doubt that the principal injustice that the Law of Return causes does not stem from the fact that it grants advantages in immigration on a nationalist basis, but rather from the fact that it grants such advantages to one nation within a state which includes members of more than one nation entitled to self-determination.[19]

The second major problem that the Law of Return creates is demographic. It poses a demographic threat not only to the Palestinians living

---

[19] Coleman and Harding, who seem to support Israel's Law of Return, also fail to appreciate the significance of this point. See Coleman and Harding, 'Citizenship, justice, political borders', p. 44.

in Israel and under its rule, or Arabs in the neighbouring states, but also to Israel's Jewish population because it grants rights of return to every single Jew. According to the Law of Return, the criteria that serve to determine who may be considered a Jew are religious criteria: that is, in order to qualify as a Jew one must either have a Jewish mother or have undergone an Orthodox conversion. Every person who meets one of these criteria has an almost automatic right *vis-à-vis* the state to enter it and to become a citizen.[20] Moreover, the state also provides him/her with financial aid to cover his/her initial expenses in his/her new home. This has always caused anxiety among Arabs living in Israel, in the territories under Israel's rule and in states neighbouring Israel. Similar anxieties are evoked among the Jewish population in Israel by the fact that certain populations in Africa and India are claimed by themselves and others to be Jewish and therefore wish to immigrate to Israel. In this context it must be noted that the Palestinian demand to include a right of return for former refugees as part of the peace agreement with Israel also creates similar anxieties among Jewish Israelis.

The three principles proposed here cannot give rise to similar anxieties primarily because they do not grant individual rights to a large population of potential immigrants. Except for the second principle, which grants group rights where immigration is expected to assist in maintaining the demographic status quo necessary for a group's self-determination, they do not confer rights to actually immigrate on individuals. Rather, they are guidelines according to which the authorities should determine immigration quotas and choose among potential immigrants. Furthermore, these are only partial guidelines since immigration policies should also be determined based on considerations concerning needs other than those deriving from people's nationality, that is, the needs both of potential immigrants and of the state's own population. These three principles do not at any stage contain demographic threats and therefore cannot be a source of demographic anxieties.

However, it is also the substance of these principles and not merely the fact that the advantages under consideration are constrained by immigration quotas which could prevent them from creating demographic threats. The first principle, let us recall, asserts that the national needs of potential immigrants must be significant within the balance of considerations according to which immigration policies are decided. This principle cannot lead to demographic threats to any particular group since it applies to

---

[20] In fact, the law is even wider, and applies not only to individuals who are themselves Jewish according to the religious definition, but also their offspring up to the third generation, even if the latter are not Jewish.

diaspora members who, for nationalist reasons, attribute significance to living where their nation enjoys self-determination. Most of the Jews who immigrated to Israel from the Soviet Union in the period right before and since the collapse of the USSR, could not have immigrated to Israel on the basis of this principle. Most of them had had little contact with Jewish culture and their motivation for immigrating to Israel was not a desire to become a part of Jewish history and culture. Rather, their immigration to Israel was primarily motivated by economic and political hardship. Therefore, the present principle cannot serve as a basis for granting them nationality-based priority in immigration. This principle could perhaps serve as a basis for the immigration of many American Jews. However, considering the extent of their involvement in American society, and the economic situation there, the odds that the Jewish component of their identity would motivate a significant number of them to immigrate to Israel are very slim indeed. Therefore, it seems that the first of the above-mentioned principles for setting nationality-based immigration policies should not become a source for demographic concern, even if it did grant individual rights to those who wish to immigrate for nationalist reasons.

The second principle grants national groups the right to encourage the immigration of their members and the right to take in the number of immigrants required in order to maintain their self-determination. As clarified earlier, if applied to inhabited areas, this principle is intended to maintain the demographic status quo within which the right to self-determination is already realized and not to create a demographic state of affairs that will enable nations to exercise this right. It therefore does not entail demographic threats.

The third principle, which deals with priorities for refugees who are co-nationals, and with efficiency- and fraternity-based priorities for co-nationals even if they are not refugees, applies, as far as its content is concerned, to much larger groups than the first two principles. Nevertheless, the demographic scope of the third principle is limited as a result of the justifications on which it is based. Recall that according to the efficiency justification, the absorption of immigrants who share a national identity with those who receive them stands a greater chance of success than the absorption of those who do not share such identity. The fraternity justification relies on the special obligations existing between national groups and their members, because of their shared identity. The present principle thus applies only to potential immigrants who in fact share the same culture and identity with the target group. The group of Jews who would be eligible to immigrate on the basis of this principle would undoubtedly include American, Russian, English and Moroccan Jews, most of whom could not have been included in the first two categories. However, it could not, for instance, include the 300 million candidates who were discovered recently in India for they share no common memory and culture with the Jews in Israel and the communities the latter originally came from.[21] Nor is there a cultural similarity between members of the group in India and those living in Israel on a level sufficient to facilitate their smooth integration into Israeli society.

Because of the age-old persecution of the Jews which culminated in the Holocaust, Israel's Law of Return constitutes an historical declaration that has important symbolic significance. In practice, however, the Law of Return should have been limited to the three principles discussed above. Yet, this is not the way the law is in fact interpreted in Israel. Moreover, according to one rather prominent interpretation of Zionist ideology (though surely not its only interpretation), the advantages granted by the Law of Return should be realized by all the members of the Jewish people. It is no wonder that this law generates fears among Palestinians. As noted above, the Palestinian demand to grant a right of return to their refugees gives rise to similar fears among Jewish Israelis. It seems to me that a distinction between the symbolic significance of such a right and its realization in practice must also apply to the Palestinian right of return.[22]

The nationality-based principles of immigration – some possible objections

The principles proposed above as guidelines for nationality-based immigration policies may give rise to various objections. This is so especially with regard to the first two principles. The first principle, according to which states must allot a portion of their immigration quotas to those immigrants who wish to live where their nation enjoys self-determination,

---

[21] Certain rabbis in modern Israel have made it their mission to discover the lost tribes of the ancient Sons of Israel. As mentioned, they recently claimed to have found some 300 million of their descendants in India.

[22] A Palestinian right of return is justified not so much for reasons of distributive justice, as was the case with regard to the three nationality-based immigration principles proposed above, but rather for reasons of corrective justice. These considerations pertain to wrongs perpetrated not so long ago in historical terms, which is why a strong case for a Palestinian right of return can indeed be made. However, this does not constitute an overriding case for a Palestinian right of return. Many Jewish Israelis live their lives within Jewish Israeli culture in the same places where the refugees used to live. The return of refugees in great numbers to these places might destabilize their lives and render it difficult for them to live within the framework of their culture. For these reasons, it seems to me that the considerations supporting the return of the refugees should not be regarded as decisive. Many of the arguments presented in this book could be used to support this claim.

is problematic because, in order to be carried out, it requires states to probe into the motives of potential immigrants. There are important reasons, mainly substantive ones regarding privacy, but also technical and evidentiary reasons, why this is undesirable. The problems to which the second principle gives rise are even more serious. According to this principle, national groups may allow into their homelands the number of members that is required for their self-determination. This immediately gives rise to questions such as how many members a group requires in order to realize its right to self-determination? Since the answer to this question is context-dependent, it gives rise to a further question: Who should have the authority to make a decision on this matter? The power to decide such matters could either be granted to international bodies or could be left to the authorities of the state in which a given group enjoys self-determination. Both solutions could be questionable. The first is somewhat utopian. With regard to the second solution, it is not difficult to imagine the magnitude of practical problems (not to mention the theoretical ones) which the respective state authorities would face in deciding on the above question, especially in states where more than one group enjoys self-determination. It is not difficult to imagine how certain groups enjoying self-determination in a state together with other groups enjoying the same right might manipulate this principle, or the bitterness that would be created as a result of such manipulation. However, the question is whether these objections to the proposed principles are conclusive. The objection to the first principle was that the implementation of the principle involves invasions of privacy and gives rise to problems of evidence. It could perhaps be argued that a person who might potentially benefit from the principle must decide on his or her priorities with regard to privacy on the one hand and cultural-national aspirations on the other. His/her predicament is similar to that of conscientious objectors regarding military service. Some liberal states grant exemptions to conscientious objectors, despite the fact that this involves procedures that might infringe on the privacy of potential benefactors. They have to reveal details about their lives that would convince the relevant officials of the sincerity of their objection. Conscientious objectors thus have to decide whether their conscience comes before their privacy. It seems that if liberal states allow this practice with regard to conscientious objection, they can also afford to allow it in the context of the first principle of return suggested here.

The objection to the second principle, that which grants national groups a right to allow into their homelands that number of members required for their self-determination, seems more powerful to me. However, it must be remembered that not allowing any priorities in immigration on a national basis where the population required for a group's self-determination decreases means the loss of the group's self-determination. This means that members of the group will not be able to live their lives within their culture. The possibility of assimilating into the majority culture of the state where the group in question has decreased in size will then become a serious one for the group's members. Is it justified to assist them in attempts to avoid this condition and thus avoid assimilation and the loss of their distinct identity?

Brian Barry claims that '[W]e cannot simply assume that conditions in which there are incentives for assimilation are necessarily unjust. Even if the institutional background satisfied the demands of justice, it may well still be that the culture (for example, the language) of a group puts it at a disadvantage in pursuing ends valued by its members.'[23] This is surely correct. However, the crucial question is what institutional background would satisfy the demands of justice for purposes of evaluating decisions to assimilate. Is it sufficient, as Barry seems to hold,[24] that institutions refrain from forcing people to assimilate or from causing them to do so by stigmatizing them and discriminating against them? Or do institutions have to allow and even support certain sorts of positive action such as the action allowed by the second immigration principle, so that people's culture does not deteriorate to a condition which provides them with incentives to assimilate? After all, people may hold complex preferences. They may prefer to adhere to their original culture and not assimilate on the condition that this culture is viable. At the same time, if this culture is not viable, they may prefer to assimilate rather than adhere to their original culture. Let us assume that an attempt to enhance a culture's chances to be viable should be made if the means for doing so do not infringe basic human rights and are not too costly. Accordingly, if a particular homeland group is assimilated because its self-determination is not supported by such measures, then this assimilation can be said to have occurred within an institutional background that does not satisfy the demands of justice. In other words, Barry's claim that '[W]e cannot simply assume that conditions in which there are incentives for assimilation are necessarily unjust', obscures important issues raised by cultural nationalism and multiculturalism. If my arguments in this book are correct, then national groups must be allowed to take the measures required for their preservation as long as these measures do not significantly violate the human rights of either members or non-members. The second nationality-based

---

[23] Barry, *Culture and Equality*, p. 75.   [24] *Ibid.*, pp. 75–6.

immigration principle meets this qualification. This is in contrast to such measures as prohibiting exit from the group, or prohibiting its members from associating with other groups and cultures. In sum, the implementation of the second nationality-based immigration principle might cause serious practical problems. However, refraining from implementing this principle might cause serious injustice.

6   Nationalism, particularism and cosmopolitanism

In the last few chapters I discussed several demands that cultural nationalism makes in the public domain. The purpose of the present chapter is mainly to consider some demands that cultural nationalism makes in the private domain. In the first part of the chapter I will discuss the position according to which people are permitted or even required to demonstrate a measure of partiality and special concern for their national group and its members. I will argue that this partiality can be accommodated within the framework of ethical universalism, the position according to which ethics is about 'individuals with their generic human capacities, considered . . . as standing apart from and prior to their relationships to other individuals'.[1] I will reject the thesis according to which such partiality could be accommodated only within the framework of ethical particularism. According to ethical particularism, ethics is about agents 'which . . . are already encumbered with a variety of ties and commitments to particular other agents, or to groups or collectivities',[2] ties and commitments which they are born into or into which they grow involuntarily. Later in this chapter, I will discuss the relationship between cultural particularism and cultural cosmopolitanism. The former is the view that it is good for people to be immersed in one particular culture. The latter is the view that it is good for them to shape their lives by means of ideas, texts, customs etc. that they gather from different cultures. I will argue for at least one sense in which these doctrines could be compatible. I will conclude the chapter by noting that the nationalism presented in this book is compatible not only with the two sorts of universalism/cosmopolitanism mentioned so far, namely, ethical universalism and cultural cosmopolitanism, but also presupposes a third kind of cosmopolitanism pertaining to distributive justice. According to this type of cosmopolitanism, the basic unit for implementing distributive justice is the entire world rather than individual states.[3]

[1] D. Miller, *On Nationality*, p. 50.   [2] *Ibid.*
[3] For a similar distinction, see Coleman and Harding, 'Citizenship, justice, political borders', pp. 35–8. The present distinction between the particularist and cosmopolitan

148

Ethical universalism and national particularism

The position according to which morality requires or at least permits people to demonstrate special concern for their national group and its members is accepted by many writers who at the same time hold the view that people ought to be concerned about people as such and not just as members of any particular group. Both ethical particularists and ethical universalists believe that the two positions are reconcilable. The dispute between them is not so much about the compatibility of the two positions, but rather about the appropriate framework for accounting for it. Particularists argue that their position is more consistent with human nature and with social reality than the universalist position. According to them, people are by nature motivated to act on the basis of the ties and commitments into which they are born. The world is in fact divided into communities whose members interact with one another and take part in projects that are unique to their respective community. According to particularists, the ideals of ethical universalism do not take the psychological reality of human beings and the social reality of human organization seriously enough.[4] In contrast, universalists argue that particularism is logically incoherent and is inconsistent with the fact that moral thinking, like all branches of thinking, requires general categories.[5] They also argue that ethical particularism leads to immoral consequences because it allows people to consider only those close to themselves and to ignore the needs of humans as such.[6] Particularists argue that their position could accommodate the universalist concern for people in general, while universalism could not accommodate the particular commitments which people have to their national group and its members. On the other hand, universalists argue that it is particularism which could not accommodate universalist concerns for people in general and that it is universalism which could accommodate the concern of particularism for special ties.

As noted above, I will join the universalist position and will argue that particularism cannot seriously accommodate the universalist's concern for people in general, while universalism is equipped with several strategies to accommodate certain particularist commitments that people have

---

approaches to distributive justice is also included in Sidgwick's account of his distinction between the national ideal and the cosmopolitan ideal of political organization (Henry Sidgewick, *The Elements of Politics* (New York: Kraus, 1969), p. 309).

[4] D. Miller, *On Nationality*, chap. 3, makes such claims in the name of moral particularism.
[5] See, e.g., Thomas Hurka, 'The Justification of National Partiality', in McKim and McMahan (eds.), *The Morality of Nationalism*, p. 143.
[6] See, e.g., Martha C. Nussbaum, 'Patriotism and Cosmopolitanism', in Joshua Cohen (ed.), *For Love of Country: Debating the Limits of Patriotism – Martha C. Nussbaum with Respondents* (Boston: Beacon Press, 1996), p. 5; Poole, *Nation and Identity*, p. 154.

to their national group. I shall deal mainly with two such strategies, those which David Miller has named the 'useful convention' strategy, and the 'voluntary creation' strategy. According to the 'useful convention' strategy, considerations pertaining to moral division of labour explain why members of a national group incur special obligations *vis-à-vis* one another which they do not incur towards people in general.[7] Since most people can care only for a limited number of other people, efficiency requires that they concentrate on those people with whom they have kinship ties or some other close relationship. According to the 'voluntary creation' strategy, members of national groups have special obligations towards one another that they don't have towards all other people, because they choose to belong to the group. They have such obligations in the same way that promisors have special obligations towards their promisees that they do not have towards other people. Whether these strategies succeed or fail in accounting for the particularist nationalist obligations depends on what we expect them to account for. Are they meant to justify *obligations* of partiality or sometimes just *permission* to be partial? What are the permissions and obligations that they are meant to establish? Are they permissions granted to the group's institutions to be partial towards its members, or obligations of members towards other members in matters pertaining to the group? Or are they obligations that require partiality among members in private dealings? Do we expect each of these strategies to account for all these permissions and obligations, or do we expect them to account only for some, and then only sometimes or partially? It seems that if the system of particularist obligations and permissions that need to be acknowledged in various contexts is adequately qualified, and if we expect different universalist strategies to account for various sorts of particularist priorities in the complex manner implied by the current questions, then the 'useful convention' and the 'voluntary creation' strategies do not completely fail. In what follows I will discuss mainly two types of special obligations: the special responsibilities which people have towards their groups, and the special obligations which the institutions of a given group have towards group members.

Partiality towards one's group

The claim that the members of a national group may demonstrate partiality and may even be required to demonstrate partiality towards their

---

[7] D. Miller, *On Nationality*, pp. 51–2, 62–4. As implied by its name, mainly utilitarians support this argument. See e.g., Sidgewick, *The Methods of Ethics*, p. 431, and Robert Goodin, 'What Is So Special about Our Fellow Countrymen?' *Ethics* 98 (1988), 663–86.

group, its prosperity and its integrity is hard to dispute. Consider the following example of two military units, one of Israeli soldiers who beat up a Palestinian civilian and another of Palestinian soldiers who also beat up a Palestinian. If I conceive of my Israeliness as an important component of my identity this will mean that I must have a sense of special responsibility for the behaviour of the Israeli unit and not for the Palestinian one. This would imply choosing to prevent the Israelis rather than the Palestinians from continuing to beat up their respective victims. Such a preference is an expression of my Israeli identity in the same way that granting preference to friends over non-friends is part of the meaning of being a friend. Without such expressions of partiality it is not at all clear what group membership means. The question of what the special responsibilities that constitute one's belonging to a group are could be contested. However, it can hardly be contested that such responsibilities are required in order to grant some substance to group membership. At first glance, it seems that such special responsibilities cannot be justified in terms of the 'voluntary creation' strategy. For most people, their national belonging is not something that they have chosen but rather something they were born into and grew up with. However, a closer look reveals that this does not entail that the responsibilities which a group's members owe their group are not a matter of choice. Since responsibility for one's national group is a normative issue, normative considerations should be used to determine whether people have such responsibilities rather than the empirical fact that most people's national affiliation is a result of their place of birth or upbringing. If, however, it is true that people should not be forced to identify with the national groups into which they were born and/or within which they grew up, and that they should be left free to decide whether or not they wish to do so, then their responsibilities towards their group are ultimately a matter of choice. In other words, despite the fact that most people belong to the national groups into which they were born, the special responsibilities which are associated with such affiliation should not be ascribed to people without their voluntary identification with these groups and without their viewing this affiliation as forming a significant part of their life or identity.

Some people might doubt the soundness of these claims. They would argue that they entail a view according to which people could choose to identify with the national group into which they were born and have responsibilities towards it in the same way that they could have chosen to identify with any other national group and thus have been responsible for it. They would argue that putting the national group into which a person was born on one and the same level as any other group from the perspective of one's responsibilities towards such groups disregards an important component in how one conceives the special responsibilities people have towards their national groups. Just as people have responsibilities towards the particular parents to whom they were born or by whom they were raised, and just as one cannot choose any parents in order to fulfil these responsibilities, so it is in the case of the responsibilities people have towards national groups. They must fulfil this special responsibility towards the national group within which they were born and the responsibilities in question are not voluntary.

While one of the objections implicit in the argument under discussion seems to be justified, the other is not. The justified objection is that which protests against blurring the distinction between people's choice to identify with the national group into which they were born and/or within which they grew up as opposed to the option of choosing another group. The unjustified objection is that which presumes that people's normative position in relation to the group within which they were born is similar to their normative stance *vis-à-vis* their parents. Namely, it requires their concern for the group and denies that they have moral freedom not to be concerned about the group. The first objection is justified because there are certain strong amoral and moral reasons to identify with the group in which people were born and/or grew up in which apply to them involuntarily, whereas no such reasons hold for other groups. The amoral reason pertains to the fact that people's identification with the group in which they were born or grew up in does not require extensive efforts of acculturation that are necessary when people choose to become members of other groups. It also does not require acceptance by members of other groups. However, this surely does not mean that people necessarily have a duty to identify with their original culture. It merely constitutes one reason due to which other people have a duty to allow them to identify with their original culture. Other reasons which justify the first objection noted above are the moral reasons people have for identifying with their original culture, which derive from people's interest in their endeavours, as discussed in Chapter 2 above. This interest explains the interest people have in the historical existence of their culture, which creates moral reasons for people to identify with their ancestral culture. Thus, people do not only have important amoral reasons to belong to the culture within which they were born or grew up, but also moral reasons to do so. The fact that people are confronted with these reasons and considerations is clearly not a matter of choice. In this respect, their normative position *vis-à-vis* the culture they were born into or within which they were raised is similar to their normative position in relation to their parents, and differs from their position in relation to other cultures.

However, the second objection assumes that a person's normative position with regard to the national group within which he was born or grew up is identical to that regarding his parents, where he has filial *obligations* and is not morally free to disregard these obligations. Yet in the case of the relationship between people and their original culture, the special reasons applying to this relationship do not entail a *duty* of loyalty to this culture if they do not choose to identify with it, whereas in the case of one's parents, the reasons applying to this relationship entail certain duties. Whether or not moral reasons to act in a certain way are reasons for imposing a duty to act in this way must be the result of balancing between two groups of considerations. On the one hand, there is the intensity of the values from which these reasons derive combined with the danger to these values if people do not act according to them. On the other hand, one must consider the harm to people's freedom if duties are imposed on them to act in these ways.[8] If the duty of loyalty to one's parents is not recognized, various facets of one's parents' welfare would be detrimentally affected. On the other hand, although imposing the obligation that people be loyal to their parents (for example, by assisting them through ailments) might constrain their freedom to some extent, this would usually pertain to limited aspects of their lives for limited periods. It therefore seems that the moral reasons that people have to care for their parents and be loyal to them are reasons that justify imposing certain obligations on them. However, this situation does not apply to people's normative position regarding their original cultures. The value that might be damaged if people are not loyal to their original cultures is the value of preserving these cultures and the interest people's ancestors had in the continued existence of these cultures. The continued existence of these cultures is not really threatened if some members leave the culture. On the other hand, the constraint of personal freedom that would result from imposing duties of loyalty to people's original culture is necessarily significant. It affects many aspects of their lives and is lifelong. It seems therefore inappropriate to conceive of the moral reasons which people have to identify with their original cultures as imposing duties of loyalty to these cultures. However, it does not follow that people *never* have special obligations towards their original cultures. It only follows that if they have such duties, this is because they voluntarily choose to belong to this culture. This is analogous to the special responsibilities which people have towards their

---

[8] For example, the sanctity of life justifies a duty not to kill humans because the act of killing is certainly detrimental to this value, and also because the constraint under discussion does not impose a serious limitation on freedom. In the same way, the sanctity of life does not impose on people a duty to save two other people's lives per week.

friends. In other words, the fact that people have special *reasons* to identify with their original culture, which they do not have for identifying with other cultures, and the fact that these reasons apply to them involuntarily, does not entail that they have an obligation to identify with their original culture. However, from this it does not follow that if they identify with their original culture because of these or other reasons, they do not have special responsibilities towards it. For example, I have a special reason to identify with Jewish culture, namely, the fact that I was born into it, grew up within it, and because the endeavours of my ancestors were carried out within this culture. These reasons could not apply to my possible identification with other cultures. From this, however, it does not follow that I have an obligation to act on these reasons. Nevertheless, if I choose to act on them, if I identify with the Jewish people and consider myself as belonging to the Jewish people, then this entails special responsibilities. Such special responsibilities can be accommodated by ethical universalism in the same way that it accommodates the special responsibilities of love and friendship. In the same way that loving someone or being someone's friend means, among other things, giving them priority compared to others, so it is with any culture with which a person identifies. Feeling responsible for the group and having preferential attitudes towards it, in certain areas, are constitutive of such identification.

This basis for special responsibilities, namely, the fact that these responsibilities are a constitutive component of some sorts of relationship and affiliation, must be distinguished from another source of such responsibilities, namely, a common history. According to Thomas Hurka, such histories are a source of the special responsibilities within relationships of love and friendship and also within nations. 'I love my wife... as the person who nursed me through that illness, with whom I spent that wonderful first summer... These historical qualities focus my love on my wife as an individual.'[9] According to him, these historical qualities are a source of special responsibilities. He draws an analogy between the marital relationship and the special responsibilities to which its history gives rise, and the special responsibilities among the members of national groups. Historical qualities of the sort Hurka discusses, that is, having lived together with other people and sharing a history with them, could serve as a basis for special responsibilities. However, these must be distinguished from the responsibilities following from the very meaning of ties such as love and friendship. The latter define the tie itself and are independent of its having a history. They cease to exist when the relationship is over, despite the fact that its history cannot be eliminated. On

[9] Hurka, 'National Partiality', p. 150.

the other hand, the responsibilities arising from a common history can exist only after the relationship has accumulated a substantial history. They can also survive at least some time after the relationship has ceased to exist (provided it has not been terminated for reasons that have to do with the misbehaviour or wrongdoing of one of the parties). In other words, people can incur special responsibilities to their lovers from the moment they fall in love, even before the relationship has produced a history, for love means, among other things, preference for the love object over other persons. On the other hand, people may have special responsibilities for their former lovers and friends, at least for some time after the relationship has ended, for reasons that derive from the history of the relationship. The responsibilities in question are entailed by the values of fairness and gratitude. These responsibilities should be distinguished from those that define relationships. While the former could survive the relationship, the latter are independent of any history.

The partiality of institutions towards group members

An additional justification for the partiality that group members are permitted to demonstrate towards their group pertains to pragmatic considerations regarding the moral division of labour and conventions of efficiency. In the example mentioned earlier, I could justify the priority I attribute to rescuing the victim of the Israeli military unit over rescuing the victim of the Palestinian unit, not only because of my Israeli identity, but also because my being an Israeli makes my judgement regarding the Israeli unit's act as criminal more likely to be correct than my judgement concerning the Palestinian unit. Since it is better to prevent activities the wrongness of which one is more certain about than to prevent activities one only suspects to be evil, I would do better to prevent the former act. A justification of this type could also work in the case of the special responsibilities which officials have towards members of their respective nations, as opposed to members of other nations. For example, most people would not deny that Sweden's officials must give priority to the welfare of Swedish citizens over the welfare of Frenchmen. This could be justified by invoking the fact that Sweden's officials are more familiar with the needs of the Swedes than with the needs of the Frenchmen. They are closer to the members of their nation both mentally and physically and therefore are better positioned to respond to their needs.

David Miller has argued that considerations like the above cannot account for these particularist responsibilities because there are cases in which such responsibilities exist while considerations pertaining to efficiency in the division of labour do not apply. For example, he claims that the Swedish government must give priority to the welfare of Swedes not only over the welfare of the French, but also over the welfare of the Somalis. Considerations of efficiency could hardly justify this, since Somalia's government has not succeeded in providing for the Somalis' most basic needs. It is reasonable to believe that if the Swedish government stepped in, the predicament of the Somalis would improve substantially. However, what this argument shows is that considerations of efficiency could not serve as a basis for all particularist preferences. This argument does not show that considerations of efficiency cannot be used to justify *any* particularist priorities. With regard to the Swedish–Somalian example, perhaps national institutions should not prefer the non-basic needs of their own members to very basic needs of the members of the poorest nations. The fact that they actually demonstrate partiality in such cases is not necessarily because this is really justified, but because there are reasons excusing them for doing something which is unjustified. For example, although the striking gap between the poorest people in Sweden and many Somalis could constitute a reason for Sweden to allocate more funds to poor Somalis than to lower-middle-class Swedes, the Swedish government may refrain from supplying aid to the Somalis because there is no way to determine why Sweden, rather than Norway, for example, should provide aid to the Somalis in question. Similarly, if Sweden does decide to support Somalia, then why not also support Zimbabwe or Burkina Faso? If Sweden decides to support Somalia, this might discourage the Somalis from taking responsibility for their own fate. In cases where aid is provided to the victims of serious natural disasters, members of aid-providing nations do not usually complain about their government's activities, which seems to support the present argument. Perhaps such complaints are rarely made, first, because the victims of natural disasters are not considered responsible for their predicament and, secondly, it is usually the case that natural disasters occur one at a time. Thirdly, the burden of providing aid in cases of natural disasters does not usually fall on one state only.

It should perhaps be noted that similar considerations apply in cases of groups of people that are smaller than nations. In the case where a physician's son is suffering from a cold and his neighbour's son is suffering from a snake bite, it seems that the physician must give priority to the neighbour's son over his own son. In a different case, a person is free to buy his son a piano even if the neighbour's son is in need of items that are far more basic, such as a pencil for school. This does not refute the moral of the snake case. It merely confirms the claim that when differences in the needs of the parties in question are due to systemic features and are not the consequence of an unexpected crisis, people are free to prefer their relatives over strangers. However, this is not because it is intrinsically justified that they do so, but because it is often very difficult to decide who and how to aid people who are not relatives.

This brings us back to the 'voluntary creation' strategy and to the example of Sweden and Somalia. The Swedish government's preferential policies regarding the welfare of Swedes as opposed to that of French or Somali people could also be accounted for in terms of the voluntary creation strategy. The current world order seems to lack an efficient system of global distribution that would enable rich countries to share the burden of assisting the poorer nations. It also lacks a system that would provide incentives for poor countries to improve their lot. Thus, it seems that citizens of any particular state are justified in their expectation that those who choose to serve them should primarily serve their needs and interests. Those who serve as officials ought to know all this and could therefore be viewed as having voluntarily choosen to serve the needs of their group members rather than the needs and interests of people belonging to other groups. In the same way that universalism can acknowledge the obligation of promisors to provide money or other goods to their promissees even if there are people who need them more urgently, it can also acknowledge analogous obligations of officials to their group members. The fact that national groups are not voluntary associations but historical entities is irrelevant here, because the relationship under consideration is one existing between the group and its voluntarily functioning officials. Thus, this relationship is one that is voluntarily created. It is important to note also that in view of the lack of an efficient system of cosmopolitan justice, officials functioning in national institutions have reason to give priority to the needs of members of their respective nations over non-members' more basic needs. This does not entail that these officials have no obligations regarding the establishment of an international system of cosmopolitan justice. When established, such a system would bring about a change in the expectations of their peoples. This is entirely analogous to the family context. Parents have a duty, or are at least allowed, to prefer their children over other children, even if other children only need a pencil while their own might want a piano. At the same time, they have an obligation, or at least strong moral reasons, to take steps to ensure that a system of justice is established within their society which would prevent situations in which they are able to buy their children a piano while other parents are unable to buy their children a pencil.

Unlike the special responsibilities of group members towards the group, and those of the group institutions and officials towards members of the group, the 'voluntary creation' strategy and the 'useful convention' strategy cannot justify special obligations that individual members have to prefer members over non-members. However, I doubt whether such duties should at all be recognized.[10] Miller seems to think otherwise: 'if my time is restricted and two students each ask if they can consult me, I give priority to the one who belongs to my college'.[11] However, is it desirable to give such priorities? It seems that we ought to distinguish here between a case in which the needs of the two students are the same and a case in which their needs are not the same. In the former case, the teacher needs some procedure for reaching a decision on whom to help, and the fact that one of the students is a member of his college provides him with such a procedure.[12] However, the more interesting cases are of the second type. These are cases where kinship provides reason for permitting or even demanding preferential treatment of the members of one's group even if their needs are lesser than those of non-members.[13] I am not at all sure that such duties exist between co-nationals. It seems that the opposite is the case. Think, for example, of a Hungarian who decides to give a lift to another Hungarian who was lightly wounded and who refuses a lift to a severely wounded Frenchman, just because the former is a compatriot.

I hope to have shown that certain special responsibilities owed by members of national groups and their institutions can be accounted for by the 'useful convention' and the 'voluntary creation' strategies. These are not the only strategies that can be used for this purpose.[14] If they succeed, then the particularist's charge that universalism does not consider the psychology of human beings and the social reality of human organization

---

[10] See also Richard W. Miller, 'Cosmopolitan Respect and Patriotic Concern', *Philosophy and Public Affairs* 27 (1998), 206–7.

[11] D. Miller, *On Nationality*, p. 65.

[12] I owe this point to Daniel Kofman. It should be mentioned that in some cases facts of the type under discussion might provide reasons for preferring the stranger rather than the relative. For example, consider the case of a government minister who has to decide between an offer made by his brother and one made by a non-relative for a project under his jurisdiction. If the offers are the same, it seems that ultimately he should choose the non-relative.

[13] Miller's example could be interpreted not as an individual's obligation to prefer other individuals belonging to his own group over individuals belonging to other groups, but as an example of the special obligations of the group's officials to act according to such priorities. Such a case is similar to the obligations of governments to prefer their own citizens to the citizens of other countries. Miller says that his example is of a case in which the teacher has no official obligation towards the student. However, it should be remembered that officials are quite often regarded as having official duties even if they do not in fact have such duties. This could constitute sufficient reason for them to behave as if they do indeed have these duties.

[14] For other strategies, see R. Miller, 'Cosmopolitan Respect', and Moore, *The Ethics of Nationalism*, chap. 2.

seriously enough is a mute charge. This charge cannot compete with the charge that universalists make against particularism, namely, that it is logically incoherent and that it leads to immoral consequences because it accustoms people to thinking only of those close to themselves and to ignore the needs of human beings as such.

Particularism cum universalism

As noted above, particularists could attempt to refute the latter charge. They might argue that their position could accommodate the universalists' general concern for humans since people are born not only into their national group, but into a variety of groups among which is humanity in general. In view of this, '[t]here is nothing in particularism which prevents me from recognizing that I stand in *some* relationship to all other human beings by virtue of our common humanity and our sharing of a single world'.[15] However, this argument does not really demonstrate that particularism can accommodate the concerns of universalists, since it overlooks important differences between the duties that we associate with our duties towards humans in general, and the duties which are the principal concern of particularism. In referring to obligations within groups such as families and nations, we mean obligations people owe others not just because these other people are *family members* or *members of a nation*, but mainly because they are members of *their* family or *their* nation. We think of the special responsibilities they have towards their family members or compatriots which they do not have towards humanity in general. The obligations under consideration are those that in more technical terms are called agent-relative. In contrast to this, when we think of the duties humans have towards other humans we think of the duties they owe others as members of *the human* race, not as members of *their own* race. The duties under consideration are agent-neutral rather than agent-relative. In order for our obligations towards humans to be similar to particularist obligations, we must think of our obligations towards other men and women as owed to them not as members of the *human* race but rather as members of *our own* race. Thus, we do not have such obligations towards cats, for example, not because there are important differences between humans and cats, but rather because a cat is not 'one of us'. However, this is not the kind of thinking that underlies the ordinary discrimination against other mammals usually practised by people.

---

[15] D. Miller, *On Nationality*, p. 53.

Moreover, if it were the case that other humans belong to *our* race which is the reason by virtue of which we 'are not prevented', to use Miller's expression, from acknowledging special obligations towards other humans, then in the same way we 'are not prevented' from acknowledging special obligations towards, for example, the groups that share the same skin colour, income or gender. It goes without saying that acknowledging some of these categories as bases for special responsibilities is morally undesirable. In order to avoid such acknowledgement, those who argue for a particularist basis for our obligations to other humans must point out the generic differences between membership in the human race on the one hand, and the other memberships, by virtue of which members in the human race are not prevented from acknowledging mutual obligations towards each other, and members in the other groups are prevented from so doing. By pointing out these differences, one concedes to universalism. For one must thus admit that a general characteristic of the human race, or the value of the partnership among its members, is a morally relevant characteristic which justifies acknowledging mutual obligations among humans. One must also admit that the lack of this or an analogous characteristic in skin colour or gender groups prevents the members of these groups from acknowledging a parallel obligation. By conceding to all this one acknowledges that general characteristics by virtue of which individuals form a class, or general characteristic of the ties among individuals, are sufficient or at least necessary to serve as bases for moral obligations among them. One becomes a universalist, or a universalist-*cum*-particularist, rather than particularist-*cum*-universalist.

Cultural cosmopolitanism and particularism

As noted above, the dispute between moral particularists and moral universalists is not so much about the compatibility of their respective normative concerns. Moral universalists usually do not think that their concern for humanity in general excludes particularist concerns among friends, family members and members of nations. Moral particularists do not necessarily think that their insistence on emphasizing the partiality which people and societies duly demonstrate for their relatives and members exclude a moral concern for humanity in general. Rather, their dispute is about the appropriate framework for accounting for these various concerns. In contrast to this, both cultural particularists and cosmopolitans tend to reject one another's ideals and believe their two positions to be incompatible. In what follows I will argue that the interpretation of cultural nationalism for which I have argued in this book makes it possible to speak about at least one sense in which the ideals of cultural particularism and cultural cosmopolitanism are not mutually exclusive. I will argue first for their compatibility on the theoretical level, and then for their practical and institutional compatibility.

Cultural cosmopolitanism and particularism – the theoretical conflict

In an article, cited in Chapter 2, Jeremy Waldron states that '[there] are two visions to be considered ... [t]he cosmopolitan vision and the vision of belonging and immersion in the life and culture of a particular community ...'[16] The ideal of the cosmopolitan vision is a person who 'refuses to think of himself as *defined* by his location or his ancestry or his citizenship or his language.... He is a creature of modernity, conscious of living in a mixed-up world and having a mixed-up self.'[17] The person in question does not belong to a particular place or a particular culture. His identity is composed of elements gleaned from various cultures. The vision of cultural particularism is the opposite of this. It is 'the vision of belonging and immersion in the life and culture of a particular community espoused by the proponents of Article 27 [of the International Covenant of Civil and Political Rights]'.[18] According to this article, 'in those states in which ethnic, religious or linguistic minorities exist, persons belonging to such minorities shall not be denied the right, in community with the other members of their group, to enjoy their own culture, to profess and practice their own religion or to use their own language'.[19] After presenting these two alternatives, Waldron claims that they do not represent two lifestyles that 'old-fashioned' liberalism could easily accept as part of a pluralistic world: 'some like campfires, some like opera; some are Catholics, some are Methodists'.[20] Rather, in his view, they represent two opposed and mutually exclusive perceptions of human nature and of the basic human needs that ultimately dictate the contours of the social order.

Note that Waldron is making two different claims. The first claim is that those who support the cosmopolitan vision do so on the basis of an interest entailed by human nature, as do those maintaining the particularistic vision. According to Waldron, the supporters of these two visions think that they are sustained by basic and universal human interests rather than by the accidental desires of particular individuals. The second claim is that these two visions are profoundly opposed to each other, in the sense

---

[16] Waldron, 'Minority Cultures', 759.
[17] *Ibid.*, 754   [18] *Ibid.*, 759.   [19] *Ibid.*, 757.   [20] *Ibid.*

that, if one is correct, there would be strong grounds for rejecting the other, and vice versa. If cultural nationalism ought to be interpreted as I have argued in Chapter 2, namely, as based on people's interests in their identity and endeavours, then Waldron's first claim that these visions are based on fundamental interests rather than on the accidental desires of particular individuals must be accepted. However, as I shall show below, this claim must be interpreted in a way that totally undermines his second claim according to which only one of these visions can plausibly be assumed to be correct. The interests people have in their identity and endeavour – interests which cultural nationalism is based on – are interests which derive from their nature as human beings. They do not derive from accidental desires and are shared by all humans. However, there is no unified way to satisfy these interests for all people. Those whose cultural identity and the culture of their endeavours is national and particularist would need to be rooted in their national culture in order to satisfy their identity and endeavour-based interests. Those whose cultural identity is cosmopolitan, would need a cosmopolitan lifestyle in order to satisfy the same interests. The interest at stake in both instances is the same, namely, the interest in culture because culture forms part of one's identity and because one's endeavours have been realized within this particular culture. According to this reading, it is clear that both cosmopolitanism and nationalist particularism do not derive from two mutually exclusive or even different conceptions of human nature. Rather, they represent one conception of human nature with different realizations for different individuals. For most people living today this conception manifests itself as their interest in their national culture. For a minority it manifests itself as their interest in a cosmopolitan culture. As both cosmopolitanism and particularism could be supported by one and the same conception of human nature, it appears that Waldron's second claim concerning two mutually exclusive conceptions need not necessarily be accepted.

Of course, the claim that nationalism and cosmopolitanism are derived from two mutually exclusive conceptions of human nature is not new. The rejection of cosmopolitanism as opposed to human nature is a recurring motif in the history of nationalism, and one repeatedly alluded to by the present-day communitarian thinkers attacked by Waldron. According to this approach, nationalism satisfies not people's need to adhere to their culture because it is a component of their identity, but rather their need to belong to national groups because they are groups with a common language, collective memories, a common territory and history.[21]

---

[21] In this connection, Waldron (*ibid.*, 756) refers to Herder's thesis as cited by Berlin (Isaiah Berlin, 'Benjamin Disraeli, Karl Marx and the Search for Identity', in Berlin, *Against the*

This interpretation of nationalism does indeed imply the rejection of cosmopolitanism and unquestionably entails the accusations that nationalists have hurled at cosmopolitans throughout history, namely, that they are rootless, inauthentic, alienated and detached. However, why should we endorse this conception of nationalism? What reason is there to regard it as derived from a basic human need to belong to local cultures? Waldron's argument seems to presuppose that nationalism stems from the need to belong to a local culture.[22] His main criticism against nationalism is that it is possible to lead a satisfactory life outside the framework of a particular nationality, that is, to live a cosmopolitan life. According to Waldron, the very fact that such a life is possible means that the need satisfied by a particularistic nationalist life is not so basic. 'Suppose . . . that a freewheeling cosmopolitan life, lived in a kaleidoscope of cultures, is both possible and fulfilling. Suppose such a life turns out to be rich and creative . . .'. If this is the case, he says, then 'it can no longer be said that all people need their rootedness in the particular culture in which they and their ancestors were reared in the way that they need food, clothing and shelter'.[23] However, in order to show that the political value of nationalism cannot be attributed to particularism as such, and certainly not to the particularism of nationalism as such, it is not necessary to resort to the possibility of a satisfactory cosmopolitan life. If nationalism really stemmed from a basic human need for a particularistic national culture rather than the identity-based and endeavour-based human need to cleave to one's culture, it would not be as crucial to allow people to belong to *their* own particularistic cultures. Their need for cultural membership could be fulfilled through any particularistic culture that would allow for a satisfactory life. A Frenchman's need for a particularistic culture could then be met by turning him into an Italian, and an Inuit's by turning him into a Frenchman. Needless to say, this is not what cultural nationalism means. Cultural nationalism insists on people's interests to adhere

---

Current, p. 257). According to Berlin, Herder sees the human need that accounts for nationalism as 'the need to belong to a particular group, united by some common links – especially language, collective memories, continuous life upon the same soil'. Others, says Berlin, have added 'race, blood, religion, a sense of common mission, and the like'. As Berlin presents it, Herder's position is based on the need to adhere to a kind of nationalist particularism which includes life on common soil. It is therefore different from the interest in nationality as interpreted in this study. It should be noted, however, that the particularism of nationalism as interpreted by Herder himself, at least Berlin's Herder, is certainly not the particularism of race and blood.

[22] There is yet another even more extreme interpretation of cultural nationalism, according to which people's interest to be immersed in their own national culture is not due to the universal human desire to belong to a local territorial culture. Rather, this interpretation of cultural nationalism denies the universality of human nature. See Chapter 1, pp. 21–2.

[23] Waldron, 'Minority Cultures', 762.

to their culture of origin. If, as I have argued in this book, this interest derives from a basic human need people have to adhere to their identity and to the culture in which it was shaped, then it need not necessarily be a need to adhere to a particularistic culture. Particular cultural identities need not be identities with the particular characteristics of nationalism. A person's cultural identity could be cosmopolitan. The interests that people can have in their cultural identity when it is cosmopolitan are not necessarily different in substance and depth from people's interests in their cultural identity when it is national.

Cultural particularism and cosmopolitanism – the practical conflict

There is a limited number of social realities which could confer meaning and substance on the actions and endeavours of each individual cosmopolitan. There is a limited number of languages, a limited repertoire of collective memories and a limited repertoire of meaningful careers, within which individual cosmopolitans are capable of pursuing a meaningful life. Cosmopolitans might therefore not have specific interests in the continued existence of any one particular culture. They would, however, have an interest in the existence of some components of some of these cultures, since these would enable them to lead meaningful lives.

Since a cosmopolitan cultural identity does not involve sharing collective memories and a clearly defined territorial homeland with many other people, the measures one might take to promote the interests cosmopolitans might have in their cultural identity would be different from those adopted to promote the interests of those whose cultural identity is national. Needless to say, the right to political self-determination, or the protection of a particular language, or special privileges regarding immigration to a particular territory – all these crucial rights, which were presented in the above chapters as usually required for protecting people's interests in their national belongings – are alien to a cosmopolitan context. Furthermore, since cosmopolitans put the eggs of their cultural identity in many baskets, very few special measures would be required in order to secure the minimal cultural conditions necessary for their freedom and self-respect. In view of the relatively high socioeconomic status, kinds of talent and character of people likely to become cosmopolitan, it is possible that almost no special measures will be required. Consequently, and also perhaps because of humanity's pressing economic needs, it may not be necessary or appropriate to grant cosmopolitans any special rights for the protection of their cultural identity, save the right not to be humiliated because of that identity or coerced into changing it. However, it does not follow that a cosmopolitan cultural identity cannot in principle be considered an identity deserving protection, nor that people's interest in their cosmopolitan cultural identity is less essential to them than people's interest in their national cultural identity. It also does not follow that there are no circumstances in which it might be appropriate to take special measures to protect people's interest in their cultural identity, when it is cosmopolitan. Such measures would be designed to preserve the link between the specific cosmopolitan and the cultural fragments that shape his/her identity, and preserving these fragments or part of them.

Of course, cosmopolitans have additional interests which nationalists do not have. Apart from their interest in the existence of the cultures which are the source of the elements that serve to construct their particular cosmopolitan mosaic, they also have an interest in the existence of political conditions that would allow them to live within the framework of this mosaic, perhaps even adding to it. In any case, they have an interest in ensuring that their lives not be limited to only one component of this mosaic. In other words, they have an interest in preventing any attempt to restrict them to one of the cultures that comprise their individual identity. The institutional framework suggested in this book for protecting people's interests in adhering to their national cultures is also meant to facilitate an environment that would protect the cosmopolitan interests under discussion. The thesis for which I argued in Chapter 3, according to which the right to self-determination ought to be interpreted as a sub- and inter-statist right, and not as a right to an independent and homogeneous nation-state, is based, on the one hand, on rejecting the idea that states must be culturally homogeneous, and on the other hand, on supporting the continued existence of cultures in the states that coincide with their homelands. The cultural homogenization of the world's states would impose limitations on the ability of cosmopolitans to pursue their cosmopolitan lifestyles. However, protecting those who want to adhere to their national culture by means of a sub-statist right to self-determination, which implies a multicultural conception of states, does not impose such limitations. Not only would it allow cosmopolitans to adhere to their cultural mosaic (and to constantly extend it if they wish to do so), it also protects their interest in the continued existence of at least part of the components of their cultural mosaic. In other words, in addition to protecting the interest of those whose cultural identity is national to adhere to their culture and preserve it, the sub- and inter-statist conception of self-determination also protects two kinds of interests cosmopolitans might have in their cultural identity: their interest not to belong to one particular local culture, to continue having a complex cultural identity, and, on the other hand, their interest in preserving at least part of the components of their cultural mosaic.

A note on cosmopolitan and particularist approaches to distributive justice

In the first part of this chapter I argued that, if duly constrained, the particularistic obligations and permissions characteristic of cultural nationalism could be accommodated within the framework of moral universalism. I then argued that the cultural particularism of this type of nationalism does not exclude the possibility that cultural cosmopolitanism might be a way of life suitable for many people. It is perhaps appropriate to complete the present chapter with a few remarks concerning the relationship between the nationalism discussed in the previous chapters and a third debate pertaining to cosmopolitanism versus particularism, namely, the controversy of the cosmopolitan versus the particularist approach to distributive justice. Moral universalism/particularism provides answers to the question of whether the subjects of moral thought are individuals encumbered by a variety of ties and commitments or whether they are abstracted from such ties. Cultural cosmopolitanism and particularism provide answers to the question of whether people should shape their lives by means of materials that they have selected from different cultures without being rooted in any of them, or whether it is desirable for them to be rooted in one particular culture. In contrast, the argument between the cosmopolitan and the particularist approaches to distributive justice pertains to the question of what the basic units for implementing this type of justice are. According to the cosmopolitan approach, the entire world is the basic unit in which distributive justice should be implemented. The goods to be distributed are those of the whole world, and the individuals who are to benefit from the distribution of these goods are all human beings. According to this approach, states merely have an intermediary and administrative role in supervising the production and distribution of these goods. According to the particularist approach, the goods which are the objects to be distributed are those within the state's territory, and the individuals who have the right to benefit from the distribution of these goods are those individuals who live in this territory.

As in the case of the moral universalism/particularism debate discussed above, I believe that the cosmopolitan position is also the correct position in the debate regarding distributive justice. Many reasons for this are beyond the scope of this book. However, it should nevertheless be noted that some of the main positions taken in this book presuppose the cosmopolitanism rather than the particularist approach. This is the case with regard to the sub- and inter-statist conception of national self-determination, my discussion of nationalism and immigration and the justification presented for the distinction between self-government and polyethnic rights.

The sub- and inter-statist conception of self-determination presupposes a cosmopolitan approach to distributive justice since self-determination is interpreted as a right the beneficiaries of which are not only people living in the state where a given national group enjoys self-determination but also members of the diaspora of the nation in question. The same holds with regard to the position I have taken on the issue of nationalism and immigration. The justification for granting priorities in immigration to potential immigrants who are members of national diasporas to the state where their core group enjoys self-determination presupposes the possibility of the morally significant existence of groups whose members have common interests and ethical obligations towards one another even though they do not all live within the territory of their homeland. The claim that the state coinciding with their homeland should grant them some priorities in immigration presupposes that states ought to consider and serve the interests in self-determination of people who are not their members.

A cosmopolitan approach to distributive justice also underlies the justifications adduced in this book in favour of the distinction between self-government rights and polyethnic rights. According to one such justification, due to global territorial scarcity, not every sub-group of every national group can be granted self-government rights. We should therefore aim to grant at least one sub-group of every national group in the world such rights – preferably the sub-group living in the homeland. All other sub-groups, regardless of whether they were created by voluntary emigration or in any other way, are entitled only to polyethnic rights. According to the second justification, self-government rights provide national groups with better means for their self-preservation than polyethnic rights. The main purpose of polyethnic rights is to allow individual members of national groups to adhere to their original culture, but not necessarily to secure the preservation of the culture itself for future generations. Granting self-government rights to national groups in their homelands also serves the interests of their diaspora members in the historical preservation of their group. The latter must therefore be content with polyethnic rights. Both justifications presuppose that granting a group more substantial rights in one part of the world could compensate it for the meagre cultural rights it enjoys in other parts of the world. Thus, both these justifications for the distinction between self-government rights and polyethnic rights presuppose that the entire world is the basic unit for the distribution of cultural rights. In sum, cultural nationalism as presented in this study does not only allow for the possibility of cultural cosmopolitanism or presuppose ethical universalism. It also presupposes a cosmopolitan approach to distributive justice and conceives of states as having derivative rather than primary status with regard to how justice should be applied within the world.

7 Conclusion

A liberal version of cultural nationalism differs from non-liberal versions in two main dimensions. One pertains to the nature of the justifications it can provide for attributing value to national groups, while the other pertains to the normative conclusions that can be drawn from the value ascribed to nations. With regard to the first point, liberalism cannot ascribe value to national groups under the assumption that such groups have normative priority over their individual members. Liberalism can acknowledge the value of national groups only if it is based on fundamental interests of their individual members and if these interests are interests that could in principle be held by all human beings. These interests must take precedence over the value of the national group, and not vice versa, as is the case in non-liberal cultural nationalisms. With respect to the second point, the central values of liberalism are freedom and equality. A liberal version of cultural nationalism is therefore incompatible with chauvinism, which is a form of nationalism that acknowledges the value of one national group only and denies the equal value of all other national groups. Needless to say, liberal nationalism cannot condone methods such as ethnic cleansing or forced assimilation in order to advance the interests of any particular national group. Neither can it support other means which many national groups in fact do practise in the name of self-preservation which do not take into account similar interests that other national groups might have. It also cannot ignore fundamental interests that members of their own group might have which pertain to issues other than nationality. The cultural nationalism presented in this book fulfils the above conditions. It is justified by individual interests that all people in principle could have in their respective national groups, while the demands it makes are compatible with the requirements of freedom and equality.

Previous attempts in the last ten to fifteen years to present a liberal version of cultural nationalism have taken either a defensive approach, attempting to refute liberal attacks on nationalism, or tried to show that liberalism can provide justifications for at least some sorts of nationalism.

Miller, and to a lesser degree Tamir and McCormick[1] are examples of the former approach, while Kymlicka and Raz are examples of the latter approach.[2] The latter writers have concentrated mainly on showing how prominent liberal values such as freedom and self-respect could support nationalist tenets such as the principle of national self-determination as well as people's interests in adhering to their culture. The former group of writers were not so much intent on showing that these tenets could be justified by fundamental liberal values. Rather, they mainly attempted to refute typical liberal charges against nationalism. For example, Miller argues that national myths are not as condemnable as many liberals claim they are.[3] Similarly, Tamir attempts to demonstrate that liberalism has itself committed at least some of the sins its proponents have criticized nationalism for, for example, the sins of particularism and of ascribing value to groups whose membership is determined by birth and not by choice.[4] The present book mainly takes the second of the two approaches outlined above. Specifically, in Chapter 2, I partly rejected the criticism directed by some writers against Kymlicka's argument that national cultures are for many people a precondition for their freedom. In addition to this argument I argued that many people need their culture because it is the framework within which their plans and various projects are realized and exist.

It is common among writers on nationalism to try to predict the future of nationalism. Writers reacting to the crimes committed in the name of nationalism by completely rejecting it, also tend to believe that in a world undergoing a process of globalization, nationalism will eventually cease to play an important role.[5] Others who react to the crimes committed in the name of nationalism by attempting to find benign versions of it tend to be less sceptical about its future.[6] In both cases, the historical prediction and the normative position are mutually reinforcing. If nationalism is about to perish, why bother with its benign versions? My claim that nationalism's present importance results from its current role in shaping many people's identities, and from the fact that it currently provides the framework

---

[1] D. Miller, *On Nationality*; Tamir, *Liberal Nationalism*; Neil McCormick, 'Nation and Nationalism', in Neil McCormick (ed.), *Legal Right and Social Democracy* (Oxford: Clarendon Press, 1982), pp. 247–64. Canovan's *Nationhood and Political Theory* should perhaps be added to this list.
[2] Kymlicka, *Liberalism, Community and Culture*; Kymlicka, *Multicultural Citizenship*; Raz, *Ethics in the Public Domain*, chaps. 6 and 8.
[3] D. Miller, *On Nationality*, pp. 35–41.   [4] Tamir, *Liberal Nationalism*, chap. 6.
[5] Eric J. Hobsbawm, *Nations and Nationalism since 1780*, 2nd edition (Cambridge University Press, 1992), chap. 6.
[6] See, e.g., D. Miller, *On Nationality*, chap. 7; Tamir, *Liberal Nationalism*, p. 167; Smith, *Nations and Nationalism in a Global Era*, chap. 6.

within which people's endeavours attain substance, implies that it must be taken seriously regardless of its future. People's national affiliation is important today because it currently plays an important role in the identity and endeavours of very many people. There is no guarantee that this will continue to be the case. If it continues to play an important role in the identity and endeavours of a smaller number of people, then it will perhaps play a less significant role in the world's political and institutional agenda.

The foundations of cultural nationalism as interpreted here have served to justify political arrangements in which the state is not the political organ of a particular nation. However, these political arrangements allow people to live their lives within their respective cultures and to govern themselves within them. These arrangements, discussed in this book under the heading of the sub- and inter-statist conception of self-determination, could be accused of being impractical and utopian, since they require that many states and the major holders of political power in the world stop viewing themselves in the way they currently do. They require states to cease regarding themselves as nation-states, and demand that the strong national groups in the world cease viewing themselves as 'owning' their nation-state. It is unrealistic, so the charge might continue, to expect strong national groups to accept this demand and act according to it.

One way of responding to this charge is to plead guilty but then to stress the fact that the statist conception and the civic and non-cultural conception are no less demanding and therefore impractical and utopian. The statist conception demands that non-dominant national groups come to terms with their marginal normative status, while the civic conception requires even more, namely, that small and weak national groups assimilate into the majority in the state they live in or at least cease to live within the framework of their own cultures. The chances for either of these demands to be accepted peacefully and for these two alternatives to be implemented successfully are no greater than those of the sub- and inter-statist conception. If my arguments in Chapter 3 are accepted, one could claim that the latter conception is at least just. Since the implementation of neither of the conceptions can be considered as guarantee for domestic and global peace, it seems desirable to act within a framework which is at least just or acknowledges the fact that attaining just solutions in these matters requires perpetual negotiation and compromise.

Another way of responding to the charge that the arrangements suggested in this book for institutionalizing cultural nationalism are impractical and utopian is to plead guilty but then to stress the fact that the two other available models for addressing cultural demands, namely, the statist and the civic models, are even more impractical. The sub- and inter-statist conception of self-determination ultimately stands more of a chance of resolving nationalist disputes around the world than do the alternative models. In order to avoid the conflicts that the statist conception has brought about in so many places, a massive redrawing of international borders as well as global demographic changes will be required, so that ultimately all and only the members of national groups live in their own nation-state. The civic and non-cultural conception of states will require that many people give up the possibility of living their lives and governing themselves within the framework of their culture and of preserving these cultures. This will entail that they give up some of their deepest attachments to their historical heritage. Unlike the statist conception, the sub-statist conception requires neither a global demographic change, nor any redrawing of international borders. Moreover, the sub-statist conception does not neglect people's interests in living their lives and governing themselves within the framework of their cultures, and their interest in the preservation of these cultures. Rather than require changes in fundamental human emotions and attachments, the sub- and inter-statist conception of self-determination merely requires changes in social institutions and constitutional arrangements.

One change of this sort pertains to international institutions which must comprise not only states but also national groups. More important than the changes at the international level are the changes that would be required at the intra-statist level which would pertain mainly to constitutional constraints. Imposing these changes on states and on the political forces within them is no more extreme and unattainable than the imposition of the constraints required by human rights, environmental law and the laws of war. In the last few decades, more and more constraints of this kind have been integrated into international morality and international law.

Whether or not the sub- and inter-statist conception becomes widely accepted depends to a great extent on whether strong national groups around the world allow its implementation in the states where they constitute the majority. As long as many states conceive of themselves as nation-states, and many national groups conceive of themselves as 'owning' states, it is difficult to demand that minority nations be content with anything less than a state. Many such groups aspire to independent statehood in order to achieve a status that is equal to that of many other groups in the world. In cases where there is bitter conflict between minority and majority groups, and where the former are persecuted by the latter, minority groups are perhaps justified in their aspiration to secede from the state and to establish a new state. This might improve the relationship between the seceding group and the group it leaves behind, and might restore the seceding group's self-respect. (This applies *a fortiori* where the oppressed group does not secede but is liberated from occupation.) However, the norm permitting secession in such cases in order to establish new states must be regarded as a norm for a transitional period to enable cultural groups to gradually adjust to the idea of a sub-statist interpretation of their self-rule. Ultimately, states must conceive of themselves as serving the interests in self-determination of all their homeland groups as well as a variety of other interests that immigrant groups might have. Under the current geodemographic conditions of the world, to conceive of states and citizenship as multinational and multicultural is probably the only morally acceptable option. Since this conception of states and citizenship is sufficient for protecting the interests that people have in self-determination, and since it is conducive to pluralism and freedom of movement, the multinational and multicultural conception of states and citizenship is also desirable.

If nationalism is identified with the claim that the welfare of *all* people *necessarily* depends on their ability to live within their ancestral culture and the claim that national units and states must necessarily coincide, then what I have said in this book could be said to argue against cultural nationalism. If, however, nationalism is identified with the claim that national culture is an important component of many people's identity and that the world must be arranged institutionally to enable people who wish to do so to adhere to their culture and to live their lives within it as much as this is morally and practically possible, then this book has indeed argued in favour of cultural nationalism.

Bibliography

Alter, Peter, *Nationalism*, 2nd edition (London: Edward Arnold, 1994).

Anderson, Benedict, *Imagined Communities: Reflections on the Origin and Spread of Nationalism*, revised edition (London: Verso, 1991).

Appiah, Anthony K., 'Identity, Authenticity, Survival: Multicultural Societies and Social Reproduction', in A. Gutmann (ed.), *Multiculturalism: Examining the Politics of Recognition* (Princeton University Press, 1994), pp. 149–63.

Bader, Veit, 'Citizenship and Exclusion', *Political Theory* 23 (1995), 211–46.

Barnard, F. M. (trans. and ed.), *J.G. Herder on Social and Political Culture* (Cambridge University Press, 1969).

Barry, Brian, 'Self-Government Revisited', in David Miller and Larry Siedentop (eds.), *The Nature of Political Theory* (Oxford: Clarendon Press, 1983), pp. 121–54.

Culture and Equality: An Egalitarian Critique of Multiculturalism (Cambridge: Polity Press, 2001).

Barry, Brian and Goodin, Robert (eds.), *Free Movement* (Philadelphia: Pennsylvania State University Press, 1992).

Bartlett, Richard H., 'Native Title in Australia: Denial, Recognition, and Dispossession', in Paul Haveman (ed.), *Indigenous Peoples' Rights in Australia, Canada & New Zealand* (Auckland: Oxford University Press, 1999), pp. 408–27.

Beiner, Ronald S., 'National Self-Determination: Some Cautionary Remarks Concerning the Rhetoric of Rights', in M. Moore (ed.), *National Self-Determination and Secession* (Oxford University Press, 1998), pp. 158–80.

Beiner, Ronald S. (ed.), *Theorizing Citizenship* (Albany: State University of New York Press, 1995).

(ed.), *Theorizing Nationalism* (Albany: State University of New York Press, 1999).

Bentham, Jeremy, 'Principles of the Civil Code', in Charles K. Ogden (ed.), *Jeremy Bentham: The Theory of Legislation* (London: Routledge and Kegan Paul, 1931), pp. 158–98.

Berlin, Isaiah, *Against the Current: Essays in the History of Ideas*, ed. Henry Hardy (New York: Viking Press, 1980).

'Benjamin Disraeli, Karl Marx and the Search for Identity', in Isaiah Berlin, *Against the Current: Essays in the History of Ideas*, ed. Henry Hardy (New York: Viking Press, 1980), pp. 252–86.

'Nationalism: Past Neglect and Present Power', in Isaiah Berlin, *Against the Current: Essays in the History of Ideas*, ed. Henry Hardy (New York: Viking Press, 1980), pp. 333–55.

Borrows, John, ' "Landed" Citizenship: Narratives of Aboriginal Political Participation', in Will Kymlicka and Wayne Norman (eds.), *Citizenship in Diverse Societies* (Oxford University Press, 2000), pp. 326–42.

Breuilly, John, *Nationalism and the State*, 2nd edition (Chicago University Press, 1992).

Brilmayer, Lea, 'Consent, Contract and Territory', *Minnesota Law Review* 74 (1989), 1–35.

Brown, Chris (ed.), *Political Restructuring in Europe: Ethical Perspectives* (London and New York: Routledge, 1994).

Brubaker, Rogers, 'Myths and Misconceptions in the Study of Nationalism', in M. Moore (ed.), *National Self-Determination and Secession* (Oxford University Press, 1998), pp. 233–65.

Canovan, Margaret, *Nationhood and Political Theory* (Cheltenham: Edward Elgar, 1996).

Carens, Joseph H., 'Migration and Morality: A Liberal Egalitarian Perspective', in B. Barry and R. Goodin (eds.), *Free Movement* (Philadelphia: Pennsylvania State University Press, 1992), pp. 25–47.

Culture, Citizenship and Community: A Contextual Exploration of Justice as Evenhandedness (Oxford University Press, 2000).

Cassese, Antonio, *Self-Determination of Peoples: A Legal Reappraisal* (Cambridge University Press, 1995).

Cohen, Mitchell, 'Rooted Cosmopolitanism: Thoughts on the Left, Nationalism, and Multiculturalism', *Dissent* (Fall 1992), 478–83.

Coleman, Jules L. and Harding, Sarah K., 'Citizenship, the Demands of Justice, and the Moral Relevance of Political Borders', in Warren F. Schwartz (ed.), *Justice in Immigration* (Cambridge University Press, 1995), pp. 18–62.

Colley, Linda, *Britons: Forging the Nation, 1707–1837* (New Haven, CT: Yale University Press, 1992).

Connor, Walker, 'Ethno-nationalism in the First World', in Milton J. Esman (ed.), *Ethnic Conflict in the Western World* (Ithaca and London: Cornell University Press, 1975), p. 19.

Ethnonationalism: The Quest for Understanding (Princeton University Press, 1994).

Danley, John R., 'Liberalism, Aboriginal Rights, and Cultural Minorities', *Philosophy and Public Affairs* 20 (1991), 168–85.

Deutsch, Karl Wolfgang, *Nationalism and Social Communication: An Inquiry into the Foundations of Nationality* (Cambridge, MA: Technology Press of Massachusetts Institute of Technology, 1953).

Dinstein, Yoram, 'Collective Human Rights of Peoples and Minorities', *International and Comparative Law Quarterly* 25 (1976), 102–200.

Dray, William H., *Philosophy of History*, 2nd edition (Englewood Cliffs, NJ: Prentice Hall, 1993).

Ergang, R. R., *Herder and the Foundations of German Nationalism* (New York: Columbia University Press, 1931).

Fichte, Johann Gottlieb, *Addresses to the German Nation*, ed. George A. Kelly (New York: Harper Torchbooks, 1968).

Gans, Chaim, 'A Review of David Miller's *On Nationality*', *European Journal of Philosophy* 5 (1997), 210–16.

Gellner, Ernest, *Nations and Nationalism* (Oxford: Basil Blackwell, 1983).

'Do Nations Have Navels?', *Nations and Nationalism* 2/3 (1996), 366–70.

Gilbert, Paul, *The Philosophy of Nationalism* (Oxford: Westview Press, 1998).

Goodin, Robert, 'What Is So Special about Our Fellow Countrymen?' *Ethics* 98 (1988), 663–86.

Gotlieb, Gidon, *Nation against State: A New Approach to Ethnic Conflicts and the Decline of Sovereignty* (New York: Council on Foreign Relations Press, 1993).

Grotius, *De Jure Belli ac Pacis*, book II.

Gutmann A. (ed.), *Multiculturalism: Examining the Politics of Recognition* (Princeton University Press, 1994).

Habermas, Jürgen, 'Citizenship and National Identity: Some Reflections on the Future of Europe', in Ronald Beiner (ed.), *Theorizing Citizenship* (Albany: State University of New York Press, 1995), pp. 255–81.

Hammar, Tomas, *Democracy and the Nation-State: Aliens, Denizens and Citizens in a World of International Migration* (Aldershot: Avebury, 1990).

Hampton, Jean, 'Immigration, Identity, and Justice', in Warren F. Schwartz (ed.), *Justice in Immigration* (Cambridge University Press, 1995), pp. 67–93.

Hannum, Hurst, *Autonomy, Sovereignty, and Self-Determination: The Accommodation of Conflicting Rights* (Philadelphia: University of Pennsylvania Press, 1990).

Hart, H.L.A., 'Are There Any Natural Rights?', in Jeremy Waldron (ed.), *Theories of Rights* (Oxford University Press, 1984), pp. 77–90.

Haveman, Paul (ed.), *Indigenous Peoples' Rights in Australia, Canada & New Zealand* (Auckland: Oxford University Press, 1999).

Hayden, Robert M., 'Constitutional Nationalism in the Formerly Yugoslav Republics', *Slavic Review* 5 (1992), 654–73.

Hobsbawm, Eric J., *Nations and Nationalism Since 1780*, 2nd edition (Cambridge University Press, 1992).

Horowitz, Donald L., 'Self-Determination: Politics, Philosophy and Law', in M. Moore (ed.), *National Self-Determination and Secession* (Oxford University Press, 1998), pp. 181–214.

Hroch, Miroslav, 'From National Movement to the Fully-Formed Nation: The Nation-Building Process in Europe', in Geoff Eley and Ronald G. Suny (eds.), *Becoming National: A Reader* (New York: Oxford University Press, 1996), pp. 60–77.

Hume, David, *A Treatise on Human Nature*, book III.

Hurka, Thomas, 'The Justification of National Partiality', in Robert McKim and Jeff McMahan (eds.), *The Morality of Nationalism* (New York: Oxford University Press, 1997), pp. 139–57.

Hutchinson, John, *The Dynamics of Cultural Nationalism* (London: Allen and Unwin, 1987).

Ignatieff, Michael, *Blood and Belonging: Journeys into the New Nationalism* (New York: The Noonday Press, 1993).

Isocrates, *Archidamus*.

Ivison, Duncan, Patton, Paul and Sanders, Will (eds.), *Political Theory and the Rights of Indigenous Peoples* (Cambridge University Press, 2000).

Kasher, Asa, 'Justice and Affirmative Action: Naturalization and the Law of Return', *Israeli Yearbook of Human Rights* 15 (1985), 101–12.

Kedourie, Eli, *Nationalism*, 4th, expanded edition (Oxford: Blackwell, 1993).

Kofman, Daniel, 'Rights of Secession', *Society* 35 (1998), 30–7.

Kohn, Hans, *Nationalism: Its Meaning and History* (Princeton: D. Van Nostrand Company, 1955).

Kristof, Ladis K.D., 'The State-Idea, the National Idea and the Image of the Fatherland', *Orbis* 11 (1967), 238–55.

Kymlicka, Will, *Liberalism, Community and Culture* (Oxford: Clarendon Press, 1989).

Multicultural Citizenship: A Liberal Theory of Minority Rights (Oxford: Clarendon Press, 1995).

'The Sources of Nationalism: Commentary on Taylor', in Robert McKim and Jeff McMahan (eds.), *The Morality of Nationalism* (New York: Oxford University Press, 1997), pp. 56–65.

Politics in the Vernacular: Nationalism, Multiculturalism, and Citizenship (Oxford University Press, 2001).

Kymlicka, Will and Norman, Wayne (eds.), *Citizenship in Diverse Societies* (Oxford University Press, 2000).

Langton, Marcia, 'Estate of Mind: The Growing Cooperation between Indigenous and Mainstream Managers of Northern Australian Landscapes and the Challenge for Educators and Researchers', in Paul Haveman (ed.), *Indigenous Peoples' Rights in Australia, Canada and New Zealand* (Auckland: Oxford University Press, 1999), pp. 71–87.

Laponce, J. A., *Languages and Their Territories*, trans. A. Martin-Sperry (University of Toronto Press, 1987).

Lichtenberg, Judith, 'Nationalism, For and (Mainly) Against', in Robert McKim and Jeff McMahan (eds.), *The Morality of Nationalism* (New York: Oxford University Press, 1997), pp. 158–75.

Lind, M., *The Next American Nation* (New York: Free Press, 1995).

Lyons, David, 'The New Indian Claims and Original Rights to Land', in Jeffrey Paul (ed.), *Reading Nozick: Essays on Anarchy, State, and Utopia* (Oxford: Basil Blackwell, 1982), pp. 355–79.

De Maistre, Joseph, *Considerations on France*, trans. and ed. R. A. Lebrun (Cambridge University Press, 1994).

Margalit, Avishai, 'The Moral Psychology of Nationalism', in Robert McKim and Jeff McMahan (eds.), *The Morality of Nationalism* (New York: Oxford University Press, 1997), pp. 74–87.

Margalit, Avishai and Halbertal, Moshe, 'Liberalism and the Right to Culture', *Social Research* 61 (1994), 491–510.

Masaryk, Thomas G., *The Making of a State* (London: George Allen and Unwin, 1927).

Mason, Andrew, 'Political Community, Liberal-Nationalism, and the Ethics of Assimilation', *Ethics* 109 (1999), 261–86.

Mazzini, Joseph, *The Duties of Man and Other Essays* (London: Dent, 1966).

McCormick, Neil, 'Nation and Nationalism', in Neil McCormick (ed.), *Legal Right and Social Democracy* (Oxford: Clarendon Press, 1982), pp. 247–64.

McKim, Robert and McMahan, Jeff (eds.), *The Morality of Nationalism* (New York: Oxford University Press, 1997).

McMahan, Jeff, 'The Limits of National Partiality', in Robert McKim and Jeff McMahan (eds.), *The Morality of Nationalism* (New York: Oxford University Press, 1997), pp. 107–38.

Mehr, Farhang, *A Colonial Legacy: The Dispute over the Islands of Abu Musa, and the Greater and Lesser Tumbs* (New York: University Press of America, 1997).

Meyer, Lukas H., 'More than They Have a Right to: Future People and Our Future Oriented Projects', in Nick Fotion and J. C. Heller (eds.), *Contingent Future Persons* (Dordrecht: Kluwer Academic Publishers, 1997), pp. 137–56.

Mill, J. S., 'Representative Government', in Geraint Williams (ed.), *Utilitarianism, On Liberty, Considerations on Representative Government, Remarks on Bentham's Philosophy* (London: Dent, 1993).

Miller, David, *On Nationality* (Oxford: Clarendon Press, 1995).

'Secession and the Principle of Nationality', in M. Moore (ed.), *National Self-Determination and Secession* (Oxford University Press, 1998), pp. 62–78.

Miller, Richard W., 'Cosmopolitan Respect and Patriotic Concern', *Philosophy and Public Affairs* 27 (1998), 202–24.

Moore, Margaret, 'The Territorial Dimension of Self-Determination', in M. Moore (ed.), *National Self-Determination and Secession* (Oxford University Press, 1998), pp. 134–57.

The Ethics of Nationalism (Oxford University Press, 2001).

Moore, Margaret (ed.), *National Self-Determination and Secession* (Oxford University Press, 1998).

Mussolini, Benito, 'Fascism', in Omar Dahbour and Micheline R. Ishay (eds.), *The Nationalism Reader* (New York: Humanities Press, 1995), pp. 222–9.

Nathanson, Stephen, 'Nationalism and the Limits of Global Humanism', in Robert McKim and Jeff McMahan (eds.), *The Morality of Nationalism* (New York: Oxford University Press, 1997), pp. 176–87.

Nielsen, Kai, 'Cultural Nationalism, Neither Ethnic Nor Civic', *The Philosophical Forum* 28 (1996–97), 42–52.

'Cosmopolitan Nationalism', *The Monist* 82 (1999), 446–68.

Nimni, Ephraim, *Marxism and Nationalism* (London: Pluto Press, 1991).

Nozick, Robert, *Anarchy, State and Utopia* (Oxford: Basil Blackwell, 1974).

Nussbaum, Martha C., 'Patriotism and Cosmopolitanism', in Joshua Cohen (ed.), *For Love of Country: Debating the Limits of Patriotism – Martha C. Nussbaum with Respondents* (Boston: Beacon Press, 1996), pp. 2–17.

O'Leary, Brendan, 'Insufficiently Liberal and Insufficiently Nationalist', in Brendan O'Leary (ed.), 'Symposium on David Miller's *On Nationality*', *Nations and Nationalism* 2/3 (1996), 444–51.

O'Neill, Onora, 'Justice and Boundaries', in Chris Brown (ed.), *Political Restructuring in Europe: Ethical Perspectives* (London and New York: Routledge, 1994), pp. 69–88.

Perry, Stephen R., 'Immigration, Justice and Culture', in Warren F. Schwartz (ed.), *Justice in Immigration* (Cambridge University Press, 1995), pp. 94–135.

Philpott, Daniel, 'In Defense of Self-Determination', *Ethics* 105 (1995), 352–85.

Poole, Ross, *Nation and Identity* (London and New York: Routledge, 1999).

Rawls, John, *A Theory of Justice* (Cambridge, MA: Harvard University Press, 1973).

Raz, Joseph, *The Morality of Freedom* (Oxford University Press, 1986).

Ethics in the Public Domain: Essays in the Morality of Law and Politics, revised edition (Oxford: Clarendon Press, 1994).

Raz, Joseph and Margalit, Avishai, 'National Self-Determination', in J. Raz, *Ethics in the Public Domain: Essays in the Morality of Law and Politics*, revised edition (Oxford: Clarendon Press, 1994), pp. 125–45.

Rousseau, Jean Jacques, *The Social Contract*, book I.

Schmitt, Karl, *The Concept of the Political*, trans. George Schwab (Chicago and London: University of Chicago Press, 1996).

Schwartz, Warren F. (ed.), *Justice in Immigration* (Cambridge University Press, 1995).

Scruton, Roger, *The Philosopher on Dover Beach* (Manchester: Carcanet, 1990).

Seymour, Michel, with the collaboration of Jocelyne Couture and Kai Nielsen, 'Introduction: Questioning the Ethnic/Civic Dichotomy', in Jocelyne Couture, Kai Nielsen and Michel Seymour (eds.), *Rethinking Nationalism* (University of Calgary Press, 1998), pp. 1–61.

Sharp, Andrew, *Justice and the Māori: The Philosophy and Practice of Māori Claims in New Zealand since the 1970s*, 2nd edition (Auckland: Oxford University Press, 1997).

Sher, George, *Approximate Justice: Studies in Non-Ideal Theory* (Lanham, MD: Rowman & Littlefield, 1997).

Sidgewick, Henry, *The Methods of Ethics* (London: Macmillan, 1962).

The Elements of Politics (New York: Kraus, 1969).

Simmons, John A., 'Historical Rights and Fair Shares', *Law and Philosophy* 14 (1995), 149–84.

Smith, Anthony D., 'States and Homelands: The Social and Geopolitical Implications of National Territory', *Millennium: Journal of International Studies* 10 (1981), 187–202.

The Ethnic Origins of Nations (Oxford: Blackwell, 1986).

National Identity (London: Penguin, 1991).

Nations and Nationalism in a Global Era (Cambridge: Polity Press, 1995).

Nationalism and Modernism: A Critical Survey of Recent Theories of Nations and Nationalism (London and New York: Routledge, 1998).

Myths and Memories of the Nation (Oxford University Press, 1999).

Soysal, Yasemin Nuhoglu, *Limits of Citizenship: Migrants and Postnational Membership in Europe* (University of Chicago Press, 1994).

Stoicescu, Nicolae, *The Continuity of the Romanian People* (Bucharest: Editura Stiintifica si Enciclopedica, 1983).

Szporluk, Roman, *Communism and Nationalism: Karl Marx Versus Friedrich List* (New York: Oxford University Press, 1988).

Tacitus, *The Annals of Imperial Rome*, book IV.

Tamir, Yael, *Liberal Nationalism* (Princeton University Press, 1993).
'Pro Patria Mori!: Death and the State', in Robert McKim and Jeff McMahan (eds.), *The Morality of Nationalism* (New York: Oxford University Press, 1997), pp. 227–41.

Taylor, Charles, *Reconciling the Solitudes: Essays on Canadian Federalism and Nationalism* (Montreal: McGill-Queen's University Press, 1993).
'The Politics of Recognition', in A. Gutmann (ed.), *Multiculturalism: Examining the Politics of Recognition* (Princeton University Press, 1994), pp. 25–73.
'Nationalism and Modernity', in Robert McKim and Jeff McMahan (eds.), *The Morality of Nationalism* (New York: Oxford University Press, 1997), pp. 31–55.

Tomuschat, Christian, 'Self-Determination in a Post-Colonial World', in Christian Tomuschat (ed.), *Modern Law of Self-Determination* (Dordrecht: Martinus Nijhoff Publishers, 1993), pp. 1–20.

Tully, James, *An Approach to Political Philosophy: Locke in Contexts* (Cambridge University Press, 1993).
Strange Multiplicity: Constitutionalism in an Age of Diversity (Cambridge University Press, 1995).

Tushnet, Mark, 'United States Citizenship Policy and Liberal Universalism', *Georgetown Immigration Law Journal* 12 (1998), 311–22.

Viroli, Maurizio, *For Love of Country: An Essay on Patriotism and Nationalism* (Oxford University Press, 1995).

Waldron, Jeremy, 'Theoretical Foundations of Liberalism', *The Philosophical Quarterly* 37 (1987), 127–50.
The Right to Private Property (Oxford: Clarendon Press, 1988).
'Minority Cultures and the Cosmopolitan Alternative', *University of Michigan Journal of Law Reform* 25 (1991–92), 751–93.
'Superseding Historic Injustice', *Ethics* 103 (1992), 4–28.
'Redressing Historic Injustice', a paper presented in a colloquium on historical justice, Einstein Forum, Potsdam, 12–14 July 2001.

Webber, Jeremy, 'Beyond Regret: Mabo's Implications for Australian Constitutionalism', in Duncan Ivison, Paul Patton and Will Sanders (eds.), *Political Theory and the Rights of Indigenous Peoples* (Cambridge University Press, 2000), pp. 60–88.

Weber, Eugene, *Peasants into Frenchmen: The Modernization of Rural France 1870–1914* (London: Chatto & Windus, 1976).

Weber, Max, *Economy and Society*, ed. G. Roth and C. Wittich (New York: Bedminster Press, 1968).
'The Profession and Vocation of Politics', in Peter Lassman and Ronald Speirs (eds.), *Weber: Political Writings* (Cambridge University Press, 1994), pp. 309–69.

Wellman, Christopher Heath, 'Relational Facts in Liberal Political Theory: Is There Magic in the Pronoun "My"?', *Ethics* 110 (2000), 537–62.

Yack, Bernard, 'The Myth of the Civic Nation', in Ronald Beiner (ed.), *Theorizing Nationalism* (Albany: State University of New York Press, 1999), pp. 103–18.

Zipperstein, Steven J., *Elusive Prophet* (Berkeley: University of California Press, 1993).

Index